Democracy in the New Europe

Christopher Lord
and
Erika Harris

First published 2006 by
PALGRAVE MACMILLAN
Houndmills, Basingstoke, Hampshire RG21 6XS and
175 Fifth Avenue, New York, N.Y. 10010
Companies and representatives throughout the world

PALGRAVE MACMILLAN is the global academic imprint of the Palgrave
Macmillan division of St. Martin's Press, LLC and of Palgrave Macmillan Ltd.
Macmillan® is a registered trademark in the United States, United Kingdom
and other countries. Palgrave is a registered trademark in the European
Union and other countries.

ISBN-13: 978–1–4039–1302–9   hardback
ISBN-10: 1–4039–1302–1   hardback
ISBN-13: 978–1–4039–1303–6   paperback
ISBN-10: 1–4039–1303–X   paperback

This book is printed on paper suitable for recycling and made from fully
managed and sustained forest sources.

A catalogue record for this book is available from the British Library.

A catalog record for this book is available from the Library of Congress.

10 9 8 7 6 5 4 3 2 1
15 14 13 12 11 10 09 08 07 06

Printed and bound in China

the *new* europe
series

General Editor: Helen Wallace

University of Liverpool

Drawing upon the latest research, this major new series of concise thematically organized texts is designed to provide state-of-the-art overviews of the key aspects of contemporary Europe from the Atlantic to the Urals for a broad student and serious general readership. Written by leading authorities in a lively and accessible style without assuming prior knowledge, each title is designed to synthesize and contribute to current knowledge and debate in its particular field.

Published

Christopher Lord and Erika Harris: *Democracy in the New Europe*

Upcoming

Andrew Cottey: *Security in the New Europe*

and Daniel Wincott: *Welfare in the New Europe*

mond: *Globalization and the European Union*

Schmidt: *Political Economy of the New Europe*

Triandafyllidou: *What is Europe?*

Wallace: *Making Sense of the New Europe*

In preparation

Politics and Governance in the New Europe

Citizenship and Identity in the New Europe

Nationalism and the State in the New Europe

Europe and the World

Society and Social Change in the New Europe

The New Europe Series
Series Standing Order
ISBN 0–333–96042–4 hardback
ISBN 0–333–96043–2 paperback
(outside North America only)

You can receive future titles in this series as they are published. To place a standing order please contact your bookseller or, in the case of difficulty, write to us at the address below with your name and address, the title of the series and an ISBN quoted above.

Customer Services Department, Macmillan Distribution Ltd
Houndmills, Basingstoke, Hampshire RG21 6XS, England

Contents

List of Tables

Foreword

Europe has undergone great changes in the late twentieth and early twenty-first centuries that have radically transformed its political, social and economic contours. *The New Europe Series* aims to explore the key changes, examining not only the new patterns of European cooperation and integration but also key developments within and across countries. At the heart of these transformations lie the questions of how democracy is defined, anchored and developed across the continent. At first sight these might seem to be questions that concern mainly the post-communist countries, yet in reality the nature of democracy and democratic processes are also evolving in interesting ways in the 'old' democracies of Western Europe.

In this first volume of the series, Christopher Lord and Erika Harris provide a broad-ranging analysis of European democracy at state level and within and beyond the state. They set out some key definitions of the characteristics of democracy, assess different countries' experiences of democratic transformation, and consider ways in which involvement in the various processes of trans-European cooperation helps to anchor the consolidation of democracy. They also raise interesting issues about a range of challenges to democracy across the continent in a period in which governance, both national and European, is often contested. The European Union's own much-debated 'democratic deficit' is part of this picture.

Subsequent volumes in this series will explore other themes of contemporary European transformation and their consequences for both intra-European developments and the ways in which Europeans interact with the rest of the world. Their aim will be to provide comparative overviews of patterns of change at both the macro and the micro levels. It is a deliberate aim of the series to take a broad view of what Europe comprises, in which the specific role and character of the European Union and its impacts are only part of the story. Just as important are the questions about changes within and across countries in which contesting European models of social, political and economic life lie at the heart of contemporary developments.

HELEN WALLACE

European University Institute

Preface and Acknowledgements

Democracy has been at the vanguard of changes that have swept across Europe since 1918, 1945 and 1989. It has changed the political systems and international relations of Europe. But, above all, it has transformed the quality of ordinary lives.

This book is devoted to all those Europeans who dreamt of a future that is now our present, a future in which governments would be freely chosen by peoples. But especially it is devoted to Erika's parents, Alexander Grossberger and Terézia Grossbergerová, who, having survived the horrors of the Holocaust, lived in pre-1989 Slovakia but did not live to see the new Europe they always dreamt of.

Writing about democracy after 1989, it is easy to slip into the complacent belief that all that remains to be done is to pen 'and they all lived happily ever after' before sending the manuscript off to the publisher. That is not the conclusion of this book. Instead, we argue, that Europe now faces – and has perhaps always faced – the daunting challenge of ensuring that politics within and beyond the state are related to one another in ways that secure democratic standards.

In developing this argument and writing this book we have been helped by three remarkable people. David Beetham inspired both of us to study democracy and to do so with at least as much attention to values as to institutions. Helen Wallace – whose *One Europe or Several?* Programme funded a significant part of the research that went into this book – has been a constant source of acute insight and encyclopedic knowledge on all kinds of questions raised by the new Europe. Our publisher, Steven Kennedy, once again helped to turn various streams of consciousness into a book with a beginning, a middle and an end. We also owe special thanks to two anonymous referees whose comments on the manuscript went well beyond the call of duty.

Numerous conversations with John Erik Fossum, Andreas Follesdal and Paul Magnette helped shape key ideas behind this book. For other help over the years, we would also like to thank

David Bell, Richard Bellamy, Alan Cromartie, Ben Crum, Deidre Curtin, Renaud Dehousse, Erik Eriksen, Jan Erik Grindheim, Chris Hill, Simon Hix, Bob McKeever, Tibor Pichler, Johannes Pollak, Tatiana Sedova, John Schwarzmamel, Jo Shaw, Alex Warleigh, Antje Wiener and Oren Yiftachel.

We also acknowledge the support of the following grants. From the Economic and Social Research Council, 'A Democratic Audit of the Institutions of the European Union' (Grant No. L213272005 Christopher Lord) and Postdoctoral Fellowship (Grant No. T026271128 Erika Harris). From the British Academy, 'The Changing Context of Minority Politics: The Impact of European Integration on the Hungarian Minority in Slovakia (Erika Harris). From the Connex Network of Excellence funded by the Framework 6 initiative of the European Commission, help with participation in several research workshops.

CHRISTOPHER LORD
ERIKA HARRIS

Chapter 1

Introduction

Argument of the book

Our political leaders are elected within states but, increasingly, appear to exercise power from beyond the state. Given its delivery through the institutions of the state, it is understandable that many are anxious about the implications of globalization for democracy. This book argues that the new Europe has much to tell us about that wider debate, since the region is distinguished by an emerging interdependence between democracy within and beyond the state. Before this is dismissed as trite we should like to be clear that we are making three very strong claims that distinguish us quite clearly from what many others have written on the subject. Our first claim is that a two-dimensional experiment in democracy beyond the state is currently being attempted in the new Europe. One dimension consists of coordinated attempts to manage the European part of the international order, so that it includes only political systems that are democratic according to standards that are agreed and evaluated internationally; the other dimension consists of attempts to apply democratic standards to regional institutions beyond the state, notably the European Union. Needless to say there are important connections between the dimensions.

Our second claim is that 'democracy beyond the state' is not an oxymoron only capable of being uttered by those who misunderstand either the first or the last word in the phrase or both. To the contrary, it is increasingly difficult in the conditions of the new Europe to hold to justifications for democracy within the state without also conceding a need for democracy beyond it.

Our third claim is that neither of the dimensions of democracy beyond the state we identify is likely to prosper without the continued success of democracy within the state. Here we are certain to disappoint more postmodern readers who would prefer a bonfire of all existing categories to light a way to a heroic conclusion that democracy in the new Europe is about to go 'post-national' and 'post-state', or at least we are going to disappoint those amongst them who do not accept our further conclusion that the continued success of democracy within the state may only make it more likely that democracy beyond the state will be innovative in its normative meaning and its institutional practice.

In fact, this book is going to have a great deal to say about democracy within the state: about the ways in which the paths to democracy and statehood wound round one another histori-cally in different parts of Europe; about the continuing centrality of the state to 'democratic life' throughout contemporary Europe; and, as just indicated, about justifications for democ-ratic statehood and what those justifications might imply under present conditions. If the relationship between democracy within and beyond the state in the new Europe is our chosen focus, it is, moreover, on the basis of the deepest of respect for many of the things that were written during a European past when there was less reason than there is now to think outside the box of the state. Thus the reader will find the book littered with insights from Aristotle, de Tocqueville, Locke, Mill, Montesquieu and Rousseau, as well as appreciative references to more obvious prophets of beyond-stateness, such as Habermas and Kant, or to more contemporary thinkers such as Habermas once again, Pettit and Rawls.

Approach of the book

Before embarking on our investigation into the relationship between democracy within and beyond the state in the new Europe we need a toolkit for analysing democratic politics. The following paragraphs seek to demonstrate that any satisfactory discussion of democratic politics has to include at least the fol-lowing: a definition that clearly demarcates democracy from other forms of rule; an identification of the value choices involved in choosing one form of democracy over another; an understanding of the institutional choices available for the real-ization of democratic rule; and an appreciation of its social and international preconditions.

At its core democracy is a form of rule based on 'public control with political equality' (Weale, 1999, p. 14). One way of arriving at these minimum conditions is essentially inductive. As David Beetham puts it, it is the absence of public control with political equality that people have historically complained about where democracy has, in their view, been missing (Beetham, 1994, pp. 27–8). Yet, even if historical experience had been otherwise, a moment's reflection reveals the two conditions to be logically entailed in any notion of rule by the people. Whereas democracy is conceivable where citizens do not rule in person, it is inconceivable where they do not control those who take decisions in their name. If, however, some of the people were to count for more than others in exercising that public control, there would be an element of rule of some of the people by others of the people, rather than a straightforward rule by the people.

Whilst public control with political equality forms the core definition of democracy it is possible to have varying value preferences for how it should be delivered. Beetham thus identifies authorization, participation, responsiveness, representation, transparency, accountability and inclusion as democracy's 'mediating values'. Different people and societies prefer their democracies to put different emphases on these mediating values and combinations between them. Some prefer systems that put more value on participation than representation; some believe that responsiveness to popular preferences is essential; while others prefer decision-makers to use their own judgement, and then account for what they have done; and so on.

One reason why there is scope for honest disagreement amongst democrats is that arguments for democracy are themselves varied. They may, for example, be intrinsic or consequential. According to the intrinsic argument it is desirable in and of itself that individuals should have control over as many decisions that affect their own lives as possible. Democracy addresses the puzzle of how individuals can be self-governing – or, as Rousseau put it, as free as they were before they entered society (1968 [1762]) – even where they have no choice but to act collectively if they are to achieve their objectives. Although the conundrum can never be perfectly resolved (Weale, 1999, pp. 62–4), democracy may be special in offering the least bad fit between collective action and personal autonomy. Where there is popular control, governments have an incentive to base decisions on the needs and values of citizens, and not just on their own self-serving purposes (Pettit, 1997, p. 184). If, in addition, the preferences of voters are normally distributed, democratic forms of public control favour those representatives who pay attention to the needs and values of the median voter, whose views have the unique quality of being the least average distance from those of everyone else (Powell, 2000).

Some make the further claim that democracy is not just a technical or institutional fix that allows the least bad fit between the ideal of the self-governing individual and an inescapable need for some things to be decided collectively. It is also a source of moral improvement, of individual self-definition, and of taking the observation that politics is learning by doing to the conclusion of including everyone in the doing. It is, according to this point of view, only through the practice of citizenship, that the citizen becomes a citizen, able to understand the needs and values of the group, and not just of the self (Aristotle, 1962). One contemporary way of expressing this ancient thought is that politics enables us to 'reason publicly' (Rawls, 1993, p. 221); or, in other words, to go beyond the question 'what can *I* get out of collective action?' and ask another that is logically prior to it: 'where *we* as a group need to decide matters together, how can we do so in ways the overwhelming majority of us can accept as right?' (Habermas, 1996, pp. 159–62: our quotation marks).

In contrast, the consequentialist justification for democracy is that it delivers values other than those contained in its own definition. It is often claimed, for example, that democratic systems are better than others at protecting individual rights and avoiding the arbitrary domination of citizens by those who purport to rule them (Pettit, 1997). In addition, democratic systems may, in the long run, be associated with higher levels of economic and social development, since they create a structural incentive for governments to produce effective public policies on pain of losing office. It is also claimed, as we will discuss at some length, that democratic governments are more likely to produce a stable form of international relations by resolving their conflicts peacefully (Doyle, 1983, 1986).

Just as the values and justifications associated with democracy vary, so do institutional means of achieving it. Recent years have witnessed a proliferation in alleged types of democracy to the point at which the authors of one study (Collier and Levitsky, 1997) claim to be able to identify no fewer than 500 variants of democracy in the political science literature. But this does not mean that anything goes. First, any form of democracy has to satisfy the core definition of public control with political equality. Second, the match between democratic institutions and values has to be coherent so that the former can be justified as the best means of achieving whatever a society takes to be its preferred combination of the latter. It is models of democracy that do the work of matching choices of democratic values to choices of democratic institutions so that the second can be considered a plausible means of achieving the first. Some of the choices available are best understood by considering a number of distinctions in the study and practice of democratic politics.

Direct versus indirect

Perhaps the most familiar of all distinctions used in the classification of forms of democracy, direct democracy, is where the people themselves take major decisions of government, either in face-to-face meetings with one another or through mass processes such as referendums. The alternative is that the people exercise control indirectly through elected representatives, including, for example, elected chief executives (presidents) and elected parliaments. Whereas direct democracy speaks most directly to values of participation, self-rule and even moral improvement through deliberation of matters of public interest, advocates of indirect democracy are more likely to argue that the 'good life' is also to be found in projects outside politics which can only be pursued if democracy avoids overburdening the citizen.

Yet many who might otherwise defend representative institutions argue that it is also important there should also be some 'institution-free' means of discussing how politics should be conducted (Blaug, 2000). The central problem here is that institutions 'mobilize bias' (Schattsneider, 1960). They are hard to structure in a strictly neutral way so that all outcomes are equally probable, and they often have a certain self-confirming logic, as individuals invest in building up capabilities specific to the institutional settling. As Ernest Gellner might summarize the problem: any one set of representative institutions 'may be an excellent way of making relatively minor choices within an overall settled structure, but it cannot without circularity and absurdity be granted the capacity to choose between total social structures or value-systems' (Gellner, 1994, p. 185).

Consensus versus majoritarian

Majoritarian democracy is where decisions can be taken by a bare majority of the people or their representatives. Its proponents argue that any alternative would amount to a system of minority rule. In contrast, consensus democracy is where the aim is to align choices with the greatest number of citizens or their representatives, rather than with the preferences of a simple majority (Lijphart, 1984, p. 4). Its defenders argue that any alternative allows minorities to be excluded and is thus not really rule by the people as a whole. Moreover, there is, in their view, no defensible reason why a bare majority should act as a kind of cut-off point for collective decision if compromises can be made to accommodate a bigger majority without significantly deviating from the preferences of the bare majority. Examples of consensus democracy include super-majoritarian decision-rules (where decisions need the approval of more than 50 per cent), systems that require the concurrence of different majorities, consociational systems that guarantee the participation of many cultural segments in public decisions (Lijphart, 1979), and arrangements for the inclusion of opposition parties in some of the tasks of government (Powell, 1989).

Constitutional democracy versus popular sovereignty

According to 'popular' democracy the will of the people cannot be limited if it is to be sovereign. In contrast, 'constitutional' democracy holds that individuals have rights that limit the sovereignty of the people as a whole. Since those rights are seen as normatively and even temporally prior to democracy itself, they need to be protected as a precondition for it. Indeed, constitutionalists often regard rights as quite literally constitutive of political systems in the sense that rights cannot be violated without contradicting the basis on which individuals consent to shared institutions, thus releasing them from their obligation to the political system.

Constitutional democracy typically seeks to solve the puzzle of how to have rule by the people as a whole without arbitrary treatment of individuals by dividing power between institutions, each of which may, in turn, be subject to different modes of public authorization and control, and none of which can act contrary to the individual rights constitutive of the particular political association in which they are located. Thus written constitutions and bills of rights, judicial review of political acts for conformity with individual rights, bicameral legislatures, divisions of power between branches and levels of government are typical institutions of constitutionalist democracy (Weale, 1999).

It might seem there is a significant overlap between this theme and the last: between popular and constitutional democracy on the one hand and majoritarian and consensus democracy on the other. Whilst, however, consensus decision-rules are one means of realizing the constitutional ideal of 'non-manipulable political power' (Pettit, 1997), it needs to be emphasized that constitutional democracy protects certain rights even against the operation of a consensus. The constitutional protection of individual rights may, conversely, make groups and individuals more willing to move from consensus to majoritarian decision-rules.

Input versus output democracy/'responsible' versus 'responsive' government

For many it is important that democracy should produce policy 'outputs' that match citizen wants. Thus democratic institutions are expected to be 'responsive' to or to 'aggregate' the preferences of those they represent. Moreover, the notion societies have of what it is to be a self-governing people will usually contain expectations of what kinds of problem can be solved by democratically elected institutions. According to a very different view, however, those who value democracy do not principally do so because they believe that its policy outputs are more likely than alternative forms of government to give them what they want. Rather they value it for the worth it affords them as individuals by giving them the right to combine with others at regular intervals and as political equals to hold those who govern them responsible. Democracy is thus a set of rights, responsibilities and procedures, not a flow of policy outputs.

Indeed, it may be neither necessary nor sufficient that democracy should 'satisfy wants' (Plamenatz, 1973, p. 181). Whilst a technocracy or even a benign dictatorship might also succeed in aligning policy outputs with citizens' wants, a democracy 'may refuse to meet widespread popular demands without ceasing to be democratic' (ibid., p. 210). It may even be its 'duty' (ibid.) to behave in such a way if its public takes a Burkean attitude that representatives owe the represented their 'judgement' and not their 'obedience' (Burke, 1975 [1774]). From this point of view the most encompassing definition of democracy is 'responsible government' rather than 'responsive government' (Plamenatz, 1973, p. 210; see also Mansbridge, 2003).

Strategic versus deliberative democracy

Whether democracy is seen as an output problem (the right policies) or an input one (the right procedures), political competition between elites is essential. If responsiveness is the aim, competition provides the incentive for elites to align policy choices with citizen preferences. If responsibility is the goal, competition encourages a critique of incumbents and the organization of alternative power-holders in waiting, without whom the right of the public to throw the rascals out may be tightly constrained in practice. Either way democracies have an attractively simple means of organizing political competition. All adult citizens are allocated one vote – in line with the principle of political equality – and their would-be representatives then compete for those votes.

Yet as John Dewey famously put it, voting is unlikely to be enough on its own to make democracy an acceptable form of political rule (Dewey, 1927). He and others like him have argued that being outvoted by others, and being compelled, as a result, to abide by unwanted laws, is a harsh discipline that is only likely to be acceptable to those who first have an opportunity to state their point of view, and have it considered open-mindedly. Perhaps John Stuart Mill provides the classic statement of this position in his argument that representative bodies should provide a 'Congress of Opinions' where all points of view should present themselves 'in the light of day' and those who are over-ruled should 'feel satisfied that [their opinion has been] heard, and set aside not by a mere act of will, but for what are thought to be superior reasons' (Mill, 1972 [1861], pp. 239–40). Amongst more contemporary commentators, John Rawls (1993) has argued that democracy's commitment to political equality ideally requires that decisions should be shaped by the quality of justifications reasoned out in public, and not by distributions of private power or resources. The norms of debate that authentically achieve such an ideal of equal access and consideration for all points of view differentiate, in Jürgen Habermas's terms, the public from the private sphere (Calhoun, 1992). The sum of these views, then, is that democracy thus has a cooperative and deliberative dimension that needs to be combined with the competitive.

But still the building blocks of democratic politics are incomplete. As we have already argued, democracy is about society at least as much as it is about institutions. It requires a distinctive relationship between society and political system, as summarized by the following quotation from Zygmunt Bauman:

> Liberal Democracy is a daring attempt to perform an exceedingly difficult balancing act which few other societies have undertaken and none has quite succeeded in carrying through. Liberal Democracy in both its visionary and practical forms is an attempt to keep the state effective in its role as the guardian of the peace and the mediator between group of individual interests, while keeping the groups free to form and the individuals free to assert themselves and choose the form of life they wish to pursue. (Bauman, 1999, pp. 154–5)

Implicit in this is that democracy presupposes rights. Indeed, Habermas (1996) has argued that in democratic politics the rights of the individual and the binding force of decisions taken collectively by the people or their representatives are 'co-constituted'. There is no 'chicken and egg' problem of trying to work out which came first. Neither is possible without the other, and both are simultaneously enabled and limited by the other.

Requirements of participation (even minimally through elections), debate and rights-delivery rule out any possibility of democracy being a costless form of government, without its duties, its burdens or a need to invest in the capabilities of representatives and citizens alike (March and Olsen, 1995). The result is that democracy everywhere is likely to be imperfect and unfinished. Robert Dahl argues, for example, that most known 'democracies' are better described as 'polyarchies' (1971). That is to say, they allow the public to participate in the control of political power, but hardly, yet, as political equals.

If the control of political power when exercised from beyond the state now needs to be added to any appraisal of how far we are ruled democratically, a significant new front in democracy's 'unfinished business' (Arblaster, 1987) may have opened up before other tasks, associated with the full democratization of the state and society, have been completed. How far this is a problem is something that the new Europe has much to tell us.

The enquiry we intend here into the relationship between democracy within and beyond the state provides an original motive for studying democracy in Europe, which, to our knowledge, has not been attempted before. Yet we will also show how it throws new light on a number of questions that have been asked by others. The following are amongst them. How against once significant competition has democracy emerged as the dominant form of rule to the point at which few Europeans would consider their governments legitimate without it (Dunn, 2005)? Are Europeans, on the other hand, as agreed as they appear on what they mean by democracy and on what they understand to be its institutional and social preconditions, or have many older arguments about politics just been internalized to disputes about the proper nature of democracy? If it comes to that, are Europeans satisfied with their democracies? Above all, are European democracies changing, perhaps, as optimists would have it, towards a deeper democratization of society and of decisions taken internationally; or, maybe, as pessimists would have it, towards some combination of crisis, complacency and *ennui* that rots democracy at its national roots before allowing any prospect of its transposition to politics beyond the state?

Our progress through the foregoing topics will, we hope, give new force to the old adage that Europe is an invaluable laboratory for the student of democratic politics. On the one hand, the democratization of the south, centre and east of the continent since the 1970s has added greater variation in political systems, states, societies, economies and histories to the category of more or less democratic states to be found in the region. At a level of country comparisons, the European laboratory thus tests more of the variables in democratic politics and greater variation in the variables than ever before. On the other hand, the region is a laboratory in the still more original sense of allowing us to observe experiments with democracy 'beyond the state'. Here, we need not be too discouraged by the often-expressed concern that n = 1.

Even if on our first dimension of democracy beyond the state we take the European Union as the only significant experiment in the laboratory, we hope to show in Chapter 4 that some conceptually distinct approaches to the public control of Union institutions are being attempted in parallel. Of course, these are hardly ideal laboratory conditions in which all experiments are carried out independently of one another so that their effects can be gauged separately. But such conditions are not needed for evaluations that depend on compliance with norms rather than the measurement of consequences (March and Olsen, 1995).

Our discussion will necessarily be 'broad brush'. However, the study of democracy in Europe has reached a point at which an exercise of the kind we are attempting is as feasible as it is desirable. Both our framework and our conclusions can safely rely on a huge volume of rigorous multidisciplinary research into every aspect of democratic rule. Whether it is the justification of democratic values and their relationship to other attributes of what we understand by good government, the study of democratic institutions, the study of sociological and international preconditions for democracy, or the study of transformations and of how polities and societies become democratic in the first place, hardly a stone has been left unturned in what the academic community has done to expand understanding of our present democratic condition (or lack of it). On such firm foundations some bold interpretations can confidently be attempted.

Before concluding this subsection, two comments are in order on how we intend to locate this book in the broader study of politics. Assuming that we have identified a phenomenon that really is 'out there', many would find our chosen focus deeply unappealing. A role for democracy beyond the state would increase the distance between individuals and some of the decisions that affect their lives. In some cases, it would also test their willingness to share democratic institutions with those they may previously have regarded as 'strangers', or, in other words, members of political communities other than their own. However, it is not only the 'life world' of the citizen that would be challenged by proposals for democracy beyond the state, but that of the political scientist too. Since human actions within the state are regulated by a shared government, while those beyond it are not, the study of politics developed very different assumptions and methods for studying the two. Any suggestion that affairs beyond the state might now be governed – democratically or otherwise – implies some convergence between the two spheres of politics, and in our approach to studying them.

Second, it should by now be clear that we are interested in both ideas and practice: in justifications for democracy and means of practising it, and in discussing both in relation to the new Europe. Like others who have reflected on the problems (Habermas, 1992, 2001a, 2001b, 2005) covered by this book we are not too concerned that our analysis is of norms and widely held political values, as well as facts. First, norms do not pretend to be political practice, but a proposition of aims to be aspired to in politics. Second, political thought incapable of the reexamination of its principles, conceptual reflection and practical reform is merely a description of history and, in any case, historical facts are not always the best place from which to look into the future whose contours can be observed fairly clearly already. Analysis based on an assumption that the future will resemble the past is never more exposed to the charge of determinism than when it is being overtaken by events pointing to new directions.

In any case, only attempts to derive statements of fact from value are flawed, not attempts to evaluate the second against the first (Ruben, 1998, pp. 465–7). This insight more than any other tells us why attempts to investigate democracy through a separation of fact and value are bound to fail. It is precisely because democracy is now so widely accepted as a core standard for the legitimate exercise of political power that it would be bizarre if its study did not include some means of evaluating how democratic systems perform in fact against the democratic values that legitimate them. Moreover many 'facts' about democracy are facts of a particular kind. As the philosopher John Searle has noted we would not get very far if we tried to understand a chess piece as a piece of wood (Searle, 1990, 1995). What makes a chess piece what it is is the act it is used to perform and that, in turn, is defined by a system of rules, or, in other words, institutionally. What, then, people mean by public control, political equality, responsiveness, responsibility, representation and participation are, in Searle's terms, not just values, but the 'institutional facts' of democracy. They define the thing itself. They are facts and norms at the same time. But let us follow Wittgenstein in taking the analogy one step further. In children's games the rules change all the time (Giddens, 1984, p. 18). What remains to be seen is whether changing meanings that attach to democracy in the new Europe – or just the challenge of meeting settled meanings in changed circumstances – points to a need for democracy beyond the state. This book aims at least to make the question coherent, if not to contribute something to its answer.

In sum, then, we intend a book on the relationship between democracy within and beyond the state in the new Europe that ambitiously, even immodestly, is aimed simultaneously at the comparativist, the political theorist and the student of international relations. Our message to each of these three audiences is that our chosen topic is of the greatest importance to the continent in which we live but the three disciplines for which you are responsible are currently talking past each other even though you have no hope of making sense except together. As the book progresses it moves from laying the groundwork to combining familiar findings and new ones into arguments that have not been made before, at least not quite in the form they are made here. Yet we hope to do all this in a way that will be accessible to the student and all informed readers.

Plan of the book

We open our investigation into the relationship between democracy within and beyond the state in the new Europe deep inside the state itself. Chapter 2 shows how the original application of democracy to mass societies in Europe depended on such attributes of statehood as sovereignty, territoriality, identity and hierarchy. It also discusses the role of European nation-states in solving what is probably the best-known riddle of democratic politics: there can be no democracy without an answer to the question 'who are the people?'. Yet this is the one question that cannot be answered democratically, since the issue of who should count and who should not has to be settled before any democratic procedure is used. Only by understanding just how, in these various ways, state, nation and representative democracy have been so intimately connected in Europe's past can we grasp why it is so significant that democracy beyond the state has come to feature in the academic debates, and practical politics, of the new Europe.

Chapter 3 turns to an analysis of the diversity of democracy within European states in an effort to demonstrate that there is no prospect of finding a uniform starting point for discussion of how democracy within and beyond the state should best be related in national experience with democratic practice. We highlight this diversity through familiar categories of comparative politics, considering, along the way, how far different states of the new Europe make use of direct and indirect democracy, presidential and parliamentary representation, proportional and less proportional electoral systems, and principles of constitutional, consensus and majoritarian democracy. We give special attention during this chapter to varying modes of subnational democracy, in order to highlight a point that will be picked up in our subsequent analysis: any relationship between democracy within and beyond the state in the new Europe will almost certainly also have implications for the practice of democracy beneath the state. The chapter then concludes with a brief discussion of whether, quite regardless of present *levels* of diversity in European political systems, the *direction of change* is towards convergence or greater divergence.

In Chapters 4 and 5 we analyse how far there is already evidence for the practice of democracy beyond the state in the new Europe. We set out a two-dimensional view of democracy beyond the state: the one dimension consisting, as seen, of attempts to extend public control to shared institutions at European level (Chapter 4) and the other of attempts to coordinate the management of the European part of the international system so that it consists only of democracies (Chapter 5). The first dimension is investigated in Chapter 4 through an analysis of how far, and in what ways, democratic standards have been applied to the European Union. The second is examined in Chapter 5 through an analysis of coordinated democracy promotion mainly directed at those parts of the new Europe that were not democratic before 1989. Chapter 5 concludes with some comments on why it is so important to understand democracy beyond the state in the new Europe as two-dimensional in the way we do.

Chapters 6–8 contain the core argument of the book that the prospects for democracy within and beyond the state depend on one another in the new Europe. After discussing indicators and debates about the quality of contemporary democracy, Chapter

6 concludes that in much of the new Europe institutions within and beyond the state are already mutually implicated in the delivery of democratic standards; or, as we put it, they face a problem of 'joint supply' in which neither level has exclusive control over its own democratic performance. Chapter 7 then develops a case for democracy beyond the state through our own distinctive take on democratic peace theory, on globalization and on the normative insufficiency of the state in the face of universal values. Chapter 8 then concludes the book as a whole with the converse argument that any democracy within the state will nonetheless depend on the continued success of democracy within the state: first, for the constraint of power; second, for political community; and, third, for democratic capabilities. In sum, then, we intend to reach our conclusion through an empirical assessment of current practice, but also through consideration of core justifications for democracy itself and of what their realization is likely to require in the circumstances of the new Europe.

Chapter 2

Democracy Within the State

Many texts remark that democracy was first practised in Europe by those ancient Greeks who lived in the city state of Athens. If this is meant to suggest that democracy is an ancient part of Europe's heritage it is misleading. If we take universal adult suffrage to be the key threshold countries have to pass on the way to being fully democratic, it is almost as much a novelty to have democracy anywhere in Europe as it is to have it more or less everywhere. In the 1830s, the French political thinker Alexis de Tocqueville (1968 [1839]) needed to look outside Europe to the United States to study the curiosity of universal suffrage, or what he thought to be universal suffrage. During the remainder of the nineteenth century many European countries moved towards universal male suffrage but it was only after 1918 that many allowed women the vote.

In fact, only 14 out of 46 countries of the new Europe have been continuously democratic since 1945. Newcomers to democracy arguably include Switzerland which only allowed women to vote after 1971; Spain, Portugal and Greece which were governed by authoritarian military dictatorships until the 1970s; and the countries of Eastern and Central Europe, whose communist governments may have called themselves 'democratic' before 1989, but whose publics neither had free and fair elections nor much choice over their economic and social systems.

This chapter is about democracy's political apotheosis. 'Apotheosis' may not be the best of terms for the success of a form of government that dethrones gods and kings in favour of a sovereign people. Yet there are not many terms that are equal to introducing what, as John Dunn (2005) puts it, is the 'astonishing story' of how one word, democracy, 'has won the verbal competition for ultimate political commendation' (pp. 13–15). In what follows we argue that the force of its legitimating ideas, its functional performance as a system of government and the power of its friends all played an important part in democracy's

16

success in Europe; or, to be more precise, in the success of liberal democracy. In the third and fourth sections of the chapter we then show how much it mattered that the state provided liberal democracy with its institutions and the nation (albeit more problematically) provided it with its 'demos' or defined sense of political community. However much developments may point to possibilities of democracy beyond the state, democracy within the state is the only serious starting point for discussion of democracy in the new Europe.

The rise of democracy in Europe

One reason for its late arrival was that democracy had to overcome significant hostility in most parts of Europe before it could establish itself as a widely supported form of rule (Dunn, 2005, p. 71). Many doubted its practicality. Others predicted it would produce bad government by substituting the unstable for the stable, the capricious for the traditional, and the mood swings of the mob for the accumulated wisdom of those accustomed to rule. Still others feared that it would amount to little more than theft. Majorities would be able to expropriate and abuse minorities, and likely victims would include those elites responsible for established hierarchies of church and state and society's real wealth producers, the thrifty and the industrious.

One of the most forthright statements of the view that there are limits to the fitness of the people to rule themselves is to be found in a text that actually advocated democracy provided it was limited to competitive elections between leaders better able to decide than the people themselves. As Joseph Schumpeter formulated this argument, 'the typical citizen drops down to a lower level of mental performance as soon as he enters the political field. He argues and analyses in a way which he would readily recognise as infantile within the sphere of his real interests. He becomes a primitive again' (Schumpeter, 1943, p. 262).

Indeed, even more obvious shapers of European democratic thought than Schumpeter benefit from being read as somewhat guarded champions of the democratic cause, at least in comparison with what democracy subsequently achieved. Jean-Jacques Rousseau (1712–78) did not advocate democracy for what we would recognize as states or large-scale modern societies, but for small communities. When, a century later, John Stuart Mill (1806–73) provided a classic statement of the view that democracy was, nonetheless, possible in mass society through representative government (1972 [1861]), reservations were still apparent. Mill's arguments for universal suffrage sometimes seem as concerned to discipline (ibid., p. 216) what is worst in the people as they are to develop what is best in them. Likewise Mill's deeply held belief that representative bodies should only have a power of ultimate control, and that they should otherwise accept that they are 'radically unfit' for the 'function of governing' (ibid., p. 239) demonstrated that he was not intent on making an unconditional case for democracy, but on showing that it could after all be reconciled with his otherwise elitist conviction that government is best left to those who know how to govern (Ryan, 1974, p. 215). In believing that the challenge of the age was to make democracy safe, and not just to embrace it, he was in agreement with his equally remarkable contemporary, de Tocqueville (1805–1859), who put the point thus: 'the first duty on those who now direct society is to educate democracy . . . to purify its mores; to control its actions; gradually to substitute understanding of statecraft for present inexperience . . . and blind instinct' (1966 [1839], p. 9).

Yet thinkers like Mill hold the key to why democracy often seems to be an older part of the European political tradition than it really is. In inventing what was to become the dominant brand of democracy in Europe – liberal democracy – Mill and others sought to balance the right of the people as a whole to make collectively binding decisions with the rights of groups and individuals. As Alan Ryan (1974, p. 191) puts it, Mill's belief was that 'in the last resort the majority should get its way, but it ought not to do so without a struggle'. The striking of this balance between the rights of the majority and those of the individual was eased by the appropriation of materials from Europe's pre-democratic past. The idea that rule should rest on the consent of at least some of the governed assembled together pre-dates the definitive territorial settlement of European peoples to the extent that it is to be found amongst the Germanic peoples who participated in the *Völkerwanderung* before the middle of the first millennium (Davies, 1996, p. 222). The notion that the individual is the ultimate unit of value in any social and political order owes much to what John Gray (not all too sympathetically) describes as Christianity's 'cult of person-hood' (2002, p. 58). The idea that political power is something that has to be controlled and delimited by the rights of both individuals and communities has firm roots in the constitutionalism of seventeenth- and eighteenth-century Europe (Montesquieu, 1989) and even the republican era of ancient Rome (Skinner, 1978).

Altogether, then, far from putting consent, representation, individual rights and the constraint of the powerful at the centre of European thought, the distinctive contribution of liberal democracy was to adapt those preexisting values to the principle that *all* adult citizens should count as political *equals* in their realization. Yet many doubted that fully democratic societies could evolve straightforwardly from pre-democratic political forms. Prominent amongst them were the followers of Karl Marx (1818–83), who for much of the past 150 years has dwarfed the likes of his near neighbour in mid-nineteenth-century, London, John Stuart Mill, in the political imagination of European academics, political actors and publics.

Although the pre-1989 political systems of Central and Eastern Europe are probably better classed as non-democratic, they continued until the end to justify themselves by turning Marx's coruscating attack on 'bourgeois notions of freedom, culture and law' (1973, p. 83) into the critique of liberal democracy that it failed to come to terms with the revolutionary restructuring of society that would be needed if the power relations of pre-democratic societies were not simply to be reproduced in supposedly democratic ones. The fragility of democracy in much of Europe between 1918 and 1989 did not arise from any straightforward dispute between those who sought to affirm or deny that political power should only be exercised on behalf of the people. Of the great twentieth-century ideologies, both liberal democracy and communism were agreed in rejecting ideas that had been hugely influential for most of European history, namely that the exercise of political power could be justified by God, inheritance or tradition. Where they parted company was with the descent into non-democratic politics of those who believed that 'people's republics' required deeper social transformations than anything liberal democracy had to offer.

Indeed, it was precisely because liberal democracy and communism were agreed that political power could only be legitimate if exercised on behalf of the people that their mutually exclusive claims for how this should be done automatically implied the non-legitimacy of the other form of government (Bobbitt, 2002, p. 215). Thus to the charge that liberal democracy cannot ensure the equality needed for democracy, its defenders counter-charged that there is no democracy beyond liberal democracy. Isaiah Berlin, for example, argued that once ideological justification is sought for putting the 'imagined' interests of the people before their freely expressed 'empirical' preferences there is no limit to the self-serving and arbitrary forms of rule that can be substituted for democracy. 'I am in a position to ignore the actual wishes of men or societies, to bully, oppress, torture them in the name of their "real" selves' (Berlin, 1969, p. 133).

It would be naive, though, to believe that the triumph of liberal democracy was one of ideas only. It was, also, one of performance and of power relations. To understand this we need to consider what is right and what is misleading in the view that democracy in Europe came in effortlessly on a tide of social modernity. Anthony Giddens has portrayed modernity as the replacement of face-to-face relations based on traditions with interactions with strangers at a distance through abstract systems (1991, p. 80). Such a change captures much of what has happened to European societies since the eighteenth century. Markets, far-flung communications networks, standardized languages and educational systems, and, eventually, collectivized welfare systems gradually played larger roles in how livelihoods were earned, risk was managed, and understandings of the world were formed.

Yet market exchange – probably the centrepiece of all the other developments – depended crucially on another abstract system: a form of law that had two features. First, it was stripped down of its traditional elements and depersonalized so that all those entering into market transactions with strangers could be confident that it would apply to all persons in a like situation (Habermas, 1996, p. 83). Second, it enjoyed high and reliable levels of enforceability.

The interdependence between successful markets and effective law, in turn, presupposed a certain kind of state: strong, clean and capable enough to provide the legal certainty and the many other public goods without which markets could not function

(Wolf, 2005, pp. 61–4); yet restrained enough to ensure that it would not be predatory. After all, many other parts of the world had come at least as close as post-eighteenth-century European countries to take off into market relations, only to have the power-holders of the moment smother economic development through fear or greed (Hall, 1985).

Parts of Europe found this balanced trajectory in their own traditions of limited government. Given limits on their coercive power to extract resources, many European states could only tax and legislate by consent. With the development of market relations, those states had to include new wealth producers in the means of securing consent for taxation if they were not to be under-resourced relative to the societies they governed. This meant widening the right to vote for representative bodies.

Although by no means everyone at the time conceived such extensions of representative institutions as steps towards full democratization, they gained momentum in that direction by meeting a further challenge in adapting to modernity. As just seen, the forms of law required by modernity presuppose uniformly high levels of enforcement. In sophisticated societies whose members are often able to thwart public authority at little cost to themselves, uniform enforcement is, in turn, unlikely without legitimacy. Yet, because modern laws seek to regulate new kinds of relationship, their makers cannot easily rely on what has historically been one of the main sources of legitimate rule-making, namely tradition. Following Habermas (1996) we might say that the decisive advantage of using democratic institutions to regulate modern, post-traditional, societies lies in the simplicity with which they solve the challenge of how to make compulsory rules legitimate: they allow individuals to see themselves as authoring their own laws through representatives.

Also important, however, in promoting conditions for the earliest development of mass democratic politics in Europe was the external dimension of the state: that is to say, the character of the European state system and not just of its individual states. Interstate competition in Europe had long limited how far states could dominate their own peoples without losing some of the most talented and resourceful sections of society to their rivals (Hall, 1985). Then, from the end of the eighteenth century, success in war and steps towards democratization became intertwined. Philip Bobbitt takes up the story. Revolutionary France 'democratized' war by blending the mobilizing ideals of *peuple* and *patrie* together to raise larger armies than those typical of European states before 1789 (2002, p. 152). As other European states sought to raise similarly large armies over the next one and a half centuries they were forced, once again, to seek the more active cooperation of wider sections of society. Moreover, publics conscripted into mass armies, and societies bound more closely together into 'communities of fate' by patterns of 'total war' that eroded differences in the dangers faced by combatants and non-combatants, were more likely to develop those feelings of solidarity needed for democratic politics. Thus, paradoxically in the light of much contemporary thinking, democracy was not an antidote to war in the sweep of European history, but both parent and child of it (see also Dahl, 1989, p. 247; Therborn, 1977).

In sum, then, liberal democracy prospered on a virtuous circle of beliefs originating in the European enlightenment, of developing yet legally defined markets, of capable yet restrained states, of interstate competition and even of war itself. At one level it prospered because it was functional: it helped adapt relations between state, society and economy to modernity so that each could strengthen the other in a symbiotic relationship. At a second level it benefited from power relations within and beyond the state which, we will emphasize in a moment, were particular in their nature, combination and sequencing. At a third level it developed a canon of political thought that supported the view that democracy was a rightful source of political power whilst powerfully undermining the claims of all alternatives.

Yet the complacency of the image should not hide the fact that the virtuous circle was easily and often broken. As Eric Hobsbawm relates the story of the interwar period:

> In 1918–1920 legislative assemblies were dissolved or became ineffective in two European states, in the 1920s in six, in the 1930s in nine, while German occupation destroyed constitutional power in another five during the Second World War. In short the only European countries with adequately democratic institutions that functioned without a break during the entire inter-war period were Britain, Finland (only just), the Irish Free State, Sweden and Switzerland. (Hobsbawm, 1994, p. 111)

It follows that whatever its deeper roots in modernity, democracy was only stabilized in the new Europe after 1945: first, in the north and the west; then, in the 1970s, in the south; and, then, in the centre and the east from the period 1989–91. Crucially each of these waves underscored just how far democracy in Europe has long depended on a supportive pattern of international relations. Debates between those who believe that after 1945 European democracy was saved from without by the protective blanket thrown about it by the United States under the pressure of the Cold War and those who claim it was saved from within by European integration and the resources it created for a new social compromise based on welfare states miss how far those two processes depended on one another (Lord, 1995). No less misguided are those who feel a need to debate whether democracy was extended to the centre and the east of the continent by the success of the West in winning the Cold War or by the new dynamic given to European integration from the mid-1980s. Once again a bit of both has to be the only sensible answer: a new freedom to choose democracy with the vanishing of the Soviet threat to intervene by force to sustain communist regimes (the 'Brezhnev Doctrine') and a process of European integration that was sufficiently attractive for threats of exclusion from its benefits to be a deterrent to non-democratic politics both played their part in post-1989 democratic transitions in East and Central Europe, as we will see in Chapter 5.

Democracy and the state

We said in the last section that liberal democracy built on pre-democratic political forms. In this section we show how it matters that it was the nation-state that became the vessel for democracy throughout Europe, even though the political systems of the region range from those that approximate ideal types of both statehood and nationhood to those that are problematic on both counts.

The state is classically defined as an administrative hierarchy that uses a monopoly of legitimate violence to apply a uniform body of law to a defined territory. It can coerce us to do what we would sooner not do. But, unlike other coercive bodies – a gang, a racket or a mafia – a state is capable of legitimacy, or, in other words, of having an acknowledged right to exercise its power that is so persuasive that we, as citizens, have an obligation to obey it. Indeed, the rules of other bodies that structure our lives give way to those of the state in the event of conflict between the two. On account of this ultimate power to regulate all other relationships in society, we describe the state as 'sovereign' (Beetham, 1991). Since, moreover, individual states belong to a system of states, the laws we follow are normally uniform right up to the boundaries of some precisely demarcated territory, at which point our state ends and another begins.

By what peculiar alchemy is the state thought to have made it possible to apply democracy to mass society? In this section we consider how the aforementioned attributes of statehood – sovereignty, defined territoriality and administrative hierarchy – helped transform democracy from a decision-rule used by small communities to a system of government employed by mass societies. In the next section we then show how quite apart from any role played by its own characteristics the state delivered other preconditions for mass democracy through its relationship to nationhood.

Sovereignty

European historical experience shows that the sovereign character of the state can be harnessed in at least four ways to the development of democratic politics.

First, state sovereignty can provide a means of realizing popular sovereignty: a government elected by the people can pass laws with the approval of a legislature representative of the people that ultimately override other sources of organized power, bureaucratic, judicial or economic.

Second, the state can help stabilize the rights needed for democracy (Walzer, 1983). The state can make rights 'positive' (that is, effective) by giving them the force of law, and it can locate them in a defined group of 'mutual identifiers' who are prepared to accord rights to one another. Habermas's view that the popular will and individual rights are 'co-constructive' of democracy (1996) implies that the role of state sovereignty in giving the force of law to individual rights needed for democratic politics (freedoms of speech and assembly) is as important as its role in giving the force of law to measures passed by representatives of the people as a whole.

Third, the sovereign nature of the state can help motivate mass democracy. The sovereignty of the state over other relationships in society means those representing different values and interests have an acute interest in ensuring they are at least as well organized as their rivals in relation to any democratic process that allocates power within the state. This competitive logic motivates them to encourage the participation in elections of their supporters, and to organize their appeal in a manner that simplifies and coordinates choice for citizens who are otherwise unknown to one another. Indeed voter participation is motivated by some combination of the 'high stakes' nature of state politics and a sense of 'civic obligation' that goes with feelings of national identity.

Fourth, the state can nurture the capabilities needed for democratic rule. Most would agree that these include basic capacities of citizenship such as a minimal level of understanding of the political system (March and Olsen, 1995). According, however, to the social democratic critique of liberal democracy, equal and effective participation also requires that all citizens have access to minimum standards of economic and social welfare (Beetham, 1993). Thus the role of the European state in fashioning democratic citizenship may have been mediated through welfare provision and social security, as much as through civic education and social capital formation.

Hierarchy

The hierarchical character of the state lends itself to the delivery of one of the two defining attributes of democracy. To the extent that the state is hierarchical in nature the people or their representatives can secure public control through the simple and straightforward act of electing a political leadership to head up the state administration. The elected political leadership can be meaningfully held responsible for all acts of the administration on the assumption that, whatever the day-to-day patterns of delegation, they can always be changed at the behest of the centre. In anticipation of its own prospects of reelection, the elected political leadership will also be in a position to order the bureaucracy to align policy with its own assessments of public opinion. Under albeit idealized conditions of rational expectations, perfect competition in the political system and normally distributed one-dimensional preferences, this will encourage a significant alignment of public policy with the views of the median voter (Powell, 2000).

Territoriality and Congruity

Democracy assumes a 'symmetrical' or 'congruent' relationship between ruler and ruled (Held, 1991, pp. 198–9; Patomäki, 2003). Where a system of rule does not include as equals all those whose lives it affects deeply, the excluded will experience it as a form of domination, even if it is hugely successful in delivering democratic ideals to its full members. Where, on the other hand, voting rights are accorded to those who are not obliged to follow the laws of the political unit, the 'median citizen preference' by which power is controlled and policy guided in a well-functioning democracy (see Chapter 1) will, arguably, be distorted by the very unrepresentativeness of those who are able to participate without any concern for the consequences of their choices. Once again, the state has historically offered a simple solution: many of its decisions apply uniformly and impartially to a defined territory.

Democracy and the nation state

Every democracy needs agreement on who are the people. Otherwise there is no way of defining to the satisfaction of all who should be included or excluded from democratic practices such as voting and deliberation. Many European states have answered the question 'who are the people?' through their relationship with nationhood. Although the aim of this book is to understand how democracy can be practised beyond the frame of national identity, we need to understand how and why nation, demos and democracy came to be so closely bound together in Europe's past.

The universality of nationalism and the particularity of the nation

In considering the interplay between identity, state formation and demos formation we have to concede that: (a) the nation state is often seen as the most successful form of community in the modern world (Bauman, 1999); (b) no matter how much we may reject the idea that the nation state should be the main framework for democracy, solidarity and sovereignty, it is still difficult to think about political community outside the frame of the nation state (Debeljak, 2003, p. 156); and (c) nationalism, of a sometimes violent kind, has often been the basis for the construction of a community with a sense of being a national community. The events since the end of the Cold War have surely removed any trace of doubt that identity in our world could be apolitical. The Yugoslav conflict, East Timor, • Rwanda, Israel–Palestine, September 11 and the current debate on the EU Constitution illustrate that nationalism is not easily rivalled when it comes to arousing popular passions.

The basic message of nationalism is that belonging to a nation, its existence and its survival are of supreme importance to its members and the rights they share as members of humanity (Harris, 2002, p. 51). Even where, as is usually the case, one's life is largely influenced by more immediate groupings and relationships of family, gender, profession status or religion, 'the nation' is often considered an important source of personal identity (Miller, 1995, p. 82). The world is divided into nation states. Hence, 'the nation' plays the distinctive role of situating the individual in the world or humanity and, moreover, it exercises a considerable influence over one's opportunities and choices in life, if not, at times, over life itself.

The first claim of nationalism is that the cultural and historical distinctiveness of a nation entitles it to existence as a separate territorial and political entity. Thus, nationalism must be viewed as an action-orientated programme, 'designed to render the boundaries of the nation congruent with those of its governance unit' (Hechter, 2000, p. 7). The paradoxical observation that 'particularity is a potent universality' (Hardt and Negri, 2000, p. 105) underscores how the universal appeal of nationalism lies in the particularity of each nation. The specificity of each nation lies in the emotional investment that it can extract from its members and in the solidarity that it can inspire. Like other communities, nations are often bundles of other commonalities. Yet each nation is distinctive in how it blends objective and subjective commonalities – territory, language, history, economy, politics and culture – into collective consciousness (Hroch, 1993,

p. 4). The reflection of the objective in collective consciousness alone would not be able to sustain the myth of continuity and durability necessary for the financial and emotional investment into 'the nation' that states have often had to rely on for their survival.

The second claim of nationalism is to be able to speak for a national group. Demands may vary in content, gravity and urgency, but the claim is always in the name of justice (redressed or not yet addressed) and the 'right of the people'. The general aim is that 'the people' be in charge of their collective destiny. 'In charge' means government by its own people, either in its own state or through a substantial degree of autonomy within a state. The key to a proper understanding of nationalism's appeal must be sought in this democratic thrust. Once out of the hands of philosophers, poets and collectors of local customs and in those of political leaders nationalism becomes a much-used tool for attaining and preserving political legitimacy.

The nation as we know it – as the locus of sovereignty – is a relatively modern construction. Throughout the sixteenth and seventeenth centuries the endless wars between the states of the day produced a need for international law rooted in the sovereignty of states. Yet the legal concept of the state which emerged from the Peace of Westphalia (1648) pre-dates nations as political entities. Only later was the nation perceived as the subject of sovereignty as new relationships between ruled and rulers were sought as an answer to the breakdown of traditional societies and new ideas of Enlightenment in the eighteenth century. Only later still was the political organization of the state wedded to the spiritual meaning of the nation; from then on, the Westphalian state was much more than a territory and a polity. It was also invested with the principles of popular sovereignty and self-determination, thus creating a nation state. A prefix 'nation' endows the state with a further quality. It implies that 'the people' who are the 'participants in constituting and maintaining the state' (Migdal, 2004) are united in their allegiance to the pursuit of common goals based on shared cultural understanding.

To political thinkers such as Mill, the nation state and its cultural homogeneity were a precondition for democracy, well demonstrated by the claim that members of the same nationality (for example, language and literature) should be united under the same government, 'and a government to themselves apart'. Indeed, Mill believed 'that free institutions are next to impossible in a country made up of different nationalities' (1972 [1861], p. 361). The particularistic claims of national communities and universalistic principle of democracy have sustained nationalism and its main historical achievement – the modern nation state. The claim, however, was always ideal. Countries were more often than not made up of different nationalities, not states 'for and of one nation', but rather 'non-nation-states' (Brubaker, 1996, and Migdal, 2004 respectively) that included other national groups. Democracy too has struggled with competing notions of 'the people'. More than one hundred years after Mill, we are still preoccupied with the same challenges of understanding how the nation state, democracy, cultural diversity and self-determination can and should interact. In the paragraphs that follow we trace the sometimes reinforcing, sometimes contradictory relationship between democracy and nationalism as they emerged as dominant ideologies.

Making history: from the local ethnic community to 'the nation'

Generating an identity is an integral part of human nature, a psychological necessity, but how this necessity has come to be associated with national identity has to be sought in the role of the nation state. Nations surfaced in modern Europe and America from about the seventeenth–eighteenth century, but their roots go back to a combination of earlier developments. One was the rise of literacy associated with the wider availability of printed material. It would be a long time before localized communities of people who did not move much or come into contact very often with strangers would be capable of imagining themselves as bound to those strangers through historical and cultural ties. When that change did come, it was with the help of literacy and a community of language that allowed the nation to be 'imagined' into existence (Anderson, 1983). The technological advances, the spread of commerce and the militaristic expansion of states throughout the seventeenth century accelerated the shift from local and at most regional ethnic community to a nation.

Michael Mann identifies three phases in this process: militarist, industrial and modernist (Mann, 1995, p. 46), stretching through the eighteenth to the twentieth century and all of which affected the character of nations, their size and their nationalism. The British and the French nations were almost coterminous with their state so that the idea of the nation reinforced the state. The nations within the federal Austrian, Ottoman and Russian empires had to subvert existing states in order to become states of their own. There was also a third kind of nation. The German and Italian nations were also founded on an ethnic principle, but, instead of needing to extricate themselves from a larger whole, they created themselves through the unification of small states and principalities into which they were initially splintered. Such differences in the processes by which Europe's nations were formed, do not, however, justify the over-employed yet misguided assumption in the study of nationalism that civic nations are to be found in the West of Europe and ethnic ones in the East (Greenfeld, 1992; Özkirimli, 2000). The evolution of European nations is rather a matter of history, not geography. The emergence of new postcommunist democracies in Eastern Europe demonstrated that civic and ethnic features are typically mixed in the construction of a nation state (Harris, 2003).

With states came taxes, administration, public office and armies, and with armies came conscription and stories of conquests and defeats, more centralization and more mobilization of popular sentiments. At the same time, language assumed a major importance. This was the time of the codification of languages – some of the official Central and Eastern European languages date precisely from that time – prior to which people spoke only local dialects or the language of the ruling aristocracy. Sometimes language became the instrument of revolt – as in the case of the 1848 revolutionaries who claimed that it was their language that stopped them getting the top jobs in public service. Yet as European states asserted a monopoly of education, the teaching of codified languages through a universal school system became the means by which nation and state were coupled together.

Thus, the picture of cultural identity entering the political arena, aided by technological, commercial, military and state expansion, emerged more clearly throughout nineteenth-century Europe. The process was unplanned and almost unnoticed, but with it came a series of new meanings. Nations were felt by their members to be political communities with a right to govern themselves, and where that right was, in turn, acknowledged by outsiders it brought a right to participate in the 'great drama of history' (Berlin, 1972, p. 19). So, the principle of nationalism entered international relations and altered international law.

If circumstances required it, the nation could tolerate armed conflict in its defence, because 'peace', wrote the founding thinker of the sovereign nation, Jean-Jacques Rousseau can be 'incompatible with freedom' and 'one must choose' (Rousseau, in 'The Government of Poland' [1771], cited in Benner, 2001, p. 168). Yet it is important to reiterate that the abuse of nationalism through terror, genocide, war and expulsion was not as prominent in the nineteenth century as disastrous consequences stemming from the disregard of national movements or hostility towards them. Had the democratic intentions of early nationalists been rewarded at least with the federalization of states – where there were obstacles to the creation of single states – modern history would probably look very different.

Political and cultural nation in search of one another

The Declaration of the Rights of Man drafted by the French National Assembly to mark the first anniversary of the Revolution opens with the words: 'the principle of sovereignty resides essentially in the Nation. No body, no individual can exercise any authority which does not explicitly emanate from it' (Declaration of the Rights of Man, 1790).

No amount of cultural heritage could have ever given 'the nation' its authority and legitimacy had it not been invested with the idea so memorably expressed through the Declaration of the Rights of Man that it is through a nation that a people can rule itself (Connor, 1972). The idea of the democratic nation is rooted in the Enlightenment and, particularly, the ideas of Rousseau. Despite academic consensus that modern usage of the word 'nation' derives from Rousseau, his thinking is better considered as the main influence on one stream in the political ideology of the nation – the democratic and political conception of 'nation'. In fact his major contribution in conceptualizing democracy as a community of participating citizens with equal rights could apply to any form of human association, not just one based on cultural commonalities (Greenfeld, 1992, p. 7). Yet because shared culture – for all its untidiness – happened to be the main basis for human organization at the time, the idea of a community of equal citizens united in a struggle for political rights was taken to be equivalent to a doctrine of national self-determination that bestows on each self-differentiating people a right to rule itself (Connor, 1972).

The people: demos or ethnos?

All political ideologies claim to speak in the name of 'the people', but none as persuasively as nationalism and democracy. This has earned them a pivotal place among ideologies of modernity. Yet in spite of their historical and ideological congruence, there is a constant tension between them. This paradox can be partly resolved by pointing out that nationalism and democracy just address different aspects of rule by the people (Harris, 2002). Whilst nationalism provides one possible answer to 'who' the people are, democracy is less concerned with the addressee and more with delivery: less with who the people are than with the 'political principles' of 'participation, inclusion and political equality' needed to achieve a 'just rule' of the people by them-selves. A core difficulty, however, is that nationhood and democracy cannot avoid all possible tensions by each, as it were, concentrating on its own contribution to rule by the people. Either may come into conflict with the other by doing what is expected of it. The following paragraphs explain.

To summarize so far, any exercise of democracy requires a prior legitimate political unit, because neither competition nor cooperation can take place without a clear definition of who is in the game and where the physical boundaries of the 'playing field' (Schmitter, 1994, p. 65) are. In modern times, the predominant principle for defining boundaries – and who the 'players' (people) are – has been 'nationality'. Thus discussions about who and what constitute the nation have preoccupied democratization processes, and a world of increased democratic ambitions has also been one in which national questions loom large.

Indeed international politics often assumes that political rights to democratic self-rule are vested in nations. But there are at least two interpretations to how the national unit is defined. The 'nation' can be an aggregation of citizens in the state, united by the attachment to that state and the legitimacy of their regime (demos), or the 'nation' can claim to be a political expression of an ethnic group (ethnos). In the latter case the ethnic group can be the dominant nationality of the state, or it may be a minority. The establishment of states, the prevalence of either 'ethnic' or 'civic' principles for the definition of the 'nation', is characterized by a degree of historical contingency and open to interpretation, to which democratic theory offers no solution.

National self-determination is a principle that holds that any self-differentiating people has the right to rule itself (Connor, 1972, p. 331) and thus can make ethnicity the ultimate measure of political legitimacy. The overlap between 'demos' (the polity) and 'ethnos' may, however, be incomplete. It can and usually does leave some residual people out of what is considered 'the nation'. Fundamental to democracy are equal political rights guaranteed by citizenship, yet the organizing principle of ethnicity can prevent some members of the polity from inclusion (for example, Palestinians in occupied territories in Israel, immigrants everywhere) in the citizenship and decision-making rights of their country of residence. Even where citizenship is awarded it may not guarantee full inclusion and participation without equal social and economic conditions and protection from discrimination. It does not require too much imagination to see that democratic principles may be lacking where nationalist principles decide who the citizens are.

Thus, legitimacy of the nation state has always been entangled with two principles whose long-term compatibility is doubtful: a civic principle of democracy and an ethnic/national principle of self-determination. Yet a couple of points are worth making. First, all kinds of nationalism may offer a solution to the problem of defining the membership of a democracy, but civic nationalism is inherently closer than ethnic nationalism to democracy's own civic principles of equality and inclusion. Second, the enduring appeal of nationalism, its role in politics and international relations and its compatibility with democracy are very different issues that need to be distinguished in understanding and overcoming its negative side.

Political unity and cultural diversity

The foregoing difficulties in reconciling the two components of rule by the people – the felt right of each people to rule itself and the need for reasons of democratic principle to include even those who are not members of a particular people on a basis of equal rights – mean that the question of 'political unity' in its literal sense of defining what should be the units by which we govern ourselves as human beings is often at the centre of political contention.

In tackling this problem it is important to be aware that cultural diversity itself takes diverse forms. David Miller distinguishes three kinds of social divisions: first, ethnic cleavages that condition political competition without members of different groups questioning their continued living together under a shared polity and within a common territory (US Italians); second, rival nationalities which seek to control all or part or the territory of the state to the exclusion of others (Northern Ireland or the rivalry between Serbs and Croats in Bosnia in the 1990s); and, finally, 'nested' nationalities that inhabit territorially distinct parts of the same state, itself seen by many as an additional focus of national identity (Belgium, Spain, the UK) (Miller, 2000, pp. 125–41). This latter and preferable case, according to Miller, is the one where people belong to two communities (a smaller and a larger), but share national identity in the sense that they share common history over a considerable period of time. The point to emphasize is that rivalry does not exclude future cooperation, that social divisions can be overcome. In Miller's terms rival nationalities can become 'nested' ones or just soften into mutually respecting ethnic cleavages with time. Indeed many of today's 'nested' nationalities have been 'rivals' in the past, just as many 'rivals' have reached a point when society has been fractured beyond those categories (as in the Israeli/Palestinian conflict).

So how can units of political rule accommodate diversity? In what follows we argue that any solution has to begin with the state, yet it cannot stop there. It also has to consider alternative ways of guaranteeing diverse cultural identities by dividing the power of the state from within and constraining it from without. Power, despite the much-propagated view that the state has sacrificed its predominance to global economic and political interdependence, is still about significant control of the national state. It is the state that controls the territory and has the supreme authority to impose rules and forms of behaviour, and demand taxes and, in case of war, sacrifice of life. States and nations are linked by a need for mutual reinforcement. On one hand, the national leaders cannot impose any desired behaviour without the significant control of the state which in order to increase or maintain its legitimacy then reinforces the nation. On the other hand, the national culture along with national education and the physical protection of citizens is thought to be best safeguarded within nation states. The relationship between the state and the nation is deeply involved; it rests on a sense of trust, cohesion and common objectives in return for safety and belonging.

Yet, in a world where so many national groups are demanding some form of self-government, Mill's solution that each national grouping should have a 'government to itself' and itself apart cannot always mean that each should have a 'state to itself and itself apart' (Mill, 1972 [1861], p. 361). Thus now, as then, solutions have to include; first, unitary states that govern themselves along multicultural lines by allowing assured rights of representation for each cultural or ethnic segment; second, states that are explicitly federated into their cultural–territorial groupings; and, third, an international dimension that, as a condition of the states system itself, allows minorities guarantees, constrains individual states from denying democratic rights to minorities, and offers them choices of arena so that they can redeem their rights externally as well as internally.

If they are constructed in a way that the one is not threatening to the other, a common identity based on shared institutions can often be sustained in parallel with the diverse and divided identities of many cultures living under the same system of government. Here, we need to distinguish two forms of identity. The first is culturally based identity which suggests that there is something special about a group of people who can be grouped together because they have certain things in common (Mason, 1999), usually expressed in terms of a distinct language, religious practice, or history. The second is polity-based identity, so-called for at least two reasons: first, the polity is a place of residence, and, second, aspects of the polity may in and of themselves inspire identity. The latter notion, polity-based identity, does not mean that one identifies with all aspects of it, and with every other member of the polity. Membership in the polity (citizenship) does not entail an absorption in it, but participation, compliance with its rules, cooperation and commitment to its institutions. Here, paradoxically, liberals, democrats and nationalists all tend to share the same fear that citizenship, thus described, is too 'cold' and abstract to bind the community together in a more meaningful way (Harris, 2003).

Being a part of a polity may indeed not be enough on its own to satisfy the more subjective elements of belonging, but does not exclude cooperation and political willingness. By the same token a passionate sense of identification with one's nation may bring about a sense of disenchantment with its current form and institutions. (Eurosceptics mention the loss of national identity and national sovereignty as the main argument against the EU.) The pragmatism and the willingness to compromise in order to direct the common fate in the best possible direction can be preferable to culturally based identity which is prone to block compromise in the face of conflicting interests. At the heart of polity-based unity is the accommodation of conflicting interests, whatever their nature, whilst unity based on cultural homogeneity is not a guarantee of either political unity or political cooperation (Harris, 2003). It is a mark of our times that the doctrine of national self-determination, for all its emancipatory credentials, has become a challenge not merely to the integrity of states, but to democracy itself. Democratic solutions are not easily found where the very principle of the accommodation of cultural diversity sought through constitutional arrangements (whether multicultural, federal, confederal, consociational or a combination of those) is viewed as a denial of democratic principles.

Nation-building and non-nation state

The true controversy of the relationship between democracy and cultural diversity is rather banal and lies in the obvious: most states comprise more than one national group and thus are 'non-nation states' (Migdal, 2004). Nevertheless, in nearly all cases one national group has the preeminent authority to assume the dominant position in the distribution of rewards and cultural values and is, as it were, the most favoured ethnic group. Others become minorities (with the exception of a few, for example, in Belgium or Switzerland) and thus national/ethnic groups which define themselves, or are defined as a separate cultural entity from the official culture of the state. Related to these definitions is the distinction between 'nation-building' and 'state-building'. The former denotes policies rooted in the deliberate effort to construct an overarching collective identity aiming at cultural homogeneity based on a putative common sentiment (mostly ethnic); the latter stands for a complementary project, but aims at social solidarity rooted in loyalty to the state, its institutions and its interests. Historically, those two processes tended to be coterminous – both seeking to cement the loyalty to the state which then in return protected the nation.

This ideal type of state-building has hardly ever existed; rather, national historians, scholars and national leaders colluded in the myth of the nation state, where national unity and state legitimacy formed the political organization of modernity. The fact that the nation state has been a successful formation, hence assumed to be the best available, should not lead us to believe that nation-building and state-building are necessarily compatible processes, even if they are historically and politically overlapping. The former pertains rather to nationalism, the latter to democracy.

It is significant that in international discourse these two processes are too often conflated and post-conflict reconstruction efforts are often referred to as nation-building when it would be much more appropriate to speak of state-building – that is, the restoration of social solidarity around the institutions of the state, preferably a democratic one. Obviously, the clash between the administrative and the political thrust of statebuilding and the cultural preoccupation of nation-building is less relevant if there is a congruence between the polity and the cultural nation. It is equally obvious that in the contemporary world, ethnic homogeneity is less and less possible to achieve – if it ever was.

The recent history of postcommunism in Europe offers many examples of the difficult balancing of nation- and state-building and of the consequences this may have for democratization. Multiethnic states can experience tensions or even conflict where state-building is seen to require a high level of social and cultural homogeneity, or where the dominant nation and its nationbuilding elites assume that the state is their own nation state to the exclusion of other cultures from ownership of the state. Too much emphasis on nation-building tends to inhibit internal integration of national groups within the state and aggravate the relationship between majority and minorities. Indeed, the experience of the most recent wave of transitions from postcommunism to democracy in Eastern and Central Europe suggests that the preservation of a democratic regime is arguably more difficult than its establishment, precisely because the premise of a just rule means different things to different people who all expect their interests to be served adequately by democratic rule. Thus, the compatibility of the two processes depends on many variables: political competition and whether elites conceive the state as belonging to a dominant nation; the historical legacy of interrelationships between national groups; regional politics where ethnic groups straddle one or more neighbouring states (for example, Eastern/Central Europe, Central Asian ex-Soviet republics); and other contingencies in international relations.

Conclusion

This chapter has shown that the state had a clear role in developing mass democracy in Europe. In part, this was on account of attributes of the state itself: defined territoriality, administrative hierarchy and state sovereignty respectively helped democracy deliver congruity between representatives and the represented, public control and a means of making the people sovereign. Yet, the state also made mass democracy possible through its relationship with nationhood, which provided a conveniently pre-political solution to the one question that needs to be settled by any democracy, but which, logically, cannot be answered by any one democratic procedure, since acceptance of the latter presupposes prior settlement of the very issue that needs to be decided: namely, who are the people and who, therefore, should be included and who excluded from any one democracy?

In giving so much attention to the relationship between identity and democracy within the state we have, however, already begun to uncover a disquieting problem that suggests the insufficiency of democracy within the state and argues for its transformation to include frameworks beyond the state. The importance of national identity, it has been argued, lies in culture, in language and a 'story'. The problem is that when the cultural 'story' becomes the foundation of political identity in the form of the nation state it tends to limit not only our moral obligation to others outside the state (we will return to this in Chapter 7), but also our scope for political solutions that accommodate the cultural diversity to be found within so many European states. The 'holy' trinity of the nation, state and territory (Bauman, 2003) has evidently produced some unholy conflicts and has repeatedly failed to deliver a lasting reconciliation between culturally diverse groups within the nation state. If we accept that the European (non)nation state is assuming an ideologically less homogenizing character, then both national identity and democracy need to change too. It is questionable how far either can endorse the narrow project of the nation state only. Both are under pressure to adapt to more versatile notions of community.

Indeed there may be wider reasons why democracy, if it is to answer the demands of our time, needs to be 'rescued' from the confines of the nation state (Habermas, 1992, 2001a). The trio of democracy, nation and state have clearly been profoundly changed by their mutual confrontation, but the case of the new Europe suggests that the era in which each element largely stabilized the other two, without a need for further forms of human organization, may now be drawing to an end. This is an argument to which we will return in the last three chapters of the book. First, we extend our investigation into democracy within the state by comparing the varieties of democratic political system that have developed at national level (Chapter 3). We also develop our own detailed interpretation of current practices of democracy beyond the state (Chapters 4 and 5).

Varieties of Democracy Within the State

In the last chapter we saw how states have provided the institutions of democratic rule and how nations have often provided the requisite sense of political community. If, however, politics within the state is the starting point for understanding democracy in Europe, it is important to note how varied are European states in their practice of democracy. Indeed we will show in the conclusion to this chapter that a further reason for wanting to investigate diversity in the meaning and practice of democracy at state level is that it presents a philosophical challenge for both aspects of democracy beyond the state we explore elsewhere in the book. Before turning to that discussion this chapter introduces various ways of comparing and contrasting European democracies at national level. These include the degree of direct democracy, presidential versus parliamentary forms of representation, consensus versus majoritarian democracy, and, overlapping with that last distinction, the proportionality of electoral systems. We also discuss the extent to which democracy has been constitutionalized in different national arenas and variations in the provision they make for local and regional democracy 'beneath the state'. Throughout we attempt only a summary analysis of salient patterns, though, hopefully, with sufficient references to other sources for the interested reader to find out more.

Direct and indirect democracy

Although mass representative structures – elections, parties, parliaments or elected chief executives – dominate the democratic politics of all states in the new Europe, all democratic systems depend on a continuous and lively interaction between representatives and represented (Beetham, 2005, p. 7). Thus most European countries allow some role for more direct forms of citizen participation through stakeholder networks, 'big conversations', citizens' juries, deliberative opinion polling, and, of course, referendums. The latter are used most in Switzerland and Italy, which allow citizens to take the initiative by petitioning for referendums of their own choosing (Gallagher, 1992, p. 231; Gallaher, 1976). Yet even in Switzerland only about 7 per cent of legislation is contested by referendum (Trechsel and Kriesi, 1996, p. 191). Thus it is to different ways of structuring representative institutions that we must look for our main understanding of the varieties of democracy in the new Europe.

A key difference is between those representative democracies where the executive and legislative branches of government are elected separately and those where the formation of the executive depends on a majority of an elected parliament. In the latter case, both executive and legislature are shaped by the one set of elections, albeit with important variations across states in the directness with which parliamentary elections are linked to government formation.

The most common way of directly electing an executive is to allow the public to choose a president who then designates the other members of a cabinet needed to head up a government. Perhaps the purest form of presidentialism is the United States. Apart from a need to get Senate approval, the US President has complete powers of appointment and dismissal over other leading members of the Administration, and is normally able to exercise those powers in the expectation of being able to continue in office for a fixed four-year term.

Few European countries practise such a strong form of presidentialism. Even allowing for the case of France which is much less presidential than it seems (Bell, 2002), most presidential systems in the new Europe are to be found in the new democracies formed out of the Soviet Union. Yet, amongst those states, only the constitutions of Azerbaijan, Belarus and Georgia allow a government that is designated by an elected president to survive independently of the legislature. In contrast, Russia and Ukraine differ from the US model in the crucial respect that the government of the day has to retain the support of both president and parliament to remain in office. Thus even the addition of many new democracies since 1989 has not invalidated the claim that it is the need for governments to be 'able to survive in the legislature' that makes 'European politics democratic' (Gallagher *et al.*, 1992, p. 28). It is worth noting, though, that several of the new democracies outside the former Soviet Union – Bulgaria, Croatia, Lithuania, Poland and Slovakia – have developed an idiosyncratic form of semi-presidentialism: a near monopoly of parliamentary democracy on government formation is combined with a directly elected president who is able to provide 'swift-responding personalised leadership' (Schleiter and Morgan-Jones, 2005). Given that such hybrids allow for the electoral accountability of both a key individual and whole governing parties, their defenders argue that they are better adjusted than many of the pre-1989 democracies to the contemporary reality that individual leaders may be more important than their parties in setting the direction of governments (ibid.).

If presidential systems in the new Europe are presidential in different ways, parliamentary ones are parliamentary in different ways. The common feature of parliamentary systems is that parliament and government are in some sense 'fused' or 'joined' rather than separated. Yet the nature of the join is by no means uniform across European countries. In some cases, government members are members of parliament and active in much of its work; in others, they are not. In addition, governments may dominate parliaments, parliaments may dominate governments, or the two can form a balanced relationship, or even one that varies with different conditions. Whether a parliament is strong or weak in relation to the government of the day is thought to depend on the following:

- *Powers to make or break governments.* Parliaments will be stronger the more formal powers they have to make or break governments. The frequency with which governments are terminated by parliaments – rather than elections – varies across European countries but remains high in spite of a belief that parliaments are reluctant to preempt the voters (Woldendorp *et al.*, 2000).
- *Party disciplines.* Parliaments are weaker in European countries where political parties have developed strong disciplines that can, in turn, be used to organize and control parliamentary majorities.
- *Type of government.* Parliaments vary from weak to strong as

the typical form of government in their country varies from the first to the last item on the following list: single-party majorities, multi-party majorities, single-party minority administrations, multi-party minority administrations.

- *Opposition participation versus government monopoly.* Parliaments are stronger where procedures allow all representatives – and not just government supporters – to shape outcomes (Powell, 1989, p. 113).
- *Agenda control.* Parliaments are stronger where they can control their own business, and, in particular, the agenda of what should come up for decision and debate, when and in what order (Döring, 1995).
- *Expertise.* Parliaments are stronger where they can develop forms of specialized knowledge needed to hold governments to account. A crucial factor here is how far representatives are able to divide their labours between a well-structured set of parliamentary committees, each of which can cultivate policy skills and institutional memories over time (Budge, Newton *et al.*, 1997, p. 259).
- *Veto points.* Parliaments are stronger the more veto points they introduce to a political system (Tsebelis, 1995, 1999). The number of such points increases with the proportion of legislation and other decisions that requires formal parliamentary approval; with second chambers that are both powerful and elected separately from the governing majority; and with rules that make it easier for parliaments to block constitutional changes promoted by governments.

Scholars have come up with contrasting classifications of the relative strengths of parliaments in different European states depending on the different weights they have given to items on the foregoing list. Thus the first column of Table 3.1 sets out a ranking based on the relative formal powers of parliaments and governments over the appointment and survival of the other. The second column shows, however, that the ranking changes if the parliaments of the new Europe are assessed, instead, by indicators other than constitutional definitions of their powers, including the extent of executive dominance exercised, in practice, through party systems, control of parliaments over their own business, and their own skills and resources. The Scandinavian parliaments move up the rankings, whilst the

TABLE 3.1   *How powerful are Parliaments in different European countries?*

	Formal measure of powers	Informal measure of powers
Parliament dominates government	Germany, Hungary, Macedonia	Denmark, Iceland, Ireland, Latvia, Luxembourg, Norway, Sweden
Balanced	Austria, Bulgaria, Czech Rep, Denmark, Estonia, Greece, Latvia, Luxembourg, Malta, Netherlands, Norway, Poland, Portugal, Romania, Russian Fed, Slovakia, Slovenia, Spain, Switzerland	Austria, Italy, Belgium, Czech Rep, Finland, Germany, Macedonia, Poland, Portugal, Slovenia, Switzerland
Government dominates parliament	Belgium, Finland, France, Ireland, Lithuania, France, Sweden,Turkey, UK	Azerbaijan, Bulgaria, Croatia, Georgia, Greece, Hungary, Lithuania, Malta, Moldova, Romania, Russian Fed, Serbia, Slovakia, Spain, Turkey, UK, Ukraine

Sources: For formal measure, Pennings (2000), p. 7; for informal measures, Doring (1995); Budge and Newton *et al.* (1997), p. 253.

German and several Central and East European parliaments move down a category (or two in the case of Hungary). Overall, fewer parliaments seem to enjoy a balanced relationship with their governments than a formal reading of constitutional allocations of powers would suggest.

Majoritarian or consensus?

Overlapping with foregoing variations – presidential versus parliamentary systems and strong versus weak parliaments – is the question of whether countries are majoritarian or consensus democracies. Majority decision-making works best in societies that are so homogeneous that even those who do not vote for the majority feel that it is likely to serve their own needs and values (Lijpart, 1984, p. 22). In contrast, consensus solutions – that aim at securing the agreement of the greatest possible number, rather than a bare majority (ibid., p. 23) – may be the only way of securing acceptance for collectively binding decisions in deeply divided societies. They may also be useful where a multidimensional pattern of political competition creates risks of 'cycling', or, in other words, where almost any outcome can obtain majority approval, depending on who has control of the agenda (McKelvey, 1976). Rules that require a high level of consensus in the setting of procedures or the taking of decisions help reduce the indeterminacies of outcome and the manipulation of process (Riker, 1982) to which such systems are prone.

Lijphart (1984, pp. 23–30) defines a system as a 'consensus democracy' in so far as it has the following 'majority restraining' devices:

1. Governments whose cabinets are made up of oversized majorities, that is, they include more than the minimum coalition of parties needed to secure power.
2. Sufficient separation of powers between the executive and the legislature to avoid any automatic domination of the one by a majority of the other.
3. Multi-party systems in which no one party has any prospect of forming a majority on its own.
4. Multidimensional party systems in which any cluster of parties that may form a majority on one dimension is unlikely to do so on another.
5. Proportional representation.
6. A bicameral legislature that balances key powers between the two chambers and uses one chamber to give assured representation to minorities.
7. Federalism and other forms of decentralization that often require majorities formed at any one level of a political

system to cooperate with majorities of a different persuasion at other levels.
8. Inflexible constitutions, that is, rules for changing constitutions that require a high level of agreement and/or the consent of minorities.

Lijphart goes on to note that political systems typically cluster into three groups: those that do or do not have the first five features on the above list (dimension 1); those that do or do not have the last three features (dimension 2) (198a, p. 219); and those that are consensual on neither dimension. This helps bring out some interesting subtleties in how the two approaches to democracy are mixed and matched across the region. Germany is majoritarian on dimension 2 but consensual on dimension 1. Its governments are typically minimum coalitions that are able to dominate at least one legislative chamber through well-disciplined parties. Yet it is also federal and strongly bicameral. Conversely Denmark is an example of how a democracy can be consensual on dimension 1 but majoritarian on dimension 2. Its governments are often minorities that have little prospect of dominating the legislature. Yet it is also one of the most centralized political systems in the new Europe. The clear outlier, however, is the United Kingdom which has historically gone even beyond majoritarianism to allow a single party representing what is usually – but even then not always that – the largest minority to take most of the power that matters in the political system on the basis of one set of national elections.

One of the foregoing indicators of consensus democracy – electoral systems that ensure proportionality between votes cast and representation received – touches on a distinction so fundamental as to merit separate attention. Albert Weale (1999, pp. 29–34) distinguishes between systems whose priority is to 'mirror' society by allocating seats in a representative body in proportion to votes cast by citizens and those whose priorities are accountable government and a direct link between voting in elections and the choice or dismissal of governments. By allocating *dis*proportional representation to the parties with the most votes, the latter accept that democratic institutions will be an imperfect reflection of those who vote for them, but they also reduce the role of bargaining between representatives themselves in government formation, sometimes, as is the case with the

Westminster system, to the point at which almost all governments are chosen directly by voters.

Indeed, disproportional representation may sharpen accountability in two ways: first, it reduces the chances of parties that have been at the core of unpopular governments being sustained in office by a mere renegotiation of governing coalitions; and, second, it magnifies the effects of any sanctioning of governments by their electorates. Whereas in strictly proportional systems parties will only lose representation in proportion to a decline in their vote, in disproportional systems the price of political failure is more savage. For example, in 1997, the British Conservatives lost a half of their seats in the House of Commons, although their share of the popular vote only declined by 11 per cent. A serious case can, therefore, be made for some measure of disproportional representation on the grounds that it may even make it easier for voters to 'throw the rascals out'.

Yet such arrangements also risk anomalies in the allocation of power within political systems. In addition to setting out the electoral systems used by different European states, Table 3.2 uses an index of disproportionality to show how far representation diverged from votes cast in most recent parliamentary elections. Whereas the index is close to or less than 1 per cent in some systems (Austria, the Netherlands, Sweden and Slovenia) it exceeds 10 per cent in others (France, Turkey and the UK).

Democratic constitutionalism

Philip Pettit defines constitutionalism as 'legally established ways of restraining the powerful' (Pettit, 1996, p. 173) and as an attempt to make political power 'non-manipulable'. He then goes on to argue that political systems will be constitutional in proportion to how far they are:

(a) are based on the 'rule of law' (here Pettit reminds us how the seventeenth-century thinker, James Harrington (1992), contrasted the consistency of the 'rule of law' with the capriciousness of the 'rule of men')

(b) disperse power so that it cannot be exercised by one individual or group

TABLE 3.2   *Electoral Systems in 42 European states*

	Electoral system	Index of disproportionality
Albania	AM with 2.5% threshold for lists	26.7
Armenia	AM with 5% threshold for lists	4.3
Austria	PR with 4% threshold	1.05
Azerbaijan	AM with 8% threshold for lists	n.d.
Belgium	PR	2.5
Bosnia*	PR with 0.5% threshold	n/a
Bulgaria	PR with 4% threshold	5.2
Croatia	PR with 5% threshold	7.8
Cyprus	PR	0.8
Czech Republic	PR with 5–11% thresholds	4.7
Denmark	PR	0.2
Estonia	PR with 5% threshold	2.7
Finland	PR	2.4
France	Second ballot majority run-off	15.4
Georgia	AM with 5% threshold for lists	5.4
Germany	AM with 5% threshold for lists	3.2
Greece	PR	5.6
Hungary	Mixed member proportional	2.7
Iceland	PR	1.5
Ireland	STV	5.1
Italy	AM with 4% threshold for lists	9.5
Latvia	PR with 5% threshold	4.1
Lithuania	AM	1.0
Luxembourg	PR	1.9
Macedonia	AM with 5% threshold for lists	5.8
Malta	STV	1.6
Moldova	PR with 4% threshold	7.3
Netherlands	PR	1.0
Norway	PR in multi-seat constituencies	1.9
Poland	PR with 5–8% threshold	5.6
Portugal	PR	4.7
Romania	PR with 5% threshold	2.6
Russia	AM with 5% threshold for lists	6.7
Serbia†	AM	9.0
Slovakia	PR with 5% threshold	4.1
Slovenia	PR	0.9
Spain	AM mixed system	4.1
Sweden	PR with 4% threshold	1.0
Switzerland	PR (National Council)	1.5
Turkey	PR	22.5
Ukraine	AM with 4% threshold for lists	6.0
United Kingdom	Simple majority vote	10.8

Notes: AM=Additional Member; PR=Proportional Representation; STV=Single Transferable Vote. Lijphart index of disproportionality, (average vote-share deviation of the two largest parties) calculated for the most recent parliamentary elections in the countries shown. *Bosnia-Herzogovina. †Serbia-Montenegro.

Sources: European Journal of Political Research, Political Data Yearbooks; OSCE/ODIHR election reports

(c)   subject power-holders to 'mutual sanctioning'
(d)   operate on counter-majoritarian principles and
(e)   entrench all the foregoing (Pettit, 1997, pp. 173–232)

Several of these elements overlap with consensus democracy. Yet, as argued in the Introduction, constitutional democracy seeks even to constrain arbitrary domination by those who decide by consensus. For that reason it is worth giving separate consideration to how far the political systems of the new Europe are constitutional democracies. That, in turn, requires us to distinguish two further questions that correspond to contrasting relationships between constitutionalism and democracy. First, how far do the constitutions of European political systems acknowledge and safeguard democratic institutions? Second, how far do they, on the other hand, set limits to what democratic institutions can do?

These questions would take a chapter, if not a book, of their own to answer in full, so, once again, we resort to the device of summarizing information in tabular form, whilst briefly discussing principles, patterns and illustrative cases. Table 3.3 presents a comparative analysis of aspects of constitutional democracy in four states of the new Europe. Column 1 identifies which of them have written constitutions that commit the political system to democracy and column 2 specifies procedures for elections by universal adult suffrage, as well as the powers of representative bodies. Columns 3 and 4 set out which have constitutionalized the rights of the individual and which have constitutional courts. Column 5 analyses constitutional separations of powers. Column 6 summarizes the procedure for changing the constitution. For the sake of space no attempt is made to analyse the constitutionalization of specific functional tasks, such as independent central banking.

Sub-national democracy: varieties of democracy beneath the state

Before we go on in Chapters 6 and 7 to develop our argument that democracy within and beyond the state in the new Europe now depend on one another we need to note that democracy within the state is itself a complex of layers. Many European

TABLE 3.3 Democracy and the constitution in four European states

	1. Democracy	2. Elections	3. Rights	4. Constitutional Court	5. Separation of powers	6. Inflexible constitution? i.e. arrangements for constitutional change
France	'France shall be an indivisible, secular, democratic and social republic' (Article 1)	'Suffrage shall always be universal, equal and secret' (Article 3)	Declares attachment to the Declaration of Rights of Man (1789)	Up to 60 Deputies or 60 Senators can ask Constitutional Court to rule on the conformity of legislation with the Constitution before it is promulgated (Article 61)	N.	60% of both chambers unless put to referendum under Article 11
Poland	'Poland shall be a democratic state' (Article 2)	'Elections shall be universal, equal, direct and proportional, and by secret ballot' (Article 96)	Bill of Rights	Any citizen can ask the Constitutional Tribunal to consider an alleged breach to the Constitution	Judiciary shall be separate and independent and local organs of 'self-government' shall perform functions not reserved to other authorities	Two-thirds majority of Sejm + Absolute majority of Senate

Russia	Russia shall be a democratic rule of law state	Stipulates which offices shall be elected, but not an electoral procedure	Chapter 2 lists rights	Yes. Hears cases on request of President, Duma or Federal Council (Article 125)	Guarantee of independence of local government and of the judiciary	Some Chapters can be amended by two-thirds of a Constitutional Assembly convened on 60% per cent vote of the Duma; others require two-thirds vote of citizens
Turkey	States that no individual or body shall deviate from liberal democracy	Elections for the Grand Assembly shall be every 5 years. But may be deferred by one year in a military emergency	Yes, but with qualifications and provision for suspension	Yes. One-fifth of members of Grand Assembly can request Court to review constitutionality of law. But not if decrees passed in period of emergency, martial law or war	Insecure, the Grand Assembly can authorize the Council of Ministers to make law by decree	60% of members of Grand Assembly, or 50% of votes in a referendum

Note: This table is based on the constitutional texts of the countries covered. Text in quotation marks corresponds sirectly to the original.

states have three or even four levels of elected government, variously divided into local councils/communes, counties/departments, regions and central government. In this section we first consider what subnational forms of government can contribute to democracy and then go on to compare and contrast practices of subnational democracy across the new Europe.

The allocation of significant functions to different levels of elected government connects in at least three ways to the quality of democracy. First, it affects the structure of voter choice. As seen, a common criticism of mass representative politics is its tendency to 'one size fits all' choices. One way of disaggregating choice somewhat is across different levels of government. Where the levels of government vary in their relative responsibility for different types of policy, voters can give different weight to different issues at the different levels, in the expectation that this will have some effect on policy outcomes. The case for such disaggregation is reinforced if the social and economic circumstances of public choice vary geographically across the territory of a democracy. If, for example, town and country, areas of economic advance and decline, or areas with distinctive demographic characteristics such as a disproportionate number of immigrants and retired people have very different needs, it might seem important that democracy should allow them greater scope to choose differently, subject to some need for solidarity between the different parts of the political system.

Second, multi-level governance makes it easier to match identities to institutions. Multi-level systems may alleviate what we have identified as a central predicament of democratic politics by making it easier for those who are not in full agreement on the desired unit of government to coexist nonetheless under a single set of democratic institutions. Minorities can enjoy a measure of 'government to themselves and themselves apart' within systems that otherwise allow culturally heterogeneous populations to act collectively. Although this works best where each part of a territory corresponds to a distinct cultural grouping, European political systems have, under the pressure of ethno-cultural complexity, developed other means of combining separate and shared forms of rule. Even where cultural communities intermingle, it is possible to design democratic systems that assure the representation of each segment or even require them to share power between themselves. Belgium is an interesting example that combines territorial decentralization with inter-communal power-sharing. Although the Flemish and Francophone communities are largely territorially distinct this is not the case in all localities, including several in Brussels itself. The result is that the constitution distributes powers between three territorial units (Flanders, Wallonie and Brussels) and two cross-cutting linguistic communities (the Francophone and the Flemish) with which individuals can register.

Asymmetric decentralization is another solution. Instead of all regions receiving the same powers, culturally distinct regions are given more autonomy than those which identify more straightforwardly with the polity as a whole. Whilst in principle this poses huge problems of congruity – of how to match representatives and represented in democratic decision-making – it has in recent years been one of the foremost developments in the territorial politics of the new Europe. Since the 1980s, Britain (where it is also referred to as 'devolution'), France, Italy, Russia and Spain have all taken significant steps towards asymmetric decentralization.

Third, multi-level arrangements can provide a further means of realizing a constitutional form of democracy. A de-concentration of power so that it cannot be monopolized from any one point in the political system but must, instead, be coordinated between mutually policing levels of government that are elected at different times and in different ways, is an obvious way of blending democracy with the constitutionalist ideal of avoiding domination and arbitrariness. Here Federal systems might be thought preferable to unitary ones, since their defining feature is the constitutional guarantee of regional powers of government, which can only be redesigned with a high level of consensus between the regions themselves. Yet Austria, Belgium, Germany, the Russian Federation and Switzerland are the only strictly federal states in the new Europe, though Spain, in the view of some, qualifies as a quasi-federal system (Linz and Stepan, 1996, pp. 99–115). Before, however, it is concluded from this that subnational democracy is more tolerated than it is cherished and safeguarded in the new Europe, we need to note that the federal/unitary distinction fails to pick up all variations in how powers are distributed across democratically elected levels of government. Amongst other factors are the following.

Are sub-national units of government also cultural units?

Where subnational forms of democracy correspond to culturally distinct units, and especially where they contribute to forms of territorial compromise that reinforce acceptance of the state itself, it may be hard to imagine their powers being redesigned at the whim of the centre even in unitary states.

Who has control over resources?

One key factor here is the proportion of national resources that are spent by central government on the one hand and regional and local governments on the other. Thus whilst Italy is a unitary state it has to be classified as one of the most regionalized political systems in Europe, since, as Robert Putnam points out (1993, p. 25), its regions spend almost as much of national product as the states of the United States of America. Another consideration is how much discretion subnational units have in deciding how they are going to spend money. Even those with deep pockets may find that their resources are soaked up in meeting commitments imposed on them from the centre. Others may find that they depend on grants from the centre that are only agreed on conditions that further narrow policy discretion on the ground. An interesting case here is Denmark, which though notionally one of the most unitary states in Europe, protects local government from dependence on manipulable grants from the centre by channelling the collection of some general taxation through the localities, which retain their agreed shares before passing the remainder on to the centre.

What is the distribution of legislative powers?

Unless there is some delineation of law-making powers between the levels, the policy choices of subnational levels of government may also be pre-empted by legislation passed at the centre. Federal systems usually protect against this possibility in one of two ways: one is to create a competence catalogue that simply reserves different types of policy to different levels of government; the other – often known as cooperative federalism or *Politikverflechtung* – is to allow both levels of government to be active in the same area whilst, first, creating means of coordination and of dealing with conflicts and, second, stipulating rules of preemption that limit one of the levels to what has not already been decided at the other. Most federal systems in Europe follow the latter model (unlike the United States), although this may pose a problem of democratic control where it is difficult for voters to determine which level was responsible for which policy outcomes and easy for elected bodies to offload blame to counterparts at other levels of government. Worth noting, however, is that it is not just in federal systems that elected levels of government beneath the state have significant legislative powers. Scotland is an example of where such powers may even be enjoyed by the devolved regions of unitary states.

How do party structures and other power networks interact with the formal territorial organization of the state?

To set against the foregoing arguments that subnational governments can enrich and improve the democratic quality of a political system are factors that may limit the degree to which democracy is likely to operate autonomously at different levels of the same political system. Power that constitutions intend should be dispersed and divided may be re-concentrated under other hierarchies of power. The foremost example of this was the Soviet Communist Party that, arguably, extended its powers across states, let alone the different levels of the Soviet Union itself. Yet parties and other elite networks can qualify the autonomy of actors at different levels of government even in democratic systems. This interacts with a further phenomenon, that the political behaviour of voters may be connected across the levels of government: rather than treat each as an autonomous arena of political competition and choice, voters may choose to give priority to one arena over another, and to use their vote in what is for them the arena of lesser importance to express a preference or an identity that relates to the other arena. This so-called pattern of second-order voting is thought to condemn European elections to the status of as many national elections as there are member states. But in many countries voting behaviour in local government elections is likewise second-order to that in national elections. Even in a powerfully federal system such as Germany, it is not uncommon for the parties that are most associated with the federal government to lose any majority they may have in the Bundesrat as one *Länder* election after another is used to express discontent with the centre.

Convergence?

So far this chapter has analysed differences between the national democracies of the new Europe along a number of dimensions: direct versus indirect democracy, presidentialism versus parliamentary, consensus versus majoritarian democracy, and the degree and character of constitutionalism and subnational democracy in different states. It may not, however, be enough to catalogue existing differences. We may also be interested in the direction of change. In particular, we may want to know whether the democracies of the new Europe are converging in their characteristics or deepening, and even perfecting, their diversities.

One reason to expect differences between European democracies is that there are strong 'path dependences' in the development of institutions. Meanings, expectations and capabilities get to be shaped by institutional pasts. It, therefore, matters that European countries arrived at democracy in different ways. Some enjoyed steady, linear and 'organic' transitions; others became democratic through revolution or sudden change; and still others only got there through 'stop–go' democratizations characterized by sometimes brutal interruptions. Indeed, European democracies are still coloured by different experiences with pre-democratic statehood. Some were previously constitutional monarchies; others right-wing authoritarian dictatorships; and still others communist states. Some inherited strong states, and others only weak states, from their pre-democratic past. Some, as we have seen, developed as states corresponding to a single and well-defined sense of nationhood, others as multinational communities. Some have been more successful than others in stabilizing democratic rights, in developing social capital, in bringing the state apparatus within a system of public control enforced by popular sovereignty, and so on. A prominent example of how these differences continue to affect the practice of democracy is that those countries with more problematic identities, or deeper internal divisions that extend in some cases to the territorial reach and sovereignty of the state, are more likely to be constrained to use complex institutions of democratic government that put at least as much emphasis on power-sharing as on unconstrained political competition and choice.

Yet there are also factors that may make for convergence between European democracies: learning from one another's successes and failures, common challenges from an external environment, shared membership of international bodies and internationally agreed standards of democratic governance might be amongst them. The following are briefly summarized examples of how the literature has treated the theme of convergence or otherwise in the practice of democracy in the new Europe. Anderson (2002) looks for evidence of whether European democracies have become more majoritarian or consensual over time, and finds none. If, however, one of the most pronounced differences – between majoritarian and consensus systems – scarcely seems to be disappearing at all, other commentators claim that there is a convergence between European countries on more constitutionalised forms of democracy.

Diamond's concept of electoral democracy (2002) offers the particularly interesting prospect of testing whether there has been any convergence between those European countries that were and were not democratic before 1989. In brief, Diamond points to the possibility that even some political systems that satisfy the minimum procedural conditions for democracy do not guarantee the necessary individual liberties or engage with a well-developed civil society capable of structuring effective political competition and constraining the abuse of power. Ten years on, those East and Central European countries that Diamond classified as electoral democracies have gone their somewhat separate ways. Some have made significant progress in guaranteeing individual rights but do not yet have parties that seem to command public confidence as linkages between voters and the political system (see p. 139). Some still seem to be in the predicament Diamond described. Still others would seem to be in danger of falling out of the category of democratic states altogether (see p. 136).

Conclusion

This chapter has demonstrated that European states practise different forms of democracy. Picking up on three distinctions developed in Chapter 1, we have shown, first, that European states may be much the same in being predominantly representative or indirect democracies. But they differ in how far they make occasional use of mechanisms of direct democracy. Second, indirect democracy is itself variously practised. Although none is as presidential as the United States there are several European countries in which representation of the public is divided between a directly elected president and an elected parliament. Even amongst purely parliamentary systems there are variations in how far the executive, once formed, dominates the legislature, or vice versa. Third, the national political systems of the new Europe span a range from strongly majoritarian to pronouncedly consensual democratic practices. Amongst the former are political systems whose priority is not the proportional representation of citizens as much as the effective implementation of the will of the majority – or even of a large minority – as well as the severe punishment of political failure and the maintenance of a direct relationship between voting in elections and the formation of governments. Fourth, European states vary in how far they constitutionalize democracy: that is, to say, in how far the terms of democratic competition and cooperation are 'non-manipulable' by particular groups of actors seeking power within the political system. Cutting across these categories we also noted that European countries vary in how far it is the state, as opposed to subnational forms of government, that is the focus of democratic competition. European states vary quite markedly in how far allocations of value are made at the national or subnational levels; in how far the powers of the latter are entrenched so that they cannot be changed by the former; and in how far voters or those seeking their support differentiate between the two levels in the structuring of democratic choice or in responding to the democratic choices on offer.

Such differences in the practice of democracy matter. Although widely misunderstood and often used as a straw man to introduce studies such as this, Francis Fukuyama's 'end of history argument' (1989) is clearly mistaken if it is taken to mean that agreement on the need for all rule to be democratic is sufficient to resolve all possible disagreement about systems of government. Since democracy comes in many varieties, and the choice between those varieties has implications for other values, it is not uncommon for other political disputes to be internalized into conflicting claims about the proper form of democracy. This suggests particular difficulties for our topic of democracy beyond the state. To limits that diversity in the meaning and practice of democracy at national level may put on prospects of agreeing standards for democracy beyond the state has to be added the difficulty that democracy is a form of rule by others that requires trust between co-participants. Thus worries that the foundations for democracy are not equally firm – from all points of view – in all European states may limit the willingness of some to embrace democracy as a shared form of rule from beyond the state.

Optimists might nonetheless believe that whilst diversity dictates there is no prospect of any democracy beyond the state matching everyone's experience with democracy within it, those who encounter the unfamiliar when they come into contact with democracy beyond the state will accept any differences in the meaning and practice of democracy at the two levels that are justified by differences in context: by, for example, the conspicuously more transnational, tentative and contested nature of politics beyond the state. Indeed, optimists may even hope that diversity will be valued in and of itself. Different, but complementary, approaches to democracy within and beyond the state might, for example, allow different priorities to be set between justifications, values and practices associated with democracy at the two levels, and increase the chances of the two stabilizing one another by the introduction to either level of safeguards that cannot easily be institutionalized at the other. Moreover, the possibility that states that come under pressure from the outside to adopt democracy might be able to choose from a range of options could take some of the sting out of the charge that democracy promotion descends into the contradiction of imposing on a people a form of rule that is supposed to be an opportunity for them to decide how they are to govern themselves.

Yet diversity in approaches to democracy has already caused some tensions in the new Europe. The possibility that the quality of democracy in one domestic arena might affect that in another – with the added complication that those responsible for the 'negative externality' may feel that they are acting perfectly properly according to their own democratic standards that just happen to be different from those who feel adversely affected – is already present in aspects of European Union decision-making. Given that majorities of the EU's Council of Ministers and Parliament engage in collaborative law-making in which representatives of no one member state retain full agenda-setting or veto powers, member governments are already exposed to the risk that amongst those participating in the making of laws binding on them are actors from other countries whose commitment to democratic values they doubt. This was, arguably, the point at issue in the decision by other Union governments to suspend bilateral discussion of Union business with Austria, in protest at the inclusion of the far right Freedom Party (Freiheitliche Partei Österreichs FPÖ) in the governing coalition. Three years later formal provision for suspending membership rights on the grounds of violation of democracy and human rights was included in the draft treaty establishing a constitution. Were such a change to come to pass it would entail continuing limits on variations in the domestic political systems of member states, and not just conditions that restrict variation at the moment of entry.

Chapter 4

Varieties of Democracy Beyond the State: the Case of the European Union

So far we have seen how democracy in Europe grew up around the political systems of its states and, somewhat more problematically, around the political identities of its nations. Yet, as we argued in Chapter 2, democracy in Europe has always been closely affected by politics beyond the state. It is to an analysis of the present role of the international dimension that we now turn. We will argue that there are two ways in which the practice of democracy in the new Europe engages with politics beyond the state. One consists of attempts to extend democratic control to the politics of a major regional organization, the European Union; the other of coordinated efforts to promote democratic politics to all the political systems of the new Europe according to standards and methods that are agreed and monitored at the regional level. The first is the subject of this chapter; the second of the next chapter.

Who said what to whom about democratizing the European Union?

At least since the Treaty on European Union (TEU), member states have used Union treaties to confirm their 'attachment to the principles of liberty, democracy and respect for human rights' (European Commission, 1992). Democracy and human rights have likewise been identified as values for export through the Common Foreign and Security Policy and Development Cooperation (Titles V and VII of TEU). They have additionally been refined as conditions for membership (Copenhagen criteria: European Council, 1993) to the point at which the Commission has since the mid-1990s reported annually to the Council with detailed appraisals of democratic standards in a number of countries that are not even members of the Union.

Of course, there is a double ambiguity in such statements. First, from a consequentialist view – which holds that democracy is not justified by any intrinsic quality but by its consequences – it might be both defensible and coherent for member states to use the Union to advance the cause of democracy in other arenas without intending that it should be a democracy itself. Second, even if it is accepted that the Union should be democratically controlled, such an objective would be compatible with a continuum of possibilities that differ precisely in how they would take democracy beyond the state. Full democratic control of the Union could quite conceivably run through the democratic institutions of its component states without any need for democracy at the Union level, and, even were the latter to develop, the 'beyond-stateness' of the construct could conceivably vary in all the following ways: in the number and range of Union offices and institutions directly or indirectly decided by European-level elections; in the degree to which voter choice is politicized around issues relevant to the Union itself; in how far citizens of the Union see themselves as a deciding people held together by feelings of political community (a 'demos'); and in how far European Union issues are deliberated in a public sphere of open communications in which all points of view come into contact with one another on a basis of equality.

In the face of such ambiguities, the treaty establishing a Constitution for Europe attempted to go some way to specifying an agreed view of what it called the 'democratic life' of the Union. After proclaiming that 'the functioning of the Union shall be founded on representative democracy' the draft stated that 'citizens are directly represented at Union level in the European Parliament' and 'member states are represented in the European Council by their Heads of State or Government and in the Council by their governments, themselves democratically accountable either to their national Parliaments, or to their citizens' (European Commission, 2004, Article 1–46). Of note is that this latter passage is expressed in the present tense, and not as a 'will be' or a 'shall be'. Thus regardless of the eventual fate of the Constitution, it can be presumably be taken as an understanding of existing arrangements that the governments of the Union are prepared to endorse and defend publicly. Indeed, the claim that the Union operates a dual system of representation in which citizens are represented both through their national governments and the European Parliament is entirely consistent with many other statements by Union institutions and governments in recent years. This chapter considers how the two pillars of representation operate in practice.

Consent? EU treaty formation

A useful starting point is with a common confusion. The power to 'throw the scoundrels out' by removing political leaders is often treated as the be-all and end-all of public control. Given, however, that institutions systematically favour some activities and values over others (see p. 6), it is far from sufficient for the public to have control over this or that group of power-holders. They also need some control over the design of institutions in which power-holders hold their power and seek regular reelection. This need is acute under three conditions: first, where there is unlikely to be scope anyway to remove one set of leaders and substitute another; second, where institutions are contested; and, third, where they are new enough for the public to be able to control their design before they 'lock in' particular behaviours, resources or capabilities. Left any later and opportunities for public control over the design of institutions become a challenge of how best to rebuild a ship at sea.

All three conditions apply to the EU. Although some of its institutions often seem to show their age, it would be a mistake to underestimate how far the Union remains a series of parallel and partially competitive institutional experiments, or, as Philippe Schmitter puts it, 'a plurality of polities at different levels of aggregation' (Schmitter, 2000). On the one hand, this reflects precisely the difficulty of agreeing institutions to the satisfaction of all in the Union arena. At any one time the Union's design reflects a series of previous stand-offs between champions of contrasting institutional philosophies and solutions (Lord and Magnette, 2004). On the other hand, it means that choices of institutional design remain remarkably open. Sometimes they can be made by just switching attention or resources from one approach to another. They can certainly be made by using treaty changes to change the legal authority for alternative approaches.

In contrast, though, to the continuing meaningfulness of institutional choice, there can be no meaningful sense in which the political leadership of the Union can ever be chosen or sanctioned as a collective (Weiler, 1997) so long as the Union has other qualities that many consider important. If it is to remain an 'extreme consensus system', one quality of which is that parts of its political leadership are chosen and removed in its member states, those same leaders cannot also be democratically chosen or removed at Union level.

Present arrangements for the democratic control of the institutional design of the Union run almost exclusively through national democratic procedures. Any treaty change has to be agreed unanimously by the elected governments of member states and then ratified unanimously according to the domestic 'constitutional requirements' of each country (Article 48). Thus a full assessment of the contribution of national democracies to the public control of the Union requires an answer to both the following questions: how well do member states link their publics to decisions on EU treaty formation? And, once powers have been conferred on the Union by the treaties, how well is the public able to monitor and control their use through nationally elected representatives?

A useful way into this discussion is to compare national referendums and votes of national parliaments as means of ratifying EU treaty change, and, along the way, consider some problems common to both. Referendums seemingly have the advantage of allowing national publics to decide questions of EU institutional design directly and on their own merits. Yet in practice such votes are heavily influenced by considerations that do not relate directly to the public control of the institutional development of the EU. Franklin *et al.* (1994, p. 487) found that in all countries which put the TEU to referendum, 'yes' and 'no' votes were significantly correlated with the popularity of the domestic governments of the day and with patterns of partisan support within national politics. It is not only elections to the European Parliament but also referendums on the constitutional design of the Union that would seem to have the second-order characteristic of being dominated by some other political game.

Another advantage that might be claimed of referendums relates to the observation that EU Treaty changes do not simply transfer powers between the national and European levels of government. They can also redistribute powers within member states, from legislature to executive and from regions to the centre (see pp. 146–9). Indeed national governments are themselves amongst the main beneficiaries of transfers of powers to the Union, since they participate so intimately in its decisions. Where national parliaments are 'executive-dominated' and Union issues feature little in electoral politics, parliamentary ratification of treaty change means there is little constraint on governments transferring powers to the club of governments of which they are themselves a part. Referendums at least do something to take the decision out of the hands of governments, though how much depends on the discretion left to governments to determine timing, the nature of the question and even whether an issue of European integration is to be put to referendum at all. In most member states the conditions that determine the calling of referendums are unclear and suspicion remains that they are used more opportunistically than in search of authentic public authorization and control.

An argument often made for ratification by national parliaments is that treaty changes are complex deals spanning many policies and institutions. They are not, in other words, easily reduced to the simple 'yes'/'no' choice of a referendum question. Yet it is a difficulty common to both methods of ratification that once a treaty has been agreed by the European Council, a decision can only be made to accept or reject the text, rather than to amend it. Either way, the formal position is that national democratic actors have veto powers but only limited and indirect agenda-setting powers. In other words, the power to say 'no' is more evident than the power to shape the choice itself, and, even then, the power to say 'yes' or 'no' is a constrained and frustrating one where treaty changes are complex package deals in relation to whose individual elements national parliaments and publics might want to pick and choose, but cannot. For small national democracies in particular the fait accompli of a package defended by a united front of governments may weigh heavily against the uncertainty of provoking a crisis in the integration process, or even of raising questions about the continued membership of countries unable to ratify.

The crucial difference between the two modes of ratification lies in how the 'take it or leave it' choice over a final text may be softened by any law of anticipated reactions by which prior negotiations are used to align draft treaties to subsequent risks of a domestic rejection. National parliamentary ratification provides continuous and structured dialogue between the ratifier and negotiator throughout the process of treaty formation. It is possible for a national parliament to sustain influence right up to the 'endgame' of intergovernmental conference (IGC) negotiations. The European Affairs Committee of the Swedish Parliament held 'telephone conferences with the Swedish negotiators' in the final stages of the Nice negotiations (Sveriges Riksdag, 2001; see also Sverdrup, 2002, p. 128). Yet there is unevenness within and across member states in the participation of national parliaments in the negotiation of treaty changes. The British government's boast that the House of Commons debated the negotiation of that treaty for 204 hours over 23 days (House of Commons Debates, 20 May 1993, col. 381) has to be qualified by its refusal to make available to parliament what was perhaps the most important document to the Political Union negotiations, the draft treaty produced by the Luxembourg Presidency in June 1991.

How national parliaments influence treaty negotiations depends on the nature of executive–legislature relations in each member state. During treaty negotiations national governments are most likely to respond to those strands of parliamentary opinion that can most credibly threaten to be veto players in subsequent treaty ratifications. Thus Chancellor Kohl toned down his support for an ambitious package deal to extend qualified majority voting (QMV) at Amsterdam for fear that it would encroach on the competence of the *Länder* who would then oppose the reaty in the Bundesrat (Beach, 2005, p. 120). In more majoritarian systems any national parliamentary influence is likely to be confined to the governing majority and is unlikely to be deliberated or even transparent to the wider representative body. For example, the outcome of the Maastricht European Council was hostage until the last moment to a parallel negotiation between the British prime minister and a cabinet minister who would probably have resigned with significant support from the wider parliamentary party had the UK not secured an opt-out from the social chapter of the TEU (Forster, 1999, p. 92).

In contrast to the continuous but calculable pressure on governments to align IGC outcomes to national parliamentarians responsible for ratification, the appeal of referendums lies precisely in the greater element of uncertainty they introduce to the prospects of treaty ratification: with less control or information about the views and behaviour of the ratifier or even of who exactly the latter will be once the vagaries of voter participation and abstention are taken into account, governments may have to anticipate a wide range of possible objections while negotiating treaty changes. Against this complaints have been made that referendums have been used to put the same question back to the electorate until it gets the desired result, and that they have been sequenced between countries in ways designed to influence outcomes (Detlef and Storsved, 1995).

Two other developments may have softened the foregoing criticism that arrangements for reaty ratification only confer veto, rather than agenda-setting, powers on national democracies. First, the now iterative nature of treaty formation, with each round of treaty change seemingly following on the heels of the last, gives scope for rumblings of discontent associated with the last negotiation to feed into the next. Second, the EU has recently experimented with conventions to draft an EU Charter of Fundamental Rights (Schönlau, 2001) and, more recently, a treaty establishing a Constitution (Eriksen *et al.*, 2004; Magnette, 2003; Norman, 2003). A number of claims have been made for how the 'convention method' can improve democratic standards at the agenda-setting stage of IGCs. First, conventions are more diverse in their composition than IGCs and thus widen access to the agenda of institutional change. National parliamentarians are for the first time directly included in face-to-face discussions in a setting that involves their counterparts from right across the unit of shared rule. Second, the inclusion of national parliaments at the agenda-setting stage means that the treaty change they are eventually asked to ratify may still be a 'take it or leave it' choice but at least it is not one structured without inputs from themselves. Third, the convention method creates a means of setting the agenda for institutional design that is more transparent to national publics. Even where previous approaches involved extensive deliberation, they took place behind closed doors, and without any need for participants to justify their positions in public. On the other hand, the record of either convention in penetrating public consciousness was disappointing. Whilst the 'Constitution Convention' was in progress,

Eurobarometer (2002, No. 57) found that only 28 per cent of the public had heard something about it in recent months. This compared with an average awareness of the four main Union institutions of 74 per cent.

Guardians? The role of elected governments

It is one thing to note that each European Union treaty change has to be unanimously agreed by the governments, publics or parliaments of its participating national democracies. It is another to demonstrate that, once empowered by treaty, the Union takes its decisions in a manner that is either responsive or open to continuing monitoring and control. The problem, according to one element of the 'dual system of representation' that is supposed to operate in the Union, is, in part, solved by the participation of elected national governments in the Council of Ministers, and the responsibility, in turn, of those governments to their own publics and parliaments. How convincing is this claim?

If the participation of elected national governments in Union decisions is to be held out as an important means of public control it is vital that the representation of governments should be structured in a principled way that delivers a consistent and fair distribution of opportunities to control outcomes. In representing its member states the Union mixes principles of 'parity' and 'proportionality'. Parity – the equal weighting of member governments – applies to treaty changes, agreements on five-year budgets, most CFSP decisions, many Justice and Home Affairs (JHA) decisions and even some European Community ones, where, formally at least, all members have a veto regardless of their size. Likewise, all members have equal access to the rotating presidency of the Council of Ministers. Where, however, majority voting is used, each member state receives a certain minimum number of block votes, which then rise thereafter in rough proportion to population. However, the roughness – or, to be technical, the 'non-linearity' – of the relationship between representation and population is striking. Germany, for example, with its population of 82.7 million, continues to receive the same representation as Britain, France and Italy with their populations of 60 million (29 votes), whilst all four only receive two more votes than Spain and Poland (27 votes) with populations of either side of 40 million. A clear difficulty is that the allocation of voting weights has been based on bargaining and status rather than any self-conscious attempt to construct a principled system of representation (Moberg, 2002).

If questions can be asked about the consistency of representation in the Council, do the elected governments of member states at least enjoy significant controlling powers over Union decisions? Here it is useful to distinguish between the legislative and executive powers of the Union. Beginning with the former, neither rules nor practice make it easy to agree legislation without the approval of almost all the nationally elected governments of the Union. Even where QMV applies, it requires a high hurdle of 71 per cent or so of the block vote allocated to member states, and, additionally, a simple majority of member states representing at least 62 per cent of the total population of the Union. But even this overstates the risk of member states having to accept a law against their wishes. A key data set has been compiled by Mikko Mattila and Jan-Erik Lane (2001) from a total of 1,381 legislative acts adopted by the Council during the period 1994–8. This shows voting is unanimous in between 75 and 85 per cent of cases per year, even where QMV is available. Moreover, in around 60 per cent of the 15–25 per cent of cases where the Council fails to achieve unanimity, there is only one dissenting member, and in around 80–90 per cent there are only two (Mattila and Lane, 2001, pp. 40–3).

In other words, member states prefer to decide by consensus, and to legislate against the wishes of one of their number less frequently than the rules permit. In only around 1 per cent of cases is the Union's legislation passed by a minimum-winning coalition under the rules. It may, of course, be that these figures understate the true level of majoritarianism. On the one hand, consensus may be formed in the 'shadow of majority voting'. Member states rationally anticipate which of their number can form minimum-winning coalitions under QMV, extract what concessions they can, and then fall in behind the majority to avoid any domestic political costs of seeming to be on the losing side of a Council vote. Also possible is that elaborate arrangements for preparing Council decisions through working parties and then the Committee of the Permanent Representatives of member states (COREPER) allow for a high level of vote-trading in which apparently high levels of consensus conceal how far member states accept suboptimal outcomes in some areas in order to get what they want in others. Some case study evidence, however, suggests that the 'preference for unanimity' in Council voting is sincere and normative, rather than strategic. Much of it would seem to be delivered in practice through what Jeffrey Lewis (1998, pp. 291–2) describes as COREPER's 'dense normative environment . . . of diffuse reciprocity and thick trust . . . [leading on to a] consensus reflex'.

But what of the execution of Union policies and laws once they are agreed? Here too elected governments enjoy significant control, not least because much of the execution of Union decisions is in their own hands. They implement Union law within the territory of their own member states, and, although they are individually constrained in this task by guidelines issued by the Commission, the preparation of the guidelines is itself supervised by the collective of member states through a complex of committees known as 'comitology'. Indeed, there are other reasons why, in spite of its formal independence, the Commission is significantly exposed to the individual and collective influence of member states:

1. In appointing a College of Commissioners and a president every five years, member governments may alter the direction of the Commission.
2. Member governments can redesign the powers of the Commission through treaty change. Here the Commission is not entirely safeguarded by a need for Treaty changes to be unanimously agreed by all 25 member states. To the extent that overall treaty changes may in practice be shaped by just a handful of larger states (Moravcsik, 1998), whilst specific changes can be submerged into wider package deals, it would be most unwise for the Commission to rely on just one member state to ride to its rescue in defence of any single treaty power. More prudent would be for it to avoid persistent misalignments between any one policy and the preferences of clusters of member states of varying size and weight in treaty bargaining.
3. The Commission depends on the member states for resources and cooperation. Although the Union benefits from a system of 'own resources' its budget still needs to be agreed every

five years by unanimous consent of member governments, which micro-manage the deployment of resources to the extent that the Union institutions cannot move expenditures between seven closely specified ceilings. The agreement of member governments is also needed for any increase in the staffing of the Commission. A dysfunctional relationship with any one member state will likewise cause problems for the Commission in terms of implementation on the ground and provision of information needed for effective policy-making.

Yet none of these controls is without cost to member states. In addition to costs of monitoring the Commission, member states may have various 'reverse dependencies' on the Commission. Amongst the latter are needs member states themselves feel for a credible enforcement mechanism at European level, and for a body that will save them transaction costs in policy initiation and bargaining (Majone, 1996, p. 69). As Mark Pollack (1997a) has pointed out, the marginal costs will up to a certain point exceed the marginal returns to member states of reasserting control; and the Commission will, accordingly, always be somewhere in between a 'run away' bureaucracy and a subservient one (Pollack, 1998, p. 218).

Indeed, it is notoriously hard to gauge a precise measure of how member governments succeed in monitoring the Commission in practice. A primary source of ambiguity is that comitology committees hardly ever use their powers to appeal to the full Council in the case of disagreement with the Commission. Is this a sign of their success in forcing 'the Commission to take objections seriously and search for consensual solutions' (Scharpf, 2003, p. 8)? Or does it suggest that the participation of national officials in EU decision-making just compounds the problem of unsupervised administrative power by encouraging a *copinage téchnocratique* (Radaelli, 2000; Trondal, 2001, p. 39; Wessels, 1998, p. 214) in which national civil servants may nominally be designated to oversee the Commission on behalf of elected national governments yet settle down to common problem-solving with Commission officials in a process that is opaque to the public and its representatives at either level of government? These are not easy questions to answer, since the distinction between acting as 'national representatives' and transferring loyalties to the shared process may itself be elusive.

The guardians guarded? National parliaments

Who guards the guardians? The claim that elected governments contribute to a dual system of representation in the European arena by retaining significant controlling powers over Union decisions self-evidently presupposes that national governments are themselves responsible for what they do at Union level. What is clear is that European Union issues are rarely salient in national elections. To take the example of three member states where data on voters' priorities are available from recent elections, the first mention of the EU appears with the third-ranked issue in the British survey (NOP, 2001), the seventh in the Swedish (Holmberg, 2001) and the fourteenth in the French case (Sofres Poll, *Le Monde*, 10–11 April 2002).

It is possible – but by no means certain – that Union issues would be more salient in national elections if only national publics had a better understanding of how they are themselves indirectly joined to the EU's political system through their election of their own national governments. That there is a gap in understanding here emerges from Eurobarometer evidence (2002, No. 57) that the Council is the least known of the Union's four main institutions, and that its public recognition is particularly low in some of the larger member states that are best placed to influence the exercise of its powers. Indeed, more general focus group evidence (European Commission, 2001) suggests that many citizens assume that member states watch the EU from the sidelines, rather than participate as decision-makers.

Nonetheless, low electoral salience, and even limited awareness, might be less of a concern if it could be shown that public needs and values on Union questions more or less correlate with other broad dimensions of choice on which national parliaments are elected, and the latter then exercise reasonable control of what their governments do at Union level. The first condition is examined – and found to offer only partial solace – later in this chapter. The second condition is the focus of the rest of this section.

National parliaments have become more active on EU matters since the early 1990s. All now (more or less) have a European Affairs Committee (EAC). The scrutiny role of national parliaments is acknowledged in a legally binding protocol to the

Amsterdam Treaty. This requires they receive draft legislation, Commission white and green papers and communications, and all documents related to the 'creation of an area of Freedom and Justice' (mainly JHA). It further states that a legislative proposal can only be placed on the Council's agenda six weeks after the text has been sent to national parliaments.

However, even the most committed national parliaments only have the time and resources for in-depth scrutiny of 100 of the 1,500 or so Union dossiers they receive per year. National parliaments also differ in their powers to act on their scrutiny of EU decisions. Only some can issue instructions their governments arc legally or politically obliged to follow. Austria and Denmark are examples of the first; Sweden and Finland of the second, though the Dutch parliament can issue mandates on JHA matters, and the German *Länder* have to be closely associated with decisions that affect their competence. The latter are sometimes even incorporated into German delegations to Council Meetings (Bergman, 1997; Hegeland and Neuhold, 2002; Maurer and Wessels, 2001).

Yet national parliaments face formidable constraints in their attempts to control EU decision-making, some of which are the product of their own domestic political systems, others of the Union's own political system. The following paragraphs explain.

Domestic constraints on national parliamentary control

Consider the example of the Danish parliament. Generally rated the most powerful national parliament on EU matters, its scrutiny procedures have evolved as a response to an unusual question: who should determine how votes in the Council of Ministers should be used in the case of a member state where, as David Arter puts it, governments are typically so much in the minority that it is 'opposition parties . . . that in practice make decisions' (1996, pp. 119–20)? From this point of view the Danish system is better classified as an 'idiosyncracy' than as a 'model'. Its transferability to other member states is limited by the simple fact that the intended 'mandatees' (the national governments) themselves control the would-be 'mandators' (to national parliaments).

The extent to which, in executive-dominated systems, national parliaments lack control of their own agenda and business

(Döring, 1995) in ways that complicate scrutiny of EU matters is best illustrated by considering the key role of committees. A strong committee-based parliament based on a division of labour between representatives will be needed to acquire specialist knowledge of EU affairs and overcome the asymmetries of information that put parliaments at a disadvantage to governments (Krehbiel, 1991). Yet, in many member states, parliamentary committees are more likely to be controlled by the party disciplines of majority governments than vice versa. Here the British and French examples are instructive. The British House of Commons, arguably, combines one of the most painstaking with one of the most inconsequential of EU scrutiny procedures. Although its Scrutiny Committee has been praised for its identification of matters of concern to MPs, scrutiny can be taken no further than an adjournment debate on the floor of the House. Apart from being cursory, ill-attended and at inhospitable times, the government, which controls parliamentary business, usually only makes space for about 12 such debates a year. Most of those debates end without a vote and, in any case, the government majority is always available to defeat a challenge (Giddings and Drewry, 1996). How the matter is handled in the Council thereafter is a matter of executive discretion. For its part, the French Assemblée Nationale is limited by the Constitution of the Fifth Republic to just six committees, a quota it had long exhausted before serious consideration was given to creating a committee on European Union affairs. As a result the parliamentary body that deals with Union matters has to labour under the fiction that it is a mere '*délégation*' and not a committee.

The EU political system as a constraint on national parliamentary control

Even those national parliaments that overcome constraints of their domestic political systems to influence what their governments do at Union level are constrained in their overall control of Union decision-making by features of the EU's own political system. The following are examples.

First, the Council is probably the only legislature in the liberal democratic world that continues to make law behind closed doors. This raises the costs to national parliaments of monitoring the contributions of their own governments to Union decisions. Although it is now public knowledge how governments vote in the Council, national parliaments will often be less interested in criticizing their governments for reaching some kind of agreement than in assessing whether it was the best obtainable from points of view that will often differ from those of their own governments. This means it is important that national parliaments should have sufficient information to test claims by their own ministers that outcomes are tightly constrained by the preferences of other member states. Otherwise attempts to disguise a choice as a necessity can just be a device by which a national government settles a matter on its own terms, rather than those of its national parliament.

Second, there may be limits to how far national parliamentary rights can be loaded on to the EU decision-making process without it losing its problem-solving capacity. That some parliaments mandate their governments may depend on others not doing so. This argument needs, however, to be treated with caution, since there is little evidence that the member states whose parliaments have the strongest mandating power are obstacles to consensus in the Council. Thus Denmark was only the sixth most frequent 'naysayer' between 1994 and 1998, casting 'no' votes in just 5 per cent of Council roll calls and abstaining in a further 0.8 per cent (Matilla and Lane, 2001, p. 43). One reason why mandating by national parliaments may not lead to high levels of negative voting on the Council is that QMV creates a balance of constraints. Since by binding their governments too tightly they risk a policy outcome that is even further from their preferences than if they had issued no mandate at all, national parliaments often indicate a range in which it is acceptable to settle, rather than issue precise instructions (Interview, Danish Folketing official, March 2003).

A third constraint common to all national parliaments is the EU's extended policy cycle. In practice, national parliaments may want to operate both 'up' and 'down' stream to the single intervention point (the publication of a draft text) created for them by the Amsterdam protocol. To the extent that member states have already bargained with one another through the committees the Commission consults prior to drafting legislation, many documents forwarded to national parliaments already represent a compromise that governments may want collectively to defend against individual attempts at parliamentary scrutiny. A representative of the Irish Dáil to COSAC (The Conference of Community and European Affairs Committees of the Parliaments of the European Union, commonly known as 'COSAC') has complained that texts often have an air of having already 'been passed by governments' before they are forwarded to their national parliaments (COSAC, 2001, p. 33).

A converse difficulty is that the EU's complex multi-stage decision-making may drift substantially from options on which national parliaments have had an opportunity to express opinions. It may only be possible to overcome this problem by giving national parliaments rights of participation towards the end of the legislative cycle, and not just in between the publication of a Commission draft and the agreement of a common position of the Council. One Member of the Convention suggested that a certain number of national parliaments should have the right to table 'reasoned amendments' that would have to be considered in a Conciliation Committee of the European Parliament (EP) and the Council (European Convention, 2002).

A fourth constraint is that national parliaments are at best only a means of enforcing the individual responsibility of single Council members. They offer no control over the institution as a whole. The EP rightly observes that 'neither the Council nor the European Council can incur ultimate political censure, since no vote of confidence is possible either in national parliaments or the European Parliament' (European Parliament, 1997, p. 5). Not only can the efforts of national parliaments be negated where their governments are outvoted, but, even where unanimity is the rule, faits accomplis often seem to emerge from bargaining relationships of which any one national parliament can control but a part. No one has done more to highlight this problem than Andrew Moravcsik (1998). Although most directly concerned with treaty formation, his conclusions serve as a more general reminder that formal requirements of unanimity only offer limited protections to elected governments of smaller member states. Even in day-to-day decision-making, member states are effectively engaged in continuous choice as to whether they are going to pursue an objective through the Union, individually, bilaterally or through an international body other than the EU. In a pure bargaining relationship the terms of any agreement to work through the Union are likely to be closest to the preferences of those governments which have least to lose from a 'non-decision'. In Moravcsik's assessment this means that agreements can be predicted from the preferences of the larger member states alone. If correct, and if transposable, as the foregoing analysis suggests, from treaty formation to day-to-day decisions, this is a bleak conclusion for the scrutiny of Council decisions by national parliaments, where, as seen, many of the most impressive efforts are to be found precisely in smaller member states.

So far, then, we have argued that both domestic political systems and that of the European Union constrain how far national parliaments can exercise control of EU matters. But even assuming those constraints could be overcome would national parliaments be a desirable mechanism of control? Perhaps not on their own without mechanisms of representation and control at the European level to complement their efforts at the national. This for at least two reasons. First, as long as Union member states differ widely in size, as they always will do, representation through national parliaments will present an incorrigible problem of political equality: how well citizens are represented on Union issues will depend on where they live. Second, national parliaments are not the most obvious fora for deliberation at the level of the Union's political system itself. Indeed, Edmund Burke's famous question to the electors of Bristol might be asked of national parliaments with mandating powers on Union issues: 'what sort of reason is it in which the determination precedes the discussion, in which one set of men deliberate and another decide, and where those who form the conclusion are perhaps three hundred miles distant from those who hear the arguments?' (Burke (1975) [1774], p. 175).

Checks and balances? The European Parliament

In the last section we assessed how far national democratic institutions can be used to exercise public control over Union affairs. However, the mantra with which we started this chapter implies that those who exercise political power through Union institutions should be subject to not one but two 'pillars' of public control: one working through representatives of national democracies and the other through representatives directly elected at the level of the EU's political system itself. This section begins the process of evaluating the second mode of representation with an assessment of the powers of the European Parliament to exercise public control over the Commission and the Council. The next section continues the appraisal with harder questions about the capacity of the Union to develop a 'democratic politics' that – amongst other attributes – links citizens to the EU's political system via elections relevant to the Union itself.

Control through Co-decision?

Most MEPs consider that the most important of their powers is that the Council must co-decide many of the Union's laws and some aspects of its budget with the Parliament. Yet academics disagree what it is about legislative co-decision in particular that empowers the EP (Crombez *et al.*, 2000; Tsebelis and Garrett, 2000). Some hold that it confers 'agenda-setting' powers by allowing the EP to propose amendments that are 'procedurally easier for the Council to accept than to modify' (Tsebelis, 1994 p. 128). Others view any scope co-decision affords the EP to shape the Union's legislative agenda as the indirect consequence of the ultimate power of veto that the Parliament enjoys under the procedure (Crombez, 1996). Council members may accept significant EP amendments rather than 'return to go' in a lengthy legislative process that may have depended on unique windows of opportunity in domestic politics or on a complex 'logroll' between themselves.

Given that the main business of the Union is rule-making (Majone, 1996), and that the Commission frequently makes proposals in response to member governments (European Commission, 1999), the role of co-decision in allowing the Parliament to check and balance Commission and the Council in the legislative process clearly has potential to function as a significant instrument of public control. Nor is this conclusion lessened by the observation that co-decision only allows the EP to make 'bounded choices' in so far as either the Commission or the Council would at some point sooner risk losing legislation altogether than accept 'extreme' parliamentary amendments (Kreppel, 2000). Given that the Union is supposed to rest on twin principles of representation it is hardly a criticism that the EP's powers to exercise checks and balances are themselves checked by the distribution of preferences represented in the Council.

Yet the Parliament is acutely conscious that co-decision is a less than complete mechanism of public control. Not only does the Treaty only require the Council to consult the Parliament on CFSP and JHA matters, but it leaves it to the Council to decide when that obligation has been satisfied. However, even the European Community pillar is, in Paul Magnette's term (1999), only 'semi-parliamentary' when account is taken of its continued exclusion from some legislation (Maurer, 2003) and limitations on its control over nearly half the budget, including the largest item, the Common Agricultural Policy (CAP). Indeed, the Parliament complains that even co-decision confers less parliamentary control than it should on Community matters, since 'comitology' allows administrators and 'experts' to 'modify and 'supplement' – rather than 'merely implement' – measures that have been agreed by the EP (European Parliament, 1998, p. 6; 2003, p. 7).

Controlling powers over the appointment of the Commission?

In addition to granting or withholding financial resources and legislative authority, representative bodies can exercise control by participating in the appointment or dismissal of key office-holders. Since 1992 the Commission and its president have only been able to take office after a vote of approval by the European Parliament. Yet, in spite of its ingenuity, the procedure only gives the EP a limited controlling power over the appointment of the Commission. In the end, the Parliament only has a 'take it or leave it' choice over a president and College designated by member states. Absence of the 'positive power' to pick and choose means that Commissions are not representative executives in the sense of being 'equilibrium governments' so aligned in their composition, portfolio distribution and policy programme with representatives' preferences as to beat all possible alternatives in any parliamentary vote (Laver and Shepsle, 1996).

Nor is it even clear that it is easy for the Parliament to use the investiture procedure as a 'negative' or 'veto' power on the Presidency or College of Commissioners. One problem is that the EP's bargaining hand is crucially shaped by what would happen in the event of a failure to agree with member states on the appointment of a Commission. The legal position is that the old Commission would continue in office, though only as a caretaker or trustee. Such a 'lame-duck' Commission could suit some member states more than the EP.

A second difficulty is that national leaders may try to organize their own support base in the EP if confronted by any risk of being denied the Commission of their choice. A study of MEPs who voted for Santer in 1994 against the wishes of their party group, reveals that most came from national parties of government. Up to 45 members seem to have been persuaded to switch their votes, a figure that exceeded Santer's majority of 21 (Hix and Lord, 1996). Likewise Santer had little difficulty 'calling the EP's bluff' at a later stage in the procedure when, on the evidence of its committee hearings, the Parliament criticized five out of the 20 nominations to the 1995–9 Commission. He correctly calculated that even if none of the nominations were withdrawn by the member states making them, the EP would still vote for the overall Commission. The formation of the 1999 Commission likewise showed how limited is the scope for MEPs to engage in proactive 'executive shaping'. President Prodi successfully resisted suggestions from the largest group in the EP that he should use his own powers over the formation of the College to press for a Commission that reflected the 'centre-right' outcome of the 1999 EP elections (*Le Monde*, 14 July 1999). More encouraging, though, from the EP's point of view was that in 2004 it was able to force the incoming Commission president and European Council to back down in their determination to designate as Justice and Home Affairs Commissioner a nominee with a record of publicly expressed homophobic and sexist opinions.

The EP's power to Dismiss the Commission

The EP is able to dismiss a College of Commissioners on a 'double' majority (two-thirds of MEPs voting and an absolute majority of the Parliament itself, that is, 314 out of 626). The threshold is set high, since the EP's power of dismissal is intended as a safeguard against poor performance or maladministration, rather than as a means for the EP to substitute one executive for another whenever that satisfies the partisan preferences of its majority.

Until the Santer Commission resigned in anticipation of a parliamentary majority for dismissal in March 1999 many doubted that the power of censure would ever be used. Limiting factors included, first, the likelihood that a minimum-winning coalition for censure would have to include party families likely to lose out from the replacement of the Commission. Second, censure appeared to be a 'nuclear option' made unusable by the drastic consequences of its own employment (Clergerie, 1995). The Parliament was considered too dependent on a strong Commission, and too closely aligned with it in battles over the institutional shape of European integration, to emerge as a fierce and independent critic prepared to wield the ultimate sanction of dismissal. Third, the injustice of only being able to remove an entire College of Commissioners – without any discrimination of individual responsibility for underperformance or wrongdoing – was thought likely to sharpen the determination of pockets of MEPs from different nationalities or party families to protect 'their Commissioners' from disgrace by withholding the double majority needed for a censure.

On the other hand, the Parliament's power of executive super-vision may long have been more subtle and effective than the foregoing suggests. Insiders noted a tendency from the early 1990s for the Commission to respond even to remote threats of parliamentary discontent developing into censure motions (Corbett *et al.*, 1995, p. 247). A possible explanation is that a censure is procedurally easy to initiate even if it is hard to con-clude. The support of only 10 per cent of MEPs is needed to table a censure and have it debated by the Parliament. The Commission then has to divert resources to fighting off a censure that may, in the meantime, damage its reputation. The result is that the Commission may accommodate grievance even at a rela-tively low level of discontent, notwithstanding the difficulties the EP would also face in fully prosecuting a censure.

Yet, in a political system where executive power is distributed between the Commission, the Council and individual member states, the censure procedure self-evidently only allows the Parliament to pursue the former. The difficulties this can create are illustrated by the BSE (mad-cow disease) crisis in the 1990s. The EP's special committee of enquiry was clear that 'primary responsibility' lay with the British government (Reimer Böge MEP, European Parliament, Verbatim Report of Proceedings, 18 February 1997). Whilst, however, managing to extract a string of concessions from the Commission by passing an indicative motion of censure, the Parliament was unable even to get the British Agriculture Minister to appear before its enquiry (Lord, 1998a, p. 89; Shackleton, 1998; Westlake, 1997).

Moreover, many other bodies than the Commission may have powers to execute Union policy. JHA in particular has been used to set up a series of European-level agencies – Europol (police co-operation), Eurojust (prosecuting magistrates), and the Schengen Secretariat (frontier management) – that may on occasion exercise significant discretionary powers, including, for example, the initiation of joint investigations and prosecutions in cases of cross-border crime. Yet there is no parliamentary role in the appointment or censure of senior executive figures. Nor are the agencies covered by general legislation on administrative standards in Union institutions such as the regulations on the processing of personal data (European Parliament, 2001) and access to documents.

Democratic politics? Voters and parties

The last section gave a mixed assessment of how far the EU allows directly elected representatives to exercise public control and affect policy outcomes. In this section we appraise how well present arrangements connect citizens to the EU's political system by offering them choices relevant to the operation of the Union itself.

The facts are broadly these: all adult voters get an opportunity every five years to choose representatives to the European Parliament. European elections are contested between national parties, which go on to form themselves into multinational party groups once they reach the European Parliament. Although party groups change somewhat from one European Parliament to another, they normally cover most of the ideological groupings common to the member societies of the Union: Christian Democrats and Conservatives, Socialists and Social Democrats, Liberals, Greens, the Far Left and Eurosceptics. Only the Far Right has found it difficult to form a group in the EP, largely because transnational self-organization is an unlikely activity for often nationalist political parties (Lord, 1998b, p. 130). Moreover, the EP's party system has stability, cohesion and defined dimensionality. No other alignment – not even that between supporters and opponents of European integration – comes close to rivalling 'left–right' in the voting behaviour of MEPs. These arrangements are, however, open to a number of criticisms:

1. The OSCE in its report on European elections singled out for criticism precisely the absence of opportunities for citizens to vote for the formations that exercise the powers of the Parliament on their behalf (OSCE, 2004b, p. 3).
2. Participation in European elections is low and apparently declining. As shown in Table 6.2, participation in the 2004 European elections averaged only 45.5 per cent against 65.8 in 1979, 63.7 in 1984, 63.6 in 1989, 58.4 in 1994 and 52.8 in 1999. On average 20–30 per cent fewer voters participate in European than national elections. Whilst, though, the evidence for declining turnout is not always as straightforward as some of the foregoing figures suggest (Franklin , 2001), it is clear that the empowerment of the European Parliament over the years has failed to persuade voters to participate in its elections in greater numbers. We will return to this problem in Chapter 6.
3. European elections are often thought to be second-order in nature. Whilst it is questionable how far this affects turnout (Blondel *et al.*, 1998), it does mean that many of those who do vote do so on national rather than European Union issues. The implication is that European elections are far from universally about the institution that is in fact being elected!
4. Some consider it a shortcoming that the EU party system reproduces the left–right cleavage to be found at national level. In their view, this limits opportunities for voters to register choices on other dimensions, such as more or less European integration. It also, in their view, means that representation through the Parliament fails to add value to that provided by a Council of Ministers that is already formed of left–right governments.

Some commentators suggest that behind these problems lies a far deeper one: the EU simply has limited 'capacity for democracy' (Kielmansegg, 1996, p. 26). Here, interestingly enough, the difficulty would not appear to be the much-discussed 'no demos' problem. Those who do not identify with the European Union are no less likely than those who do to participate in its elections. Rather there may be other reasons why the EU is just not the kind of political system that is likely to stimulate a demand for mass representative politics. Characteristics of both the EU's policies and of its political system may reduce incentives for political competition structured around elections and parties specific to the Union itself. Although claims that the Union is some kind of 'pareto-improving' polity that largely avoids reallocating values are highly questionable (Lord and Beetham, 2001, p. 447), its limited concern with financial redistribution, its consensus decision-making and its incrementalism often mean that the gains and losses associated with any *one* decision are limited.

Why such a pattern of policy-making may only function as a weak incentive for democratic mobilization is best explained by drawing on Mancur Olson's (1965) key observation that not all those with interests in common will end up organizing to influence any political process. The marginal returns of organization have to exceed the marginal costs if a group is to cohere. Thus even if voters from different Union countries would be better linked to the EU's political system by, for example, transnational political parties structured around choices specific to the Union, such links will fail to emerge if the gains and losses from Union decisions are on the whole so diffuse that the marginal return of constructing a new pattern of representative politics is unlikely to exceed the marginal cost of continuing to use existing structures that, as seen, largely connect the voter to the Union through national parties. In contrast, the highly technical nature of much of the Union's policy, its tendency to affect a few groups intensely even if its impact on society as a whole is diffuse (Pollack, 1997b), and its segmental character in which specialized policy communities interact with 'their' Commission Directorate General (DG), with 'their' sectoral Council and 'their' European Parliament Committee, may all mean that those who have the resources to influence the Union will get a better return on their efforts by working through lobbies, thus further diverting energies away from patterns of representation that use some general approach to politics that applies across the range of issues to link society to institutions.

Not only, though, may the Union's policy outputs be of a kind that are more likely to stimulate interest groups, more than parties, to organize, but there is a further difficulty: its political system, based as it is on a divided form of government, may also dampen incentives for fierce electoral competition and choice structured around issues relevant to the Union itself. Consider the difference between national and European elections. Member states' elections allow voters to choose the executive and the legislature at the same time. European elections, on the other hand, only allow voters to choose one part of the legislative power. There is, in other words, simply a good deal less at stake in European elections. Indeed, many voters, and parties competing for their votes, may feel they can give more of their attention and resources to European than national elections, precisely because the latter, in addition to deciding who holds power in the arena of primary importance to them, has the side benefit of indirectly determining the composition of the other half of the Union's legislature, the Council of Ministers.

Other commentators are, however, more sanguine. Herman Schmitt and Jacques Thomassen (2000) have shown that, even under present arrangements, the preferences of MEPs correlate closely with those who vote for them along a left–right dimension of choice. What is key about this observation is that it implies that it may not matter that voters only get to make a direct choice in European elections between national parties or even that those elections remain to some degree second-order: voters are still aligned with their representatives along a key dimension of political choice.

Now we have little difficulty agreeing with Schmitt and Thomassen that left–right preferences are, indeed, a suitable basis for representation in the European arena. Since decisions about more or less integration are largely decided by treaty formation, the European Parliament is not mainly called upon to decide questions of more or less European integration. Rather, its main business is with how best to participate in the exercise of the given powers of the Union, and that often avoids precisely left–right choices, for example between more or less regulation.

But still there are difficulties with the notion that voters can achieve adequate representation on EU issues by making left–right selections between national parties. First, voters may have perfectly coherent reasons for wanting to be of the left in relation to one arena and of the right in relation to the other. Second, more than one choice of political party will often be equidistant from the preferences of many voters, wherever the logic of political competition encourages any measure of convergence between those competing for power in representative systems. Under such conditions, a sensible way of breaking the tie would be to assess the relative chances of different parties delivering on their promises. But that presupposes knowledge of the specific political system to which representatives are being elected.

Indeed a core reason why Schmitt and Thomassen may not allay all concerns about the adequacy of the link between voters and the EU's political system goes back to the distinction we considered in the Introduction between responsive and responsible government. Even if Schmitt and Thomassen are justified in their claim that the left–right correlation between preferences of representatives and represented is likely to promote broadly the policies the voters would themselves have chosen (see also Crombez, 2003), this does not take care of the objection that the primary objective of democratic politics is not the satisfaction of wants but the exercise of rights of public control (see p. 6). This, as it were, brings the problem of 'second-order' elections, seemingly conjured away by Schmitt and Thomassen, back in. As long as European elections are to some significant degree 'second-order', the link between the citizen and the public control of Union institutions is accidental and not systematic. Voting is neither an evaluation of rival programmes for a forthcoming European Parliament (albeit filtered through media debate rather than a close reading of manifestos) nor an appraisal of the relative performance of parties in an outgoing European Parliament. Thus both *ex ante* and *ex post* mechanisms of public control would seem to be lacking.

Conclusion

In this chapter we have reviewed attempts to extend public control to a regional body beyond the state, the European Union. Some of those attempted controls run through national democracies, which have to authorize transfers of powers to the European Union, and which have scope to monitor the continued exercise of those powers through the direct participation of their governments in Union institutions and any requirements that those governments should in turn answer to national parliaments and electorates for how they have exercised the decision rights that member states retain in Union institutions. Other controls on European Union decision-making amount to a more conspicuous attempt to construct a democracy within the European arena itself. A Parliament of representatives directly elected by all adult citizens at the level of the European Union's political system itself enjoys significant powers to check and balance the Commission and the Council amounting, in some policy areas, to either full co-decision of legislative outcomes or a more qualified co-determination of budgetary resources.

However, both forms of control encounter significant difficulties in practice. Those that run through national democratic institutions are of markedly varied quality across member states, and, yet, even where they are at their best, they run up against the difficulty of trying to control the whole through its parts (Magnette, 2005, pp. 173–4). On the other hand, controls exercised by the European Parliament, victim perhaps of their own originality and the very extent of their challenge to the way things have mostly been done before, run up against the difficulty of connecting people(s) and polity, once the connection has to be made outside the comfort zones of single states. This difficulty manifests itself through an inter-active complex of factors, including the absence of elections that are conspicuously and uniformally structured around choices relevant to the European Union's political system itself; the relatively lower, and apparently declining, levels of voter participation in European elections; the opaque connection between national parties that are used to garner votes in European elections and the multinational party groups that eventually decide how the powers of the Parliament are to be used on behalf of those they represent; and citizens' poor understanding of the EU political system. We will pick up again on these difficulties in Chapter 6.

Chapter 5

Promoting Democracy in the New Europe

The lesson of European history is that democracy depends on much more than what happens within the state: it depends crucially on the international system. Swept away before 1945, rescued from the outside, reinforced in the West as part of a process of international competition, submerged in the East as part of the same competition, and then universalized to most of the continent with the help of a pattern of power relations that removed a veto that one state put on the democratization of others (the Brezhnev Doctrine), whilst creating new inducements that only democratic states could enjoy (Schimmelfennig, 2003), the story of democracy in Europe has always been one of international relations, as well as of politics within the state.

The last chapter argued that there are, in turn, two aspects to the international democracy in the new Europe. One covers proposals for an element of shared democratic rule at European level. The other dimension – which we analyse in this chapter – consists of a common effort to shape the society of European states so that it only includes states that are democratic according to more or less internationally agreed standards of democracy. When member states agreed a European Union security strategy for the first time at the end of 2003 they made it explicit that they would act together to promote democracy and do so for reasons of their own security:

> The quality of international society depends on the quality of the governments that are its foundation. The best protection for our security is a world of well-governed democratic states. Spreading good governance . . . dealing with abuse of power, establishing the rule of law and protecting human rights are the best means of strengthening the international order. (Council of the European Union, 2003, p. 10)

Such a wish only to have democracies as neighbours has, in turn, been justified on the grounds that non-democratic government can in the modern world seemingly only be sustained by closing off contacts with other societies. Such closed societies often then descend into a spiral of economic and social underdevelopment, internal repression and erratic international behaviour. As Francis Fukuyama has put it, 'since the end of the Cold War, weak or failing states have arguably become the single most important problem of international order' (2005, p. 125).

We return to the idea that democracy can help promote peace in Chapter 7. For the moment our interest is in how democracy has itself been promoted in the new Europe as an intentional act of international policy. We begin by considering general links – intended and unintended – between European integration and the consolidation of democracy in individual states. We go on to consider how so-called 'conditionality' has been used as an instrument of democratization. Here, exceptionally, we employ a case study – of Slovakia. The reason for this is simple: others have said many useful things about internationally coordinated efforts to promote democracy in third states. Those claims now need sifting and weighing through studies of particular cases. Our own strategy is to begin with a 'lead' case study of Slovakia, whose multi-ethnic character and difficult transition from communism provided an unusually hard test of many of the issues involved in internationally concerted democracy promotion. We then go on to check that our conclusions are confirmed by a wider range of less detailed case studies of other postcommunist states.

European integration and the consolidation of democracy?

The claim that European integration had a role in stabilizing democracy within the state has been made in relation to West Germany and, to a lesser extent, France and Italy in the 1940s and 1950s; to Spain, Portugal and Greece in the 1980s; and to Central and Eastern Europe in the 1990s. A number of attempts have been made to hypothesize causal links between European integration and democratic consolidation. These cluster into the following themes.

Economic Growth

Exposure to European integration may create economic growth dividends that ease distributional conflicts at fragile moments in transitions to democracy. Alan Milward (1992) argues that the economic benefits of European integration were used to resource welfare states. That, in turn, cemented a social compromise that allowed democracy to be reintroduced to Western Europe on a firmer basis than before 1945. Scepticism that democratic institutions could ever govern effectively – widespread in many parts of Europe before 1945 – dissolved in the face of indisputably high levels of economic performance and social reconstruction between 1950 and 1973.

Pluralism

A second suggestion is that European integration promotes pluralism and the balanced state–society relationships that are needed for democracy. The EU requires its member states to maintain open and competitive markets which, in turn, promote the development of independent sources of power. Remaining competitive in a Europeanizing marketplace may also require decentralization of the state through the empowerment of regions that can cultivate more localized sources of competitive advantage.

Communications

Democracies tend to cluster geographically. The chances that democracies will have democracies as neighbours are significantly higher than random (Li and Reuveny, 2003, p. 34). Indeed, non-democratic governments often seek to close their societies, precisely because the practice of democracy in one country often triggers demands for democratization in neighbouring states. European integration has precisely the effect of increasing the visibility of societies to one another and of inviting comparisons with standards – including political ones – to be found amongst 'our European partners'.

The democratizing effect of EU entry conditions

More than stimulating spontaneous democratization through example and the clustering effects of individual democracies,

European integration has, arguably, established a normative order and a pattern of identities that favour democratic politics. In a path-breaking work Frank Schimmelfennig has used a case study of recent EU and NATO enlargements to question how far membership decisions are based on rational calculation of benefits at all. As he puts it:

> The community organizations communicate their constitutive values and norms to outsider states and tell them to what extent they have to internalize them before they are entitled to join. After fulfilling the requirements, an outsider state is regarded as 'one of us' by the community members and admitted to the community organizations. Accession to the community organizations as a full member then corresponds to a formal recognition that socialisation has been successful. (Schimmelfennig, 2003, pp. 74–5).

In another contribution, Schimmelfennig and others (2003) argue that 'democratic conditionality' is the 'core strategy' of the EU to 'induce candidate states to comply with its human rights and democracy standards'. This strategy operates on two levels: explicit and implicit. The explicit strategy is reinforced by reward in the form of full membership of the EU (2003, p. 495) and its success depends on candidate states' calculations of domestic political costs and compliance. Conditionality strategy assumes that the 'community environment' with its common ethos and the 'density of interaction' will in the longer term create a self-sustaining environment of international norms to underwrite the democratic peace (Schimmelfennig, 2003).

Democracy promotion: standards, justifications, methods and problems

There is an ongoing and important debate among international relations scholars about how exactly international organizations influence domestic policy (Kelley, 2004). Within the European continent the main external promoters of democracy are the Organization for Security and Cooperation in Europe (OSCE), the Council of Europe (CE) and the EU. Although the OSCE and CE have participated in the improvement of democracy in post-

communist states their approach has mostly been one of diplomacy and persuasion, specifically of persuading elites of the benefits of democratic credentials and compliance with international
norms (Kelley, 2004). In the case of the OSCE the main areas of
engagement involve capacity-building and institution support,
election-monitoring and development of transparent legislation
committed to international standards. Notable among these
activities is the emphasis on ethnic policies in ethnically divided
societies (such as Slovakia, Estonia, Romania and Latvia) and
monitoring of volatile border areas (Moldova, the Balkans, ex-
Soviet Asian republics and so on) by the High Commissioner on
National Minorities (Kemp, 2001). Whilst there is little doubt
that these are worthwhile efforts and that, arguably, the slow
change of beliefs is in the long term a more self-sustaining
strategy, hard cases such as we will argue, were Slovakia and
Latvia may need more than persuasion to democratize in depth
or at all. The key point is that where postcommunist transitions
were combined with the establishment of new states they stimu-
lated nationalistic mobilizations that dominated domestic politics. In the midst, for example, of soft pressures by international
organizations other than the EU to improve inter-ethnic relations, the extreme nationalist Slovak National Party (SNS)
entered the government (1994) and intensified the already
authoritarian leanings of the new state. As our case study further
illustrates, it was only the EU's initial rejection of Slovakia's candidature for membership (*Agenda 2000*, July 1997) that brought

dramatic changes to domestic politics. Thus notwithstanding its
limitations, we argue that the EU's democratic conditionality,
and especially its linkage to qualification for membership of the
Union itself, has promoted democratization from beyond the
state more effectively than the strategies of other international
organizations.

With the Copenhagen criteria (1993) conditions for entry to
the EU were made explicit. Yet, from the start democracy was
widely thought to be a condition for Union membership, as was
made clear by the reasons for refusing Spain entry in the 1960s,
and use of the southern enlargements in the 1980s to promote
and consolidate democratic transitions from authoritarian rule
in Spain, Portugal and Greece. The Copenhagen criteria that
impact most directly on democracy and human rights are those
that require: (1) stability of institutions guaranteeing democracy,

the rule of law, human rights and respect for minorities; (2) the existence of a fully functioning market economy as well as the capacity to cope with competitive pressure and market forces within the Union; and (3) an effective public administration capable of taking on all the obligations of membership (*acquis communautaire*) and administering them without corruption (Glenn, 2004, p. 5; European Council, 1993).

Moreover, arguably, as important as the criteria themselves have been the methods by which they have been enforced. Since 1993, the Commission has been required to report annually to the European Council on the progress of each applicant country towards meeting each of the criteria. This procedure has, in turn, been monitored by the European Parliament, which has written reports on the Commission's annual assessment of each accession state. It is also worth mentioning that the Constitution, if ever adopted, will take the Union beyond the screening of prospective members for democratic standards and allow the European Council to suspend existing members for fundamental violations of democratic principles or of human rights.

Yet attempts by the Union to monitor standards of democracy and then turn them into a condition for granting the wish of long-suffering societies to 'return to Europe' as full participants in European integration has provoked disquiet amongst those who quip that if it were a state applying for membership of itself the Union would fail its own tests. So why, then, has there not been more opposition to the Union assuming such a role? Part of the answer is that the institutions of the Union are not self-appointed assessors: they make their evaluations as delegated agents of the elected governments of the existing member states.

Political conditionality may also have been accepted because it gives rise to a more balanced relationship than meets the eye between incumbent and applicant states. As Schimmelfennig puts it, 'the membership rules create an obligation to grant membership' if states are recognized as satisfying constitutive norms and values (2003, p. 75). Present members of the Union cannot put applicant countries through annual inspections of standards of democracy and human rights without narrowing their own margin to refuse membership should a country manifestly meet the standards in question. That said, the Union may have some scope to raise the bar. Signs that it may be demanding 'extra conditionality' of the states that did not join in 2004 may be implicit in the postponement of the signing of accession treaties with Romania and Bulgaria (Phinnemore, 2004), whilst, in the case of Croatia, the Copenhagen criteria were quite explicitly extended by further conditions: the return of refugees, cooperation with the International Criminal Tribunal for the former Yugoslavia and the pursuit of regional cooperation (European Commission, Opinion on Croatia's Application for Membership of the European Union).

The EU's political conditionality may also have been accepted, since, to use Lawrence Whitehead's (1996) distinction between three different types of outside influence on democratization, the Union's efforts have largely taken the form of 'consent' and 'contagion', rather than 'intervention'. Post-war Germany and Japan provide examples of democratization via overt military intervention, though attempts have also been made in the past to support democratization through covert or paramilitary interventions (the support for guerrilla or any other insurgency, assassination plots, *coups d'état* and so on), economic sanctions and pressures applied through classic diplomacy. The EU's efforts at democracy promotion have rarely amounted to an unwanted intervention in the affairs of others and, even where they have, they have more commonly taken the form of exhortation and the withholding of favours (candidate status for membership or market access) rather than direct sanctioning.

What, in contrast, has made the EU's political conditionality largely consensual is that its principal instrument – the decision to link membership to democratization – does not even arise unless and until another state expresses interest in accession in full knowledge that democracy is a condition of joining the Union. Since, moreover, the process is unlikely to start unless democracy has already taken root within a given country, it usually takes the form of supporting the transition to a form of rule that has already been chosen by the internationally recognized government of the country in question.

From the point of view of pro-democracy elites in transition states the EU's political conditionality may improve both the international and the domestic contexts of their own democratization. Given that democratization appears to have a demonstration effect such that democracies are more likely to have democracies as neighbours (Starr, 1991), a group of states can expect to enjoy a 'positive externality' by democratizing simultaneously: by moving together they can lock in democracy more firmly than any could by democratizing singly (see Slovakia within the Visegrad countries, or the Baltic states). Coordination problems may, however, make such joint gains hard to attain: how does any one state in a group know that it will not be caught in a game of prisoner's dilemma in which it democratizes only to find that its democratization is more fragile than expected because neighbours have not democratized? How can it be sure that all members of the group are committed to democratizing to certain minimum standards when all actors are notoriously bad judges in their own cases? One solution might be to appoint an independent referee and allow it to award prizes to those who complete the course to standards that all can accept. From this point of view, the EU's political conditionality is not the imposition of a particular form of rule and its associated political values from outside. Rather, it resolves a problem that transition states experience collectively by a means to which they consent individually in applying for membership of the Union.

In seeking Union membership pro-democracy elites have also sought to improve the domestic conditions for democratization. As we will see in our case study of the internationalisation of Slovakia's democratization process, close scrutiny of the elections it held in 2002 prior to accession negotiations contributed to the continuation in power of a pro-democracy government in the face of severe domestic opposition. The role of European integration in providing extraterritorial support for pro-democracy elites in countries undergoing unstable transitions is just one more instance, summarized in 'new *raison d'état*' perspectives (Koenig-Archibugi, 2004), of how governments may collude in self-binding forms of international cooperation, in order to weaken domestic constraints on the attainment of their objectives. In effect they trade a loss of state autonomy for an increase in the autonomy of particular kinds of government – in this instance, pro-democracy ones – within the state.

In addition to whatever support it enjoys in democratizing states themselves, political conditionality has gained international legitimacy. Since the end of the Cold War global belief in democratic forms of governance has reached unprecedented levels. Not whether democracy is the best form of government, but how to best achieve and sustain it has become the overarching question. Democracy has been the preferred choice of government in all countries that generated their own regime changes over the past three decades, so much so that Samuel Huntington (1991) has argued that the period constitutes a distinctive 'third wave of democratization' in which democracy is just assumed to be the most legitimate form of rule. This stands in sharp contrast to previous eras in which democracy often had to compete for that status against a number of alternatives.

Moreover, an entitlement to democratic rule is widely assumed to be universal to all humanity and not a right that is limited by time or place. If, however, democracy and human rights are to be considerations in the relationship any one state has with others, political conditionality is not an unwarranted interference in the affairs of others. It is a requirement of one's own behaviour. Where they are accepted by applicant, as well as incumbent, societies, notions of democratic peace may further legitimate political conditionality. They too render the internal affairs of states a legitimate aspect of international concern. Yet there are limits and dangers. The promotion of democracy with the aim of democratic peace could paradoxically see democracies become assertive in the protection of their 'way of life' to the point of promoting hostility and insecurity in 'target' states.

A converse danger to being too assertive is that the democratic peace theory does not of itself specify a level of democracy with the result that its adherents may be satisfied with a semblance of it. What, then, is the level of democratization that the EU seems to be aiming at in stipulating criteria for candidate countries? Merely listing the intended outcomes (Schraeder, 2003, p. 31), such as the protection of human rights, global economic growth and social development and increased free trade all round, is naive. A more penetrating approach would attempt to get behind the criteria and analyse what views of democracy and of democratic transitions are implied by them.

Schedler (1998) proposes a four-point continuum along which states may move on the way to democratic consolidation: authoritarian regime, 'hybrid' regime, liberal democracy and 'advanced democracy'. Whilst we should be cautious of any suggestion of 'teleological' progression between the stages contained in such classificatory schemes, they can help us clarify the goals implicit in the EU's accession criteria. The criteria are not aimed at democratic perfection (advanced democracy). Yet they do embrace a host of issues – popular legitimacy, democratic norms, minority protection rights, human rights, the role of the military, corruption, the decentralization of state power, judicial reforms – that go beyond mere 'polyarchy', defined by Dahl (1971) as pluralistic but imperfect competition between elites mediated by elections in which all adult citizens can vote. Given, moreover, that they aim at sustainability, the EU's accession criteria are probably best described as aiming at that point on Schedler's continuum at which liberal democracy becomes firmly consolidated. This, in turn, can be defined as 'confidence that democracy will persist in the near and not so near future' (Schedler, 1998, p. 103).

A final question is whether the standards contained in the EU's accession criteria are permissive or whether they 'bias' or limit newly democratizing states in their choice of what kind of democracy they want to be.

That there are limits to political conditionality is amply illustrated by the Union's attempts to promote democracy in the new Europe. One difficulty is that several states in the region appear to be beyond seduction. Among the 27 new postcommunist states, many have deviated from the liberal democracy path towards less democratic forms of transitions with idiosyncratic features. The literature now abounds with terms designed to express the varying degrees of incompleteness or imperfection in the democratic transitions made by different postcommunist states: 'hybrid regimes' (Diamond, 2002), 'diminished subtypes' (Schedler, 1998) 'delegative democracies' (O'Donnell, 1996), 'defective democracies' (Markell, 2000), 'illiberal democracies' (Zakaria, 2003), 'pariah regimes' (Pridham, 2001).

We are a long way away from being able to establish a firm typology of these 'hybrid regimes' or of the conditions under which they evolve. Postcommunist transitions have produced results as divergent as the histories and societies from which transitions started out. Many variables explain these differences: traditions of nationhood, ethnic composition and harmony, economic conditions, communist legacies and levels of political and economic development prior even to communism itself. The 'Europeanization' of postcommunist states may even have muddied the waters of academic investigation by adding international influences – variously projected and variously felt – to an already complex patterns of factors affecting democratization. Indeed, the 'hybrids' do not just differ amongst themselves. The

EU has varied perceptions about their prospects for democratic consolidation.

The democratic standards a country is expected to meet may vary depending on which postcommunist states it is commonly compared with and that, in turn, may be a matter of geographical location and neighbourhood (Pridham, 2001, p. 70). In the case of Slovakia between 1993 and 1998, international disquiet about lack of respect for minorities, contraventions of the rule of law, attempts to intervene in the freedom of the media, 'cronyism' bordering on corruption, and disregard for international disapproval was aggravated by comparison with immediate neighbours whose transitions created benchmarks that Slovakia was failing to meet in spite of starting from conditions that were not obviously less favourable to democratization. In that sense, the inclusion of Slovakia among 'pariah' regimes, whilst unfair in comparison to Serbia or Belarus, was understandable when set against standards shown to be attainable elsewhere in Central Europe.

Beyond, however, some scope in those cases where comparison is reasonable for using the achievements of some as benchmarks for others, there are real difficulties in defining democratic consolidation to the point at which it is straightforward to identify when it has or has not been achieved. Postcommunist transitions have demonstrated that sustaining democracy may be at least as difficult as establishing it. In convincing scholars and practitioners that democracy can be 'crafted' without requiring a long organic process of transition, the 'velvet revolutions' of 1989 may even have created a false confidence in the linear nature of 'democratic consolidation'. Another difficulty, of course, is how to pick out cases where countries satisfy formal criteria of procedural democracy, whilst remaining deficient in some of its background conditions. Any danger that tests have only been satisfied superficially or temporally will, of course, become most acute once the incentives or sanctions by which they are enforced are relaxed.

EU conditionality and democratic consolation: the case of Slovakia

Until recently scholarship has been preoccupied with the domestic factors that shape democratic transitions (Schraeder,

2003, p. 23): elite competition, the evolution of political parties, political culture, economy, civil society, ethnic history and complexity (Beissinger, 2002; Bibič, 1994; Diamond, 2002; Horowitz, 1985; Stepan and Linz, 1996). The divergence in transition paths and outcomes in postcommunist states confirms the relevance of this approach. Yet postcommunism was itself precipitated and shaped by international change as much as domestic collapse, and the simultaneous accession to the EU of eight postcommunist states with very different transition histories underscores the importance of including international contexts in analyses of democratization. For reasons discussed in the general analysis of the previous section and confirmed by the case study in this, the consolidation of the new democracies of Central and Eastern Europe can only be understood as a triple process of stabilization, domestic work on the institutional and societal preconditions of democracy and international integration into a European family of states defined by its common commitment to democratic norms.

When it comes to an assessment of the EU's ability to promote democracy in postcommunist Europe, Slovakia must count as one of the best case studies of democracy promotion and political conditionality at work. In July 1997, the Opinions of the European Commission on the applications for accession (*Agenda 2000*, July 1997, p. 130) concluded that

> Slovakia does not fulfil in satisfying manner the political conditions set out by the European Council in Copenhagen because of the instability of Slovakia's institutions, their lack of rootedness in political life and the shortcomings in the functioning of its democracy. This situation is regrettable since Slovakia could satisfy the economic criteria.

Yet Slovakia joined the 'big bang' enlargement in May 2004. The accession of this previously disqualified candidate confirms that 'Europeanization' – taken here to mean a transformation in the domestic structures of a state by European frameworks, norms and rules (Green Cowles *et al.*, 2001; Harris, 2004; Olsen, 2002; Radaelli, 2000) – can be driven by the use of the EU's political conditionality to intensify democratization from beyond a state's boundaries.

Slovakia's initial exclusion from European integration resulted from the practice by the Mečiar's administration of 1993–8 of a form of 'postcommunist authoritarianism' (Krause, 2003) that subordinated democratization to national and even nationalistic issues. Yet the 1998 and 2002 elections were won by elites who were prepared to commit to constitutional order, the rule of law and respect for minorities in order to secure membership of the European Union. Although this clearly was a turning point we will see here how consecutive post-1998 Slovak governments have been better at managing European integration than domestic politics, with the result that the case study illustrates the limits, as much as the possibilities, of linking integration, the goals of local elites and in-depth democratization on the ground.

Laffan (2001) argues that the EU is a social construction that is being grafted on to the nation state. This is of particular significance when integration follows soon after the establishment of independent statehood and where there are many still unresolved issues concerning nationhood and minorities (Vermeersch, 2004). Since Laffan goes on to argue that the transforming effects of integration work simultaneously through institutional, normative and cognitive channels, they can be an acute challenge to existing identities in accession states. Obviously, this is not a question of either/or, but rather a process of merging, overlap and possible collision. Yet post communist transitions show that it is easier to erect democratic institutions, formal rules and procedures than to change historically evolved practices, norms and collective identities, and this, we will see, is precisely the condition in which the application of the Copenhagen criteria has left democracy in Slovakia.

Whilst the redefinition of collective identities and the significant change in the understanding of the role of the nation state (and its ontologically related concepts such as national identity, citizenship, territoriality and statehood) may be particularly difficult in newly independent postcommunist democracies (the Baltic states, Slovenia, Slovakia), it would be wrong to assume that in established accession states, such as Poland, the Czech Republic and Hungary, this transition is less problematic. All postcommunist states are newly independent democracies, if not in a territorial sense, at least in the sense that they have emerged from decades of Soviet domination in which sovereignty, whether popular, international or economic, was reduced to a pretence (the Brezhnev Doctrine that was used to justify the

1968 military intervention into Czechoslovakia spoke openly of 'limited sovereignty' of states within the Soviet sphere of influence). This is one of the reasons why integration dilemmas involving contradictions between national and European identity and the suspicion of being 'absorbed' into yet another supranational institution (Rijshoj, 2004) with the consequent loss of sovereignty feeds the agenda of political parties critical of the EU in Poland and the Czech Republic. Hungary, with some three million ethnic kin in surrounding states, may make less of the issue of state sovereignty, but nevertheless places identity high on its domestic agenda. It could be even argued that smaller new postcommunist democracies are more pragmatic in the 'absorption' dilemma than states with a longer tradition of statehood (see below).

Also important to note is how 'Europeanization' has become a discourse (Fink-Hafner, 1999) of expectations and challenges in the case of Eastern enlargement. Expectations amongst accession countries focus on a return to Europe, economic benefits, enculturation and entry to a club of mature democracies; whilst challenges include the impact of accession on the capacities and autonomy of their states. For Union institutions, on the other hand, the challenge is one of ensuring the adaptation of accession states to entry criteria, including those that require democratization. These expectations and challenges mean, first, that Europeanization is likely to produce divergent levels of success and satisfaction in different accession states; second, that, Europeanization often means 'Westernization' for such societies; and, third, that domestic and international politics have merged into a tight and at times uncomfortable nexus, especially for smaller or weaker accession states. Implications for democracy, sovereignty and the idea of the nation are considerable. In so far as traditional understandings of the nation, the state and its sovereignty no longer describe reality, yet retain affective power over citizens, an element of disorientation can be expected.

Political conditionality and prospects for democracy in post-1998 Slovakia

Among factors that distinguish Slovak politics from that of its Central European neighbours (Poland, the Czech Republic and Hungary) are: a considerable deviation in democratization paths that led at one stage to Slovakia's exclusion from Euro-Atlantic structures (the rejection in 1997 of its applications to both NATO and the EU); the structural instability of the party system, compounded by ethnic division in its party structure; the continuation right up until 2002 of elections deemed 'critical' to the continuation of democratization in Slovakia (Pridham, 2003); and the speed with which Slovakia experienced Europeanization once it elected a government that prioritized integration. The following paragraphs explain and expand these considerations while using them to demonstrate how Slovakia emerged as a compelling example of the EU's capacity to function as an external democratizing force.

It took five general elections to confirm Slovakia's status as a postcommunist democracy. This was longer than for any other post-communist Central European country. The Mečiar administration of 1993–8 gave priority to consolidating the independence of the recently formed state following its breakaway from Czechoslovakia. Victory in the 1998 election of forces committed to democratization and European integration led by the centre-right leader Mikulás Dzurinda ended Slovakia's experiment with postcommunist nationalism. But it was only with the 2002 election that democratization was confirmed, albeit without, even then, being fully stabilized.

Since newcomers have to incorporate Union policies and adapt their institutions to the existing supranational body before they can have a say in the further evolution of the EU (Cowles *et al.* 2001, pp. 1–7; Fink-Hafner, 2003, p. 25) the stage of Europeanization immediately prior to membership shifts foreign policy goals to the top of domestic politics and automatically draws the electorate into complex and demanding adjustments. Yet the comparatively late emergence of political forces fully committed to democracy and European integration meant that in Slovakia's case the boundary between foreign and domestic policies was broken down particularly abruptly over the short period of 1998–2004.

An understanding of precisely how European integration functioned as an external democratizing force between 1998 and 2004 requires an overview of the results of the 1998 and 2002 elections (Table 5.1). Slovak parties are large in number, fluid in their electoral support base (with the exception of the Hungarian Coalition) and continuously open to being destabilized as new

TABLE 5.1   *General elections in Slovakia, 1994–2002*

Party	1994 %	Seats	1998 %	Seats	2002 %	Seats
ANO					8.0*	15*
DÚ	8.5	15				
HzDS	34.9*	61*	27.0	43	19.5	36
KDH	10.0	17			8.2*	15*
KSS					6.3	11
MK	10.1	17				
SDK			26.3*	42*		
SDKÚ					15.9*	28*
SDL'			14.6*	23*		
SMER					13.4	25
SMK			9.1*	15*	11.1*	20*
SNS	5.4*	9*	9.0	14		
SOP			8.0*	13*		
SV	10.4	18				
ZRS	7.3*	13*				

Key
ANO	Alliance of a New Citizen
DÚ	Democratic Union
HzDS	Movement for Democratic Slovakia
KDH	Christian Democratic Movement
KSS	Communist Party
MK	Hungarian Coalition
SDK	Slovak Democratic Coalition
SDKÚ	Slovak Democratic and Christian Union
SDL'	Party of the Democratic Left
SMER	Direction
SMK	Party of the Hungarian Coalition
SNS	Slovak National Party
SOP	Party of Civic Understanding
SV	Common Choice
ZRS	Association of Workers

* Denotes a coalition party

Note: The turnout in 2002 was 70.7%, nearly 15% down on the 1998 election (84.4%), but equal to the Hungarian elections (71%) and much higher than in the Czech Republic and Poland (58% and 46% respectively).

Sources: M. Bútora and P. Hunčík (1996) *Slovensko 1995*. Bratislava, Sándor Marai; M. Bútora (ed.) (1999) *Kto? Prečo? Ako?* Bratislava; IVO; G. Mesežnikov, O. Gyárfášová, M. Kollár and T. Nicholson (eds) (2003) *Slovak Elections 2002*. Bratislava, IVO.

political parties (usually breakaways from existing parties) find it easy to form and re-form and attract significant voters. Of the four parties that formed a government after the 1998 elections – Slovak Democratic Coalition (SDK), Party of the Hungarian Coalition (SMK), Party of Civic Understanding (SOP) and the Party of the Democratic Left (SDL') – the first three were formed for those elections alone and all four, in fact, encompassed ten parties. The SOP did not even contest the 2002 elections, whilst both the SDL' and the SDK split – the former into the Slovakian Democratic Alternative (SDA) and 'Direction' (SMER); the latter into the Christian Democratic Movement (KDH) and Slovak Democratic and Christian Union (SDKÚ). In total seven important parties formed between 1998 and 2002 (for details see Harris, 2004).

Besides the dire economic inheritance, one of its greatest problems was how to maintain the unity of the 'coalition of coalitions' formed after 1998, shot through as it was by contrasting personal and party interests. Clues to the survival of the incoming coalition are to be found in two features of the 1998 election. First, the high mobilization of voters (84.2 per cent) indicated awareness that something more fundamental was at stake than a mere change of government. Second, Mečiar's HzDS won more votes than any other single party, but was blocked from forming a government. The wish to exclude Mečiar was stronger than disagreements between his opponents, as it would be again after the 2002 election when the 'winning' HzDS failed, once more, to find coalition partners.

Between 1993 and 1998 issues of parliamentary democracy, constitutionalism, European integration, independence and the rule of law emerged as deep dividing lines in Slovakian politics, compounded by ethnic division. From 1998 to 2002 the participation in government of the centre left (SDL' and SOP), the centre right (SDK) and Hungarian parties (SMK) softened left–right divisions and the ethnic cleavage (Mesežnikov in Bútora, 1999, p. 45), whilst creating a broad front of parties that were willing to be judged on the likelihood of their delivering democratization and EU accession. However, a governing coalition that was wide enough to leave few mainstream parties in opposition yet fractious enough to sap some of its own credibility encouraged further proliferation of parties. Amongst the most important of the new 'alternatives' were ANO (Alliance of a New Citizen) and SMER ('Direction'): the former a centre-right party with pro-business orientation and versatile coalition-building potential which secured its place in the government; the latter a populist leftover of the rapidly disintegrating Democratic Left (SDL'), and a vehicle for one of the country's most ambitious politicians, Robert Fico.

That maintaining the course of democracy was an issue at all in the 2002 elections indicated the fragility of Slovakia's transition. Also of concern was that some parties continued to use ethnic and national issues to mobilize support. Yet the outcome of the election was, as Pridham puts it, of 'systemic importance', in consolidating liberal democracy and ensuring that developments since 1998 could 'progress without hindrance' (2003, p. 334).

The elections were noteworthy for the attention given to NATO and especially EU accession. The Dzurinda government made the issue of accession central to its reelection by stressing that 'the integration of Slovakia' was not merely a question of foreign policy, but a 'paramount domestic issue' (*SME*, daily newspaper, Bratislava, 8 July 2002). Since, both NATO and the EU were scheduled to make their decisions in November and December 2002 respectively, the elections could hardly have been better timed from a point of view of needing to persuade prospective partners of Slovakia's continued commitment to democratization if it was to participate in the collaborative frameworks that were most likely to shape its economic and security prospects, as well as define it as a fully accepted member of the European society of states. It took only two weeks to form a coalition which, in the prime minister's words, would 'get the country into the EU and NATO' (*TASR*, 5 October 2002).

Indeed, the international community took the opportunity to leave the Slovak electorate in no doubt that the presence of Mečiar, his HzDS, or the SNS (extracts from Prime Minister Dzurinda's speech at his SDKÚ party's conference in Bratislava, 6 July 2002, available at *tasrgate@kiss.SK*) in any new formation would be a 'fundamental obstacle to Slovakia's accession to NATO' (Nicholas Burns, the American ambassador for NATO, *Domino Forum*, year 11, no. 10, 2002) and would exclude it from the Union. But this was not the only issue on which the international community expressed views: all parties were aware that the exclusion of the Hungarian minority party – the SMK –

from government after 2002 would be considered by the Union as a step back for Slovak democracy. 'We are the kingmaker', claimed, quite rightly, the SMK.

However, the 2002 election confirmed two idiosyncratic features of Slovak politics. Even if it remained in opposition, Mečiar's HzDS, once again, emerged as the strongest party. Whilst international disapproval of him almost certainly impacted on the behaviour of representatives when it came to government formation, there is no empirical evidence of whether it affected the behaviour of voters, amongst whom Mečiar's position was, in any case, weakened by other factors, such as a split in his party and the entry of a breakaway rival party (the HZD) to the electoral lists. Second, the election continued to demonstrate volatility in voter support, and a proliferation and splintering of parties. This begs the question whether Slovakia yet has a sufficiently stable party system to be classed as a fully consolidated democracy. Only one of the four parties that made up the 1998–2002 government – the SMK – returned in 2002. Although the key role in the incoming government of two new parties formed out of the previous SDK provides an element of continuity that has hitherto been lacking in Slovak politics, the continuous reformation of parties hardly indicates a political system that is connected to its population through parties with deep roots in society.

Slovakia may be a success story of democracy promotion from beyond the state, but it is also a reminder of its limitations. Some of the instabilities in Slovakian politics resurfaced as soon as EU accession was secured. In mid-April 2004, the opposition and trade unions initiated a 'recall' referendum that would have removed the Dzurinda government halfway through a full parliamentary term. Although the referendum was voided by a low turnout (35.86 per cent), it was a sign of the unsettled state of domestic politics. Mečiar won the first round of the presidential election held on the same day as the unsuccessful recall referendum. After two weeks of mutual recriminations, the second round was won by Ivan Gašparovič (previously a leading figure in Mečiar's inner circle), whose best credentials were probably that he was neither supported by the government, nor sufficiently 'known' to the EU to be considered threatening to Slovakia's continued democratic consolidation (*Pravda* 6 April 2004; *SME* 5th April 2004).

The principal reason why the presidential election turned out as it did was the lack of cohesion among the coalition partners who failed to unite behind one candidate. Not only may this be one more sign of the problems to democratic consolidation posed by a fragmented party system – voters found themselves confused by the choice on offer – it may also indicate that a coalition formed to satisfy the political conditions, including those of democratization, needed for EU accession may struggle once membership is secured.

Indeed, the beginning of the latest pre-election campaign suggests that 'critical' may be a description of the forthcoming 2006 elections too. At this early stage, the idiosyncratic features of Slovak postcommunist political competition – its combination of anti-government mobilization by opposition parties, ethnic division, fractiousness within the governing coalition and alliance-building that is both short-term and negative – seem to have returned. Paradoxically, the anti-government mobilization by the opposition SMER and the distasteful anti-Hungarian rhetoric of the re-united Slovak National Party make the still strong Mečiar's HzDS appear a moderate party with coalition-building potential; even the Party of the Hungarian Coalition does not deny that it may be willing to enter into pre-election agreements with them.

European elections in June 2004 demonstrated further signs of weakness. Although participation was low across the Union as a whole, Slovakia produced the lowest turnout of all at 16.9 per cent. 'Voter fatigue' following the recall referendum and presidential elections only a few weeks before is only a part of the story. As much as European integration has been a primary objective of the government since the last six years, there is yet to be an open national debate about the EU and the future of Slovakia within it. Lack of political identification with the EU was compounded by the dullness of the campaign. Low engagement of the population with the EU may not be exclusive to Slovakia, but it is a concern in a country with a history of populist mobilizations that have linked external frustrations with internal ethnic divisions.

National question and the EU

As seen, political conditionality risks producing only a superficial and fragile form of democratization. It is thus not enough to

insist on procedural conditions for democracy that can be relatively easily verified. Additional requirements that are less
tractable to international monitoring include a political culture
that is tolerant of minorities and capable of renegotiating identities to ensure sustainable public acceptance of international
norms of liberal democracy. The de-territorialized expansion of
democracy through transnational norms and organizations
meets its greatest challenge in dealing with the territorial politics
of the nation state, particularly the relationship between territory, democracy and ethnicity. The problem is still more acute
where nation- and state-building are themselves still ongoing
(Harris, 2002).

With European integration, national identities which have
hitherto reinforced the project of the nation state are required to
reinforce, or at the very least relate to, a very different political
project, within and beyond the national territory (Harris,
2003b). Thus more than involving the external integration of
nation states into a transnational polity, Europeanization
involves adjustments to national identities, in particular a reexamination of how different national groups within the state are
integrated with one another. The last follows directly from the
EU's political conditionality and its requirement of democratic
institutions that do not discriminate against minorities.

Such challenges to existing understandings of national identity
and majority–minority relations may be especially difficult to
handle when Europeanization follows hard on the heels of a
postcommunist transition. Early stages of such transitions typically put identity-related issues at the centre of political life in a
manner that can destabilize new democracies and interstate relations. Slovakia's integration process was nearly destroyed by
nationalist policies, mostly directed at the Hungarian minority,
whose mother country is often blamed by nationalist opinion for
the stunted development of the Slovakian nation.

The relatively high level of ethnic heterogeneity makes the
position of minorities one of the most important socio-political
issues in Slovakia. The nationalistic slant of the Mečiar administration – which discriminated against the Hungarian minority
whilst neglecting the problems of the Romany population – was
one of the reasons for the EU's rejection of Slovakia from the
initial stages of accession negotiations. The 1993–8 government
implemented a discriminatory State Language Law (1995),

reduced cultural subsidies, engineered administrative districts and introduced Slovak ethnic quotas in order to reduce the Hungarian influence at regional/local level. It also made unsuccessful efforts to enforce Slovak education in Hungarian schools.

The post-1998 administration improved the framework of minority rights. It re-instated bilingual certificates for schools that taught in minority languages and cancelled ethnic quotas in communal elections; it improved the system of cultural subsidies and minority education and ensured better mechanisms for representation of minorities, including the Romany, on government advisory bodies. Moreover, it established a long-awaited Ombudsman and a new post of Deputy Prime Minister for Minorities and Regional Development with an attached section for human rights and Romany issues. Finally, a Hungarian University opened in 2004. Although the 2002 elections provoked some disagreeable discussion of how far non-Slovaks should participate in a new government, Hungarians improved their representation with 20 seats in the new parliament, three ministries in the new government (agriculture, environment and development) and significantly, the post of the Deputy Prime Minister for Human Rights, Minorities and European Integration. That in addition to 241 mayors and a further 4,013 representatives at local government level.

Yet the degree of progress on minority issues remains open to question. First, continued recourse to anti-minority rhetoric indicates some sections of the political elite still see the exploitation of ethnic divisions as a profitable strategy for political mobilization. Second, there are no constitutional guarantees of minority rights. Indeed no ordinary laws that specifically address minority problems have been passed since 1999, with the exception of the *Minority Language Law* (1999) which brought changes to the much-criticized Language Law (1995; for details see Harris, 2002, 2004) and enabled the ratification of the European *Charter for Regional or Minority Languages*. Even that legislation, though, is at best only a half-hearted adoption of European norms it purports to ratify. The stipulation of the older and restrictive Language Law which defines the territorial reach of each minority language by the presence of an ethnic community corresponding to at least 20 per cent of the population leaves out many minorities – Romany, Polish, Czech, Ukrainian, German and Bulgarian – that rarely constitute more than 20 per cent of the population in any one locality. Moreover, the new law only regulates the right of minorities to deal with official authorities in their own language. It does not cover whole areas of social and cultural life: the media, education, courts, theatres and libraries.

Many other major issues concerning minority legislation remain open. The most important among them is the change to the preamble of the Constitution (1992) which still refers to 'the Slovak nation', thus implicitly excluding minorities from 'co-ownership' of the state. The change of the preamble has long been demanded by the SMK, together with other constitutional guarantees, the formal creation of a district corresponding to one that de facto already exists with the Hungarian majority, and a restitution of Hungarian properties confiscated after the Second World War, or at least a revocation of 'collective guilt' on the basis of which the confiscations were legally justified. The Hungarian representatives, during the seven years in government, achieved only minor compromises on some issues, but no significant victories, in spite of often positive assessments by both the Slovak public and politicians of the SMK's contribution to democratization and European integration (Harris, 2004; Krause, 2003).

It is important to stress that Europeanization of postcommunist states – where nearly without exception the national question has been politically salient – involves adapting minority policies to European norms (Tesser, 2003). Even though in the majority of cases, national elites have formally adopted the norms in question, it would be naive to assume that this guarantees a change in majority–minority relationships. After all many of the latter are grounded in a long history of mutual incomprehension to the point at which it is hard for different cultural communities not to feel threatened by one another. Rogers Brubaker (1996) has identified a 'new nationalism' in postcommunist Europe with an interlocking dynamic between 'nationalizing' nationalism of newly independent states, autonomist nationalism of national minorities and the trans-border nationalism of the 'external homelands' to which those minorities belong by shared ethnicity, but not by citizenship. This model is well illustrated by the Slovak–Hungarian relationship: Hungary emphasizes its status as 'external homeland' to the Hungarian minority in Slovakia by including amongst its foreign policy goals the interests of its ethnic kin abroad (see below), whilst Slovakia continues to view the Hungarian minority as an extension of a historically hostile state.

A similar situation arises in Romania which is residence to two million Hungarians. A good example of inter-ethnic uneasiness in Central Europe is the so-called Status Law passed by the Hungarian parliament in June 2001. The controversy lay in the extension of constitutionally underpinned 'partial' citizenship rights to ethnic kin abroad (but not in Austria). Not only were these rights to be extended on the basis of a verification document issued by Hungarian authorities to those resident in the territory of other states, but the law was enacted without consulting either Slovakia or Romania. This led to political upheavals in both states and eventually, under the pressure of the EU's Venice Commission, the law had to be changed so as to be acceptable to all parties (2003). Although, as was always going to be the case, the law effectively became redundant on Slovakia's entry into the EU, it temporarily added to inter-ethnic tension in Slovakia and Romania.

The above discussion highlights a number of considerations. One uneasy question is whether Europeanization is not, unwittingly, reinvigorating ethnicity by eroding civic affiliation to the nation state. As the Hungarian ex-prime minister and architect of the Status Law, Victor Orbán, has put it: 'from the Hungarian point of view, the EU is a possibility to unify the Hungarian nation without the modification of borders' (Radio Free Europe/Radio Liberty, 17 October 2003). Second, the Europeanization of minority rights is a double-edged sword: it has positive effects, as argued here in the Slovak–Hungarian case (similarly in Estonia and Latvia in respect of their Russian minority), but, at the same time, an instrumental attitude in which minority rights are developed to fulfil the EU conditionality criteria without encouraging broad social support for them in the majority population may impede the realization of those rights in practice. National groups in Central Europe are facing a choice between the often difficult national histories and Europe in which future cooperation could put this past to rest.

Finally, in a Central European context where nationalism is rejected on a pragmatic level but invoked easily on an emotive one, it makes sense to introduce another level that can help resolve some of those historically inspired conflicts independent of political manoeuvrings. Hence the role of the EU as a mediating factor in interstate and inter-ethnic conflicts is crucial. Thus Brubaker's triadic relationship between 'nationalizing' nationalism of newly independent states, autonomist nationalism of minorities and the trans-border nationalism of the 'external homelands' should be extended by a fourth party – the EU – which has become, if not an active participant, then certainly a mediator in the evolving relationship between national groups within the Central European region.

The purpose of our rather lengthy case study has been to investigate how far democratic consolidation in new enlargement states can be attributed to European integration. Slovakia provides a 'hard' case study of the EU's political conditionality in the region, but one that, accordingly, provides an illuminating test of its political and normative potential to promote democratization from beyond the state by specifying requirements for a consolidated democracy. However, we also need to cross-check that the issues raised are not just peculiar to Slovakia without being representative of other cases. In the next section we do just that.

Europeanization and democratization in other postcommunist states

In this section we compare Slovakia as a 'hard' case in the application of EU democratic conditionality with the Baltic states, the Czech Republic, Hungary and Poland. The comparison with the Czech Republic is fascinating, since the two states shared a pre-independence past and, since then, Slovakia has often been compared unfavourably with its former partner in terms of democratic performance. Yet the other states are also useful sources of comparison: Hungary because it is one of the most notable markers of Slovak national identity; Poland because its identity politics are, to the contrary, detached from those of Slovakia in spite of Slavic and Catholic cultural connections; and the Baltic states because, like Slovakia, they were exposed to the EU's democratic conditionality just years after reemerging as newly (re)created states with large ethnic minorities. Yet at the end of the accession process Slovakia was, at least amongst the Visegrad four (the Czech Republic, Hungary, Poland and

Slovakia) the least critical of the EU. This suggests that where the EU feels it has to play hardball with democratic conditionality there is less cost in terms of Euroscepticism.

Euroscepticism?

The new member states from Central and Eastern Europe have provided academics with rich material with which to improve our understanding of the causes and diversity of Euroscepticism (Kopecký and Mudde, 2002; Rijshoj, 2004; Szczerbiak, 2001; Szczerbiak and Taggart, 2002, 2003). Some aspects of this debate are relevant here. A degree of Euroscepticism should have been expected around the time of accession for predictable reasons. Once membership was secured, some of the drawbacks of not holding a full, critical and open public debate at an earlier stage became evident. Concerns that had previously been suppressed for fear of appearing insufficiently Euro-enthusiastic were free to emerge.

Although the divisions between its subcategories are not always clear, Euroscepticism found in new member states mostly takes the form of acknowledgement of domestic problems deriving from EU membership (Euro-realism), or of opposition to present forms of integration ('soft' Euroscepticism). Only rarely does it amount to opposition to any form of European integration ('hard' Euroscepticism). New member states are not very different to 'old' member states in that multiple forms of societal insecurity can become a platform for domestic political competition and electoral mobilization. Yet, in the final analysis, mobilization around pro- or anti-EU positions depends a great deal on elites, given that public opinion is underinformed and often uninterested.

Rijshoj(2004) has suggested that Euroscepticism can be classified as follows:

- *Identity*-based Euroscepticism, involving a perceived contradiction between national identity and European identity, combined with a fear of being 'absorbed' by the EU and losing national sovereignty.
- *Cleavage*-based, linked to the main dividing lines in society, for example, town–country, work–capital, religion–secularism. People living in the country tend to be more

Eurosceptic. Other socio-economic cleavages then follow those likely to win or lose from transformations provoked by European integration.

- *Policy*-based or 'functional Euro-realism'. This consists of opposition to single policies, conspicuously the CAP, the euro, or arrangements for the free movement of labour, and the liberalization of real estate. Indeed 'single-issue Euroscepticism' is evident on environmental and moral questions.
- *Institutionally*-based amongst those who question the legitimacy of Union institutions sometimes in comparison with their national counterparts.
- *National interest*-based on a belief that the Union is committed to goals that contradict 'core' national interests. Often provoked by attempts to negotiate a specific *finalité* to integration, this form of Euroscepticism may lead to a belief that vital national interests need to be defended even at the cost of weakening the common Union itself.
- *Experience*-based on a feeling that accession negotiations have been unfair and asymmetric and that the terms of membership are thus unjust.
- *Party*-based, formed top-down by political parties and charismatic political leaders, typically using neoliberal, anti-modern or left-populist arguments.
- *Atlantic*-based around a perceived tension between pro-Americanism and pro-Europeanism, notably in the development of the EU's Common Foreign and Security Policy.
- Finally, a *practice*-based Euroscepticism. Here we find no articulated opposition to either the EU or Europeanization, but commitments to both are defined in particular national ways that do not fit mainstream interpretations of what the Copenhagen criteria require of new members.

At least one, but usually a number, of the foregoing feature in the domestic politics of all new member states. Even in Slovenia – generally held to have been the least problematic accession state – reservations have been expressed about the liberalization of real estate and about moral and ethical implications of Western liberalism. Before, however, we look at some countries in more detail, it is important to note that, whatever its complexity, opposition to integration has largely concentrated on questions of national identity and socio-economic issues, with the former proving harder than the second for Central and Eastern European countries to manage. In most accession states, socio-economic cleavages have been successfully incorporated into domestic party politics by national elites, even if not within a predictable Western ideological framework. With the exception of the Czech Republic (longer history of industrialization and socio-economic party identification), economic policies have not emerged as the main cleavage for party alignments for the obvious reason that the market economy was the only option out of the morass of the communist economic legacy. The margins of differentiation in party politics were thus considerably constrained and as a result focused more on identity politics (Kitschelt *et al.*, 1999). Eurosceptic parties thus have every chance of being broadly 'symmetric' with an underlying identity-based cleavage structure, in contrast to established member states where they are more likely to be outliers and relatively weak single-issue parties. Any tendency for identity-based opposition to the EU to feed off already neuralgic divisions on identity questions has been further increased by the fact that East/Central European political parties have developed concurrently with the adaptation of their countries to European integration itself (Batory, 2001).

Hungary

We have argued that one of the consequences of new statehood is the salience of identity politics, often to the detriment of democracy promotion and Europeanization. It would, however, be wrong to assume the salience of identity in newly independent states only. In terms of nationalism's core doctrine – a state being in charge of its nation's destiny – all postcommunist states, after decades of Soviet control, are in fact new states. In Hungary, as in other postcommunist states, the officially declared position of all parties is largely in support of the European project, including those that emphasize identity politics. Identity, however, dominates Hungarian politics: the loss of territories following the disintegration of the Austro-Hungarian Empire left sizeable Hungarian minorities in other countries and the Hungarian national identity marked by what seems to be a pervading sense of loss and injustice – at home and in the Diaspora.

Important parties and their profile

The pendulum of Hungarian politics seems to swing between Socialists (MSZP), who governed from 1994 to 1998 with the Alliance of Free Democrats (SZDSZ), and more Conservative forces. After 1998, the coalition consisted of the Hungarian Civic Party (FIDESZ), and the Agrarian Smallholder Party (FKGP) and the small Christian–Conservative Hungarian Democratic Forum (MDF). The current government (2002) is again led by the Socialists and faces formidable opposition from the FIDESZ.

Pro-market parties include the SZDSZ (Alliance), FIDESZ and, surprisingly, the Socialists. More predictably, the populist and nationalist MIÉP (the Hungarian Justice and Life Party, a splinter party of the MDF) are openly protectionist, while the Smallholders (FKGP) are somewhere in between, choosing to accept the accession for purely economic reasons, whilst stressing the loss of national characteristics. Socialists and Free Democrats have a more cosmopolitan outlook and, whilst they express concern for the Diaspora, they usually do so in moderate non-nationalistic terms. FIDESZ, on the other hand, is becoming increasingly less 'civic' and more ethnically driven, particularly since being defeated in 2002. Although not represented in the 2002 Parliament the MIÉP has developed a form of Euroscepticism that puts it in direct opposition to Europeanization. Not unlike other populist parties in the region – such as the Slovak National Party, the Polish Self-Defence and the Czech Republican Party – it rejects foreign investment and influence and seeks re-nationalization.

Hungarian foreign policy objectives have since the early 1990s concentrated on: (a) the integration into Euro-Atlantic structures (NATO and the EU); (b) good neighbourly relations and relatedly (c) minority policy, by which is meant the representation of interests of ethnic kin abroad (Batory, 2001). Unsurprisingly, foreign policy objectives, identity politics and European integration are mutually interdependent. Whilst there is no political party that would explicitly renounce any of those foreign policy goals, some are prepared to take risks with the others in order to prioritize identity politics. Having participated in EU entry negotiations when in government, FIDESZ has, since leaving office in 2002, positioned itself as the champion of Hungarian identity by claiming that the final accession terms agreed by the Socialists failed to pay sufficient attention to the problem of Hungarian minorities in other states. Thus, whilst being careful to claim to oppose the terms on which entry was negotiated and not the principle entry itself, it has nonetheless been prepared to mobilize domestic pressures on the government, which could only be accommodated at some cost to neighbourly relations with other states. Similarly, Hungarian Democratic Forum, when in opposition, qualified its normal pro-EU position with criticism of the governing Socialists for an 'internationalist–cosmopolitan' attitude that entailed the abandonment of the ethnic kin abroad.

Although its accession was never in doubt, it is clear that identity politics occupy an important place in Hungary's domestic politics and are readily exploited for the purposes of political competition. A key point is that grounds for opposition to European integration often migrate from their actual causes. Where, for example, EU integration sits uncomfortably with national/cultural values, there are contrasting tendencies for those concerns to be euphemistically expressed as criticism of the terms of accession or the present nature of integration, and for disquiet with particular accession terms or aspects of the *acquis* to be expressed as a problem of national culture and values (Szczerbiak and Taggart, 2003). The first serves to make arguments more acceptable to opinion elsewhere in the EU; the second to make them the more profitable sources of domestic electoral gain.

The Baltic states

In Lithuania, where the constitution requires 50 per cent participation for a referendum to be valid, turnout was 63.4 per cent, in spite of high abstention by the Russian and Polish minorities. At 91%, the 'yes' vote was convincing. The other two Baltic states, Estonia and Latvia, produced a lower 'yes' vote (66.8 and 67.5 per cent respectively). Like Slovakia, Estonia was a hard case for EU democracy promotion, particularly on minority (30 per cent of the population are ethnic Russians, half still without citizenship) and institutional questions (Raik, 2003). Although often compared to Slovakia in its nationalist tendencies, Estonia was nevertheless treated more favourably by the EU which opened negotiations in 1998 in return for considerable reforms in citizenship laws and progress in the institutionalization of democracy. Yet, unlike the Hungarian minority in Slovakia, the Estonian Russians did not support accession as a means of securing minority protection or economic opportunity. Indeed, presentation of EU membership as a means of protecting Estonia as a whole from Russian influence only alienated Russian voters, and left an impression that EU accession would cut them off still further from their homeland.

The same situation could be observed in Latvia, with an even higher Russian minority (40%). Latvia, unlike Slovakia, was less criticized by the EU and OSCE for violation of democratic principles than for the poor integration of non-Latvians into its society (Schimmelfennig, 2003) and citizenship laws that discriminated on ethnic grounds (Schimmelfennig, Engest, Heiko, 2003, pp. 511–12). Instead of being linked to residence, access to citizenship was linked to overtly ethnic quotas. Only after reluctant changes to the naturalization law and the Latvian State Language Law could accession negotiations begin from 1999.

Thus the Baltic states, newly reestablished with historically complex relationships with their sizeable minorities, confirm the lessons of Slovakia that EU conditionality is a positive, if slow, external democratizing force. The last two examples, Poland and the Czech Republic, demonstrate that (a) pro-EU elites need consistent positive signals from the EU and (b) that larger well-established states with relatively good democratic credentials may, in fact, turn more Eurosceptic during the Europeanization process.

Poland

For well-known historical and geopolitical reasons (the Second World War, the role of Poland as the historical victim in its triangular relationship with Germany and Russia, the Solidarity movement tradition, the overwhelmingly Christian population and the size of the country), the EU was always committed to Polish accession. Poland was the first country in Eastern/Central Europe to 'negotiate' the end of communism and thus orchestrate its transition to democracy from below. (A similar case might be Slovenia (Harris, 2002).)

One consequence of Poland's lengthy home-grown transition was a high level of elite consensus about democratic reforms and a relatively low presence of 'old' elites seeking to divert the transition (in Slovenia, unusually, the 'old' elites instigated the democratization process; to this day Slovene politics is still dominated by the same 'old–new' elites). Hence, the implementation of economic and political reform was fairly smooth (with some problems associated with corruption), even if not as smooth as was often presented by Polish politicians to the outside world (Schoenman, 2005). Polish application for full membership was accepted as early as the Luxembourg European Council of 1994 and the date for negotiations to open was agreed for the spring of 1998.

One of the most difficult issues of EU conditionality – the minority question – played no role in a largely ethnically homogenous state. Yet, from the late 1990s onwards the support for the EU appeared to be waning. The fear of rising Euroscepticism led to a new law by which the Parliament could approve EU accession by a two-thirds majority if the referendum were to be invalidated by a turnout of less than the required 50 per cent. In the event, the fears were unsubstantiated and the Polish anti-EU mood remained just that. The EU referendum produced a 77.4 per cent 'yes' vote and a sufficient turnout of 58.9 per cent. Even though Euroscepticism did not translate into a 'no' vote, it needs to be explained. The following would seem to be the most likely explanations:

1. Fears for the loss of sovereignty of this large state (39 million) with a long and dramatic national history. Even before its accession had been completed the Polish government was prepared to court controversy in the manner of an important member state. During the EU summit in Rome (2003) it joined with Spain to block approval of the new Constitutional Treaty on account of its opposition to changes to the Council of Ministers voting rules. It also adopted a strong pro-US position on the Iraq war and signalled a strong commitment to NATO as its preferred framework for the further development of security policy.
2. A strong agricultural lobby representing a huge rural population, already fairly conservative, but also fearful of the implications of the EU farming policies on their livelihoods.
3. The constellation of political parties in the 2001 parliament which included two right-wing populist parties: the new

Catholic League of Polish Families and the populist agrarian Self-Defence; the former's Euroscepticism is rooted in issues of national and cultural identity, whilst the latter's resentments are more policy-based. The effectiveness of those two parties has been magnified by the unpopularity of the ruling Democratic Left Alliance (Henderson, 2004).

Poland is another example where the conditions of membership, rather than membership itself, became an issue, particularly when all obstacles to entry were removed. Polish EU membership was hardly ever in jeopardy – not at home and not amongst the established member states.

The Czech Republic

The EU referendum (2003) – the first in the Czech Republic, only made possible by a new constitutional adaptation for this specific purpose – registered a 77.3 per cent 'yes' vote on a 55.2 per cent turnout. The domestic political scene prior to the referendum was one of upheaval due to the inability of the Czech parliament to choose a new president to succeed Václav Havel. Eventually, Václav Klaus, the leader of the rightist opposition CDS (Civic Democratic Party), won by one vote, with the support of the Communist Party and, oddly, some members of the ruling CSDS (Czech Social Democratic Party) who were originally opposed to his candidature.

Klaus, unusually for a president of a new member state, is a severe critic of the EU. The criticism of the current EU processes follows a period of extremely good relations with the EU, inherited from times when the Czech Republic was a shining example of a successful transition to democracy, politically and economically. It was Václav Klaus as prime minister in 1996 who submitted the application for membership and continued to lead the most pro-EU, pro-free market party in the Czech Republic. The current right-wing critique of the EU is concerned mostly with three issues:

1. The lack of economic liberalism (Klaus makes much of his admiration for Thatcherism).
2. Fear of the loss of sovereignty and, consequently, resistance to supranationalism and the CFSP. The Czech Republic

opposed the bombing of Serbia which it viewed as a violation of the sovereignty of Yugoslavia.

3. A strong pro-US stance to counterbalance Germany, generally, but especially now the Czech Republic is participating in a more integrated EU. Anti-German feeling in the Czech Republic (shared by the parliamentary Communist Party to the point at which it was prepared to support Klaus, despite diametrically opposed ideologies) raises the problem for the Union as a whole of the still unresolved issue of restitutions to 2.5 million Sudeten Germans expelled from the Czech Republic after the Second World War (the same Beneš Decrees, in fact, expelled ethnic Hungarians from Slovakia to work on the land, thus vacated by the Sudeten Germans).

Despite all criticism of the EU, the only parliamentary political party that openly opposes the EU is the Communist Party. Yet Czech Euroscepticism seems to have deeper roots than the normal pre-accession apprehension that usually follows the relaxation of the regime of conditionality. The Czech Republic also defies the proposition that Europeanization is more problematic in new 'nation-building' states; on the contrary, the country has a proud history going back to a medieval kingdom and can claim to have remained the only democracy among the post-1918 states in Europe during the inter-war period. Even Euro-enthusiasts seem to find it necessary to criticize the EU. Václav Havel, for example, has often criticized the EU for its bureaucracy, its priority for economic over moral goals, and the sluggish emergence of a common European identity. When in the 1998 elections the Czech Social Democratic Party became the largest single party, its chairman Miloš Zeman also spoke of a Europe that would be not only a common market, but a community of common values and norms with a common foreign and security policy and a common social and economic policy, including a common tax system. Despite such declarations, Zeman's government was slow in the implementation of the *acquis* and engaged in xenophobic rhetoric towards Germany and Austria. In sum, the resistance to the EU in the Czech Republic seems to blur the ideological boundaries of political parties, but overwhelmingly is identity-based with some concern for economic policies.

Conclusion: political conditionality in post-accession states

This chapter has analysed how criteria agreed beyond the state – in this case the EU's political conditionality – can be used to promote democracy within particular states. The analysis suggests the following two principal conclusions:

1. Democracy promotion through the EU's political conditionality disturbs the traditional symbiosis between the nation, democracy and territory by extending the 'playing field' beyond the state's boundaries and adding an extra level of power. In the case of new democracies this form of democracy promotion involves the stipulation of international expectations of democratic transitions and their democratic consolidation.

2. Political conditionality can achieve a degree of democratic consolidation. We developed the case of Slovakia at some length precisely because it shows how the external carrots and sticks of conditionality can be decisive to democratization, especially where the latter is thought to entail inclusion of minorities, and not the untrammelled rule of the elected representatives of the majority. Yet it remains to be seen whether political conditionality can guarantee deep and stable democratization in the long term. The following are amongst connected reasons for concern:

   (a) The top-down nature of processes of democratization guided by political conditionality. These depend on national elites responding to an external incentive structure which may not be widely or equally understood by all other actors within the state.

   (b) The lack of open discussion of the criteria for democracy promotion themselves, of why they are being applied, or of what might justify them.

   (c) The speed of accession, whereby formal satisfaction of membership criteria may for a period take precedence over in-depth adaptation of society to European integration, democracy, and, we have repeatedly emphasized, the kind of identity politics that go with being a democratic state and society within the EU.

(d) Whilst Europeanization dominates the domestic political process prior to accession, post-accession political conditionality loses its grip far too quickly.

(e) One of the least anticipated post-accession issues is how to deal with any economic or political anti-climax. There is a danger that disappointments with enlargement may spill over into opposition to changes wrought by the democracy promotion that accompanied it. The risk is probably greatest in relation to those minority protections which, as we saw through the Slovakian and Baltic examples in particular, would not have been put in place without EU political conditionality. Many of those protections still fit uneasily with local ideas of how majorities and minorities should relate together in a single state. The examples studied in this chapter of states with considerable 'minority' issues suggest that European integration has contributed to the improvement of inter-ethnic relations within and beyond states. But they also demonstrate that it has not eliminated ethnicity as a basis for political mobilization.

(f) The dangers of backlash are clear. Some fear that Europeanization will weaken civic attachments and virtues associated with the state whilst putting little in their place. Whatever the truth of this claim, there is little doubt that the leap from a postcommunist democracy to a fully fledged European democracy requires yet another national adaptation. Already transforming societies are put through another transformation that is open to being portrayed as an imposed 'Westernization'. That the latter is a caricature of what is in reality a more balanced relationship between the external 'democracy promoter' and the 'target' state and society misses the point which is one of perception; and, in any case, it would be hard to deny on the strength of the evidence presented in this chapter that at least some changes brought about by democracy promotion are decidedly not 'home-grown' and most definitely fashioned from beyond the state.

Chapter 6

Assessing Democracy in the New Europe

So far we have shown that democracy in the new Europe operates at three levels: within the state, but also beneath and beyond it. But how well does it operate? The gathering pace of efforts during the 1990s to promote democracy in other countries begged a simple question: how can we tell whether a country is a democracy? Yet because democracy is widely assumed to be the sole legitimate form of government in the new Europe, and thus a critical measure of 'how well' we are ruled, we have good reason to appraise established, and not just emerging, democracies. A difference, though, between the two is that when we appraise established democracies we are more likely to look for measures of degree than kind: to ask 'how democratic is a political system?' and not just whether it is democratic; to probe 'deficits' from ideal standards, rather than the satisfaction of minimum ones.

It would require a book in itself to make a thorough assessment of democracy in the new Europe. However, the first section of this chapter shows how a preliminary debate can be structured around some core indicators. The middle section then reviews more qualitative academic debates about 'crisis or renewal?' in European democracy. The final section adds a distinctive twist that is central to the overall argument of the book. It claims that however we evaluate democracy in the new Europe we will have to adapt our methods to a problem of 'joint supply'. That is to say, at least for the 25 countries of the region that belong to the European Union, it is no longer possible to assess the quality of democracy by evaluating national and European Union political systems separately.

Applying methods of democracy assessment to the New Europe

The attempt to evaluate democratic performance is as fraught with difficulty as it is hard to avoid. We will see how even statistical measures require a great deal of interpretation. As the researcher then travels the spectrum between quantifiable and more qualitative indicators of democracy performance, measurement increasingly gives way to judgement (Lord, 2004, pp. 14–15). Sometimes, though, it is possible to limit judgements to those that can be checked or disputed by others. One example relates to the assessment of democracy's 'basic freedoms'. If provision in constitutional and legal texts for freedom of speech and association is assessed comparatively, benchmark standards soon emerge that ease somewhat the dependence of any appraisal on the personal opinion of the researcher; and, if more than one scorer is used, scores can be averaged out, or scorers with split opinions can be asked to deliberate and justify the differences in their assessments. Another example relates to the assessment of democracy's 'minimum procedural conditions' for free and fair elections. These include effective and independent registration of voters, non-interference with voters or those competing for office, equal access to party funding and the media, accurate and honest counting of votes, and so on. It is now common practice to appoint international teams – who build up expertise over time and publish reports setting out detailed reasons for their judgements – to observe elections in different countries.

Yet as Philippe Schmitter and Carsten Schneider have argued, all this is still only to scratch the surface: 'it may not be difficult to agree what Robert Dahl has called the "procedural minimum" without which no democracy could be said to exist, but underlying these accomplishments and flowing from them are more subtle and complex relations' (2003, p. 12). In other words, we will need to assess democracy's supporting conditions, and not just democracy itself. Anything less will give us an inadequate view of the robustness of any one democracy, not to mention the 'quality of democracy' (Andreev, 2005), which, so often, depends not just on the features of a political system, but on how governing institutions interact with myriad other features of state, economy, society and international context (ibid.). Many factors may, therefore, need to be tested in a fully comprehensive democracy assessment. Sergei Andreev (2005) proposes 51 indicators, David Beetham *et al.* (2002) 105, and so on. It is, therefore, in the knowledge that we can only offer an *hors d'oeuvre* here that we discuss the following indicators of the condition of democracy in the new Europe: public satisfaction with democracy, voter participation, equality of representation of women and minorities, and various scores of free and fair elections, as well as of rights directly entailed by democracy (freedom of speech and association).

Satisfaction with Democracy

As set out in Table 6.1, Eurobarometer now provides data for 28 of the 43 countries covered by this study on how satisfied publics are with democracy in their own country and in the EU. The data also measure levels of trust in what are essential institutions, processes and intermediaries for any democracy including parliaments, parties, the media and structures of civil society. The following are some points worth highlighting.

A moment's glance at the table reveals there are significant cross-country variations in overall satisfaction with democracy. When it comes to assessments of its individual components, none attracts more mistrust than political parties. This is alarming to the extent that these are the bodies responsible for persuading voters to participate in elections and for structuring their choice. The mistrust of political parties is particularly strong in Central and Eastern Europe where the notion of 'party' is often associated with the controlling bodies of the communist era that acted as arms of the state, rather than instruments of representation (Moser, 1999); and where postcommunist party structures have in many cases failed as yet to settle into something more than changing clusters of notables seeking to mobilize support in different ways for each round of elections (van Biezen, 2005). Amongst other 'intermediaries' non-governmental organizations are relatively well trusted, whilst, with some exceptions, the media is more trusted than it is mistrusted.

In contrast to the lower-than-average trust for political parties in Central and Eastern Europe, trust in the media is higher in those countries than across the new Europe as a whole. Indeed, the clear outliers, as far as trust in the media is concerned, are television in Italy and the written press in the UK, which are mis-

TABLE 6.1   *Satisfaction with democracy in 28 European countries*

Country	1. Balance of those who tend to trust their national parliament over those who do not	2. Balance of those who tend to trust political parties over those who do not	3. Balance of those who tend to trust non-governmental organizations over those who do not	4. Balance of those who tend to trust the press over those who do not	5. Balance of those who tend to trust the television over those who do not.	6. Balance of those satisfied over those dissatisfied with the working of national democracy	7. Balance of those satisfied over those dissatisfied with democracy in the EU
Austria	–4	–52	+3	+6	+26	+32	–6
Belgium	–15	–53	+16	+22	+34	+26	+24
Cyprus	–53	–32	–	+14	+33	+36	+33
Czech Rep	–54	–69	–	+29	+38	–2	+29
Denmark	+32	–25	+16	+8	+35	+82	+13
Estonia	–19	–54	–	+10	+55	+7	+30
Finland	+22	–51	–7	+ 15	+47	+54	–11
France	–18	–66	+ 1	+ 24	0	+14	+3
Germany	–31	–70	–9	–5	+ 25	+3	–5
Greece	30	–40	–14	–5	+3	+29	+34
Hungary	–32	–62	–	–37	–6	–44	+22
Ireland	–8	–41	+29	+2	+53	+47	+44
Italy	–21	–65	+5	–3	–17	–27	+9
Latvia	–50	–73	–	+10	+40	–8	+28
Lithuania	–51	–67	–	+20	+42	–48	+27
Luxembourg	+28	–23	+29	+19	+26	+63	+33
Malta	+11	–13	–	–4	+22	+1	+29
Netherlands	–6	–37	+22	+24	+41	+29	–15
Poland	–77	–83	–	+10	+18	–38	+29
Portugal	–20	–63	+22	+17	+37	–36	–6
Slovakia	–51	–75	–	+23	+42	–46	+13
Slovenia	–44	–61	–	+13	+30	+13	+40
Spain	–7	–38	+ 1	+ 27	+8	+34	+30
Sweden	+21	–53	+ 13	+21	+32	+48	–14
UK	–36	–68	– 4	–53	+17	+22	–9
EU candidate countries							
Bulgaria	–65	–76	–	–17	+ 43	–56	+31
Romania	–30	–57	–	–26	+ 52	–38	+52
Turkey	–49	–49	–	–27	– 2	–16	+37

Sources: Data from Eurobarometer 57 (2002) for column 3; Eurobarometer 61 (2004) for columns 1, 2, 4, 5, 6, 7.

trusted by a net balance of 29 per cent of the public in the former case and a massive 52 per cent in the latter.

Participation

In contrast to the Eurobarometer data, participation in elections can be taken as a test of satisfaction with democracy that is based on the real behaviour of citizens and not just on what they tell opinion polls. It is a fair surmise that dissatisfaction with democracy would soon challenge feelings of civic obligation which remain the most convincing explanation for why people vote. Indeed, there are other reasons for equating low voter participation with poor democratic performance. First, it is one of the most distinctive qualities of democratic systems that they use elections to choose office-holders and confer consent in the same act (Beetham, 1991). Second, low participation may impoverish elections as sources of information about the needs and values of citizens, and blunt incentives for those seeking reelection to anticipate the preferences of a wide cross-section of voters. To the extent that some social groups are even more likely to abstain as average participation by the population as a whole declines, low voter turnout will be associated with biases in the representative processes. Table 6.2 analyses levels of voter participation in national elections across the new Europe. It also includes data on voter turnout in European Parliament elections. Amongst points of note are the following:

1. Contrary to widespread belief, the overall figures do not indicate a universal pattern of declining voter participation. As Richard Rose (2004) puts it, there would appear to be one group of countries where significantly fewer citizens have voted in recent elections, and another where participation 'bobs up and down' from one election to another without discernible long-term trend. 'Bobbing up and down' may suggest that low turnout tends to be self-correcting where it leads to outcomes unwelcome to significant groups of voters. Thus the low turnout that let the far right leader, Jean-Marie Le Pen, through to the second stage of the French presidential elections in 2002 was followed by daily street demonstrations and a 7 per cent increase in turnout between the two ballots. Although there is usually more participation

in a second than a first round of a French presidential election, the increase in 2002 remains remarkable, given that there was no real contest after the first round limited the choice to Chirac versus Le Pen.

2. Regardless of whether participation is stable or declining overall, the 18–24 generational cohort is significantly less likely than older citizens to vote. What is less clear is whether this is a timebomb ticking away under European democracies or whether the present generation of young people will follow their parents and grandparents in becoming more likely to vote as they grow older (Bréchon, 1999). The pessimistic view is supported by those who believe democracy is most valued by those who have experienced other forms of government and easily taken for granted by those for whom non-democratic politics is a distant memory.

3. Citizens of the new European democracies are, on the whole, less likely to vote than those of countries that were democratic before 1989, a finding that casts doubt on the preceding view that democracy is most valued by those who have experienced non-democratic politics. Indeed, participation tends to be up to 10 per cent higher in countries whose voters have lived all their lives under a democratic system (Rose, 2004), though, as noted, a further complication is the low level of trust in political parties in Eastern and Central Europe.

Yet the relationship between voter participation and democratic performance is far from straightforward. There are at least three conditions under which the effective functioning and design of a democratic system may even depress voter turnout. Although lack of differentiation in the policies of those competing for power is often given as a reason for voter abstention, convergence by representatives on positions favoured by the median voter may also be taken as a sign of efficient political competition. Second, low turnout may be associated with pluralist systems of divided government. Where the branches, levels or senior offices of a political system are elected in different ways and at different times, there will be less at stake in any one election, and thus less incentive to participate, than where power in the system as a whole depends on just one election. This would seem to be a factor in low-level participation in Swiss and, of

TABLE 6.2   *Electoral participation in 43 European countries*

	1 Average turnout 1945–2001	2 Average turnout in 1990s	3 Most recent national election	4 European Parliament election 2004	5 Difference between columns 3 and 4
Albania	–	88.0 (4)	–	–	–
Armenia	–	75.4 (2)	52.7 (2003)	–	–
Austria	91.3 (17)	83.8 (4)	84.3 (2002)	41.8	–42.5
Azerbaijan	–	86.1 (1)	–	–	–
Belarus	–	60.6 (2)	–	–	–
Belgium	92.5 (18)	91.5 (3)	91.6 (2003)	90.8	–0.8
Bosnia–H	–	58.4 (2)	55.0 (2002)	–	–
Bulgaria	–	72.7 (3)	67.0 (2001)	–	–
Croatia	–	72.2 (2)	59.6 (2003)	–	–
Cyprus	89.7 (7)	92.2 (2)	71.2	–	–
Czech Repub	–	82.8 (4)	58.0 (2002)	27.9	–30.1
Denmark	85.9 (22)	84.3 (3)	87.1 (2001)	47.9	–39.2
Estonia	–	68.0 (2)	58.2 (2003)	26.9	–31.3
France	73.8 (15)	68.5 (2)	64.4 (Assembly 2002)	43.1	–21.3
Finland	76.0 (16)	67.4 (3)	66.7 (2003)	41.1	–25.6
Georgia	–	68.9 (3)		–	–
Germany	85.4 (14)	79.9 (3)	79.1 (2002)	43.0	–36.1
Greece	79.9 (16)	79.7 (2)	75.0 (2000)	62.8	–12.2
Hungary	–	67.0 (3)	73.5 (2002)	38.5	–35
Iceland	89.5 (17)	86.4 (3)	87.7 (2003)	–	–
Ireland	73.3 (16)	67.3 (2)	62.7 (2002)	59.7	–3
Italy	89.8 (15)	85.5 (3)	81.4 (2001)	73.1	–8.3
Latvia	–	78.7 (4)	71.5 (2002)	48.2	–23.3
Lithuania	–	64.1 (2)	53.9 (2002)	38.5	–15.4

Note: Bracketed figures in columns 1 and 2 indicate number of elections during the period.

course, in European elections. Yet, as seen throughout this book, there may be persuasive reasons of democratic principle, of prudence and of cultural diversity for favouring a division of powers within political systems. Third, the phenomenon of 'voter fatigue' alerts us to the possibility that participation may fall in inverse proportion to the number of elections in which voters are asked

TABLE 6.2 *continued*

	1 *Average* *turnout* *1945–2001*	2 *Average* *turnout* *in 1990s*	3 *Most recent* *national* *election*	4 *European* *Parliament* *election 2004*	5 *Difference* *between* *columns* *3 and 4*
Luxembourg	89.7 (12)	87.8 (2)		90.0	
Macedonia	–	61.9 (3)	53.6 (2004 Presidential)	–	–
Malta	88.2 (14)	92.6 (3)	96.9 (2003)	82.4	–14.5
Moldova	–	74.2 (2)	64.8 (2005)	–	–
Netherlands	87.5 (16)	76.0 (2)	80.0 (2003)	39.1	–40.1
Norway	80.4 (15)	76.9 (2)	75.0 (2001)	–	–
Poland	–	47.7 (3)	–	28.3	
Portugal	77.0 (10)	65.2 (3)	61.5 (2002)	38.7	–22.8
Romania	–	76.2 (2)	58.5 (2004)	–	–
Russian Fed	–	58.4 (3)	55.8 (2003 State Duma)	–	–
Serbia-M	–	58.9 (3)	58.5 (2003)	–	–
Slovakia	–	85.2 (4)	70.0 (2002)	16.7	–53.3
Slovenia	–	79.6 (2)	70.1 (2002)	28.3	–41.8
Spain	73.6 (8)	77.6 (2)	38.7	–	–
Sweden	87.1 (17)	85.4 (3)	80.1 (2002)	37.2	–42.9
Switzerland	56.5 (14)	44.1 (2)	45.2 (2003)	–	–
Turkey	81.3 (10)	85.4 (3)		–	–
UK	75.2 (16)	74.7 (2)	61.3 (2005)	38.9	–22.4
Ukraine	–	73.3 (2)	–	–	–
EU Average	–	–	–	45.5	–

Sources: *European Journal of Political Research*, Political Data Yearbooks; OSCE/ODIHR election report; IDEA. *Voter Turn-out since 1945, A Global Report* Stockholm, IDEA (2002).

to participate. Indeed without frequent demands on the time of voters it would not only be hard to have a democracy in which majorities elected at different times and in different places check and balance one another. It would also be hard to have a lively multi-level democracy or a system of referendums in which particular questions can be decided separately from the 'take it or

leave it' choices involved in deciding between the policy programmes of political parties.

Political equality indicators

The participation of women and ethnic minorities in democratic
politics can be a telling indicator of political equality. For the
sake of space we only analyse the former here. There are enor-
mous cross-country variations, as set out in Table 6.3, in the
likelihood of women being elected to office. The Scandinavian
countries approach – but do not quite reach – gender equality in
access to elected office, whilst the 'new' democracies have a
mixed record, and even some of the 'old' democracies such as
France and Italy remain remarkably patriarchal.

Democracy's 'basic freedoms' and its 'minimum procedural conditions'

Ratings of political systems according to their observation of
'basic freedoms' and minimum conditions for free and fair elections are to be found in the Polity-IV and, more controversially,
the Freedom House data sets. In addition, the Organization for
Security Cooperation in Europe (OSCE) has developed a widely
respected system for monitoring elections. Table 6.4 summarizes Freedom House and Polity IV data for those countries
covered by our study that are not given a maximum score for
freedom by the former organization (column 3 of the table) or
democracy by the latter (column 4). Column 1 consists of the
Freedom House index of 'political rights'. Column 2 consists of
the Freedom House index of civil liberties. Columns 5 and 6
then use Polity IV data to assess how far executives are
appointed through political competition and how far they are
then constrained from abusing their powers.

 Most of the countries that do not receive the perfect score in
one of the two data sets are from the Balkans or the former
Soviet Union. Both data sets concur that there are two countries
in the region – Azerbaijan and Belarus – where conditions for
democracy hardly exist at all. Polity IV effectively rates both as
'pseudo-democracies' that operate as personal autocracies
behind a facade of elected institutions. A key difference, though,
between the two ratings is that Freedom House is deeply con-

TABLE 6.3   *Percentage representation of women in parliaments of 42*
European countries and in the European Parliament

Albania	6.4 (40)	Greece	14.0 (28)	Russia	9.8 (35)
Austria	33.9 (8)	Hungary	9.1 (38)	Serbia-M	7.9 (39)
Azerbaijan	10.5 (33)	Iceland	30.2 (10)	Slovakia	16.7 (25)
Belarus	29.4 (11)	Ireland	13.3 (29)	Slovenia	12.3 (31)
Belgium	34.7 (7)	Italy	11.5 (32)	Spain	36.0 (6)
Bulgaria	26.3 (12)	Latvia	21.0 (19)	Sweden	45.3 (1)
Bosnia-H	16.7 (26)	Lithuania	22.0 (15)	Switzerland	25.0 (13)
Croatia	21.7 (17)	Lux	23.3 (14)	Turkey	4.4 (42)
Cyprus	16.1 (27)	Macedonia	19.2 (21)	UK	18.1 (23)
Czech Rep	17.0 (24)	Malta	9.2 (37)	Ukraine	5.3 (41)
Denmark	36.9 (4)	Moldova	21.8 (16)		
Estonia	18.8 (22)	Netherlands	36.7 (5)	European	
Finland	37.5 (3)	Norway	38.2 (2)	Parliament	27.7
France	12.2 (30)	Poland	20.2 (20)		
Georgia	9.4 (36)	Portugal	21.3 (18)		
Germany	32.8 (9)	Romania	11.2 (33)		

Figures in brackets show rank.

Source: Interparliamentary Union, data compiled on situation at 30 April
2005, available at www.ipu.org/iss-e/women.htm

cerned by the Russian Federation where, in its view, political
rights and civil liberties have deteriorated sharply since Vladimir
Putin took over the presidency in 2000. In contrast, Polity IV
continues to score Russia as a competitive political system.
Independent election-monitoring by the OSCE suggests that the
truth lies in between the Freedom House and Polity IV assessments. The OSCE portrays Russian elections as an unlevel
playing field, rather than as contests that it would be impossible
for opponents of the government to win. Worrying though it
may be that the Russian authorities use state resources to favour
pro-government candidates, and that they deny equal media
access to parties and candidates (OSCE, 2004a), this is in a different league to straightforward 'falsification of the results'
through ballot box stuffing, and use of pre-marked ballots
reported in the case of Azerbaijan (OSCE, 2003).

TABLE 6.4 *Freedom House and Polity IV scores for 16 European states*

	Freedom House			Polity IV		
	1 Political rights* 1 (best)–7 (worst)	2 Civil liberties** 1 (best)–7 (worst)	3 Freedom 1 (best)–7 (worst)	4 Polity II –10 = high autocracy; +10 = high democracy	5 XRCOMP Competitiveness of executive recruitment 3 = best	6 XCONST Constraints on the executive 7 = best
Albania	3 (3.4)	3 (4)	3 (3.7)	7 (5)	2 (2)	6 (5.1)
Armenia	5 (4)	4 (4)	4.5 (4)	5 (5)	2 (2)	5 (5)
Azerbaijan	6 (5.9)	5 (5)	5.5 (5.5)	–7 (–6.8)	1 (1)	2 (2)
Belarus	7 (5.5)	6 (5.3)	6.5 (5.4)	–7 (–7)	1 (1)	2 (2)
Bosnia–H	4 (5.2)	3 (4.9)	3.5 (5.1)	n/a	n/a	n/a
Bulgaria	1 (1.7)	2 (2.2)	1.5 (2)	9 (9)	3 (3)	7 (7)
Croatia	2 (3.5)	2 (3.5)	2 (3.5)	7 (7)	2 (2)	6 (6)
Georgia	3 (3.8)	4 (4.3)	3.5 (4.0)	5 (5)	2 (2)	5 (5)
Latvia	1 (1.7)	2 (2.2)	1.5 (2)	8 (8)	2 (2)	7 (7)
Macedonia	2 (3.4)	2 (3.1)	2 (3.2)	9 (9)	3 (3)	7 (7)
Moldova	3 (3.2)	4 (4.2)	3.5 (3.6)	8 (7.7)	3 (2.3)	7 (7)
Romania	3 (2.7)	2 (2.6)	2.5 (2.6)	8 (8)	3 (3)	6 (6)
Russia	6 (3.9)	5 (4.4)	5.5 (4.1)	7 (7)	3 (3)	5 (5)

Serbia-M	3 (5)	2 (4.7)	2.5 (4.8)	6 (6)	2 (2)	4 (4)
Turkey	3 (3.8)	3 (4.6)	3 (4.2)	7 (7.3)	3 (3)	7 (7)
Ukraine	4 (3.5)	3 (3.8)	3.5 (3.6)	7 (6.7)	3 (2.7)	5 (4.7)

* Political rights include: free and fair elections of the head of government and the legislature; opportunities for citizens to form political parties and other political associations of their choice; opportunities for opposition; absence of domination by the military, foreign powers, other hierarchies or 'economic oligarchies; accountability and transparency of governments between elections; minority rights.

** Civil liberties include: assessments of media freedom, academic and religious freedom; freedom of association and demonstration; independence of the judiciary; the rule of law and equality of treatment under the law; protection from the abuse of police powers; rights of personal autonomy and property.

Unbracketed figures are the most recent scores (for 2003 in the case of Polity IV and 2004 in that of Freedom House) Figures in brackets are average scores since 1993 (or since most recent 'regime transition' in the case of Polity IV).

Sources: Polity IV database available at www.cidcm.umd.edu/inscr/polity; Freedom House data available at www.freedomhouse.org/research.

Crisis or renewal?

It is not hard to identify a number of claims that European democracy is acutely challenged in what has hitherto been its primary habitat, the state. From the next section of this chapter onwards this book considers the widely made argument that globalization and European integration now limit the autonomy of the elected governments of European states to the point at which they are unable to meet their citizens' understandings of what it is to be a self-governing people. This section, however, considers two further problems that, arguably, interact with difficulties raised by globalization. One suggestion is that the democratic politics of many European states have failed to deal with risks of public alienation inherent in the practice of representative democracy itself. The other is that specialist parts of the state are becoming more independent of mechanisms designed to ensure their public control.

Alienation and hollowing out?

Many readers might be surprised by the levels of dissatisfaction with democracy and mistrust of its individual components discussed above. Yet at least since Robert Michels's classic depiction of an 'iron law of oligarchy' (1949 [1911]) it has been understood that the very processes by which mass representative systems make it possible to apply democracy to large-scale societies also risk alienating citizens. Of its nature, representative democracy rests on at least two kinds of specialized elite: one to organize the knowledge and capabilities needed for effective government into permanent yet responsible bureaucracies; and the other to compete for power and take responsibility for its exercise through election as representatives of the public. Under ideal conditions, the public is nonetheless able to 'rule through' both kinds of elite: bureaucracies are headed up by elected politicians grouped into identifiable political parties, which are, in turn, under constant competitive pressure to anticipate the verdict of the public in future elections. Yet it is not hard to imagine how representative democracy might deliver a good deal less than this model promises. Commentators on contemporary politics identify challenges both to the notion of democratically controlled bureaucracy and to that of perfectly competitive political parties. The following paragraphs explain.

The argument that the democratic state is in danger of being 'hollowed out' (Rhodes, 1996) is the contemporary version of the long-standing fear that the boundaries between unaccountable technocracy and representative democracy are ever insecure. The suggestion here is that with the growth of social complexity, only experts possess the specialist knowledge needed to make effective policy. Power, accordingly, passes away from hierarchies that link each level of a bureaucracy to a controlling political leadership. Instead it is increasingly found in the networks and policy communities in which experts huddle together to solve problems. These are often informal, without authorization, regularized control by democratic bodies, or even precise definition. The experts that people them may not only be anxious to resist accountability demands from the political leadership of their own institution that go against the consensus of their own policy community. They may also be in a position to do so, first, on account of asymmetries of information (they just understand the problem better than those who purport to control them) and, second, because only they can deliver the collaboration of other network participants which is so important to the solution of co-ordination problems faced by all.

What, though, of the idea that political leaders are linked to voters through political competition? Here difficulties arise even if democratic competition is efficient. Whilst it is easy to imagine political parties having an incentive to compete for the median voter – who, under fairly undemanding assumptions of normally distributed and uni-dimensional preferences – can be relied upon to be the least average distance from all other voters, this benign outcome can only be secured through a convergence in the policies of parties to the point at which it may be hard to distinguish between them. The 'alienated voter' may see this as a restriction of choice even though it does not so much remove voter choice, as anticipate it.

A second difficulty is that highly competitive political systems may be unable to deal with 'time-inconsistency' problems (Kydland and Prescott, 1977). It is unclear what incentive such systems offer governments to deal optimally with problems whose solutions impose more costs than they offer benefits within the time horizons needed for reelection. Thus in the 1970s – before independent central banking became the rule – it was common to ask whether democracies geared to short electoral cycles cause inflation and debauch public finances. Thirty years on there is concern that even if democracies could coordinate themselves internationally they would struggle individually to impose the sacrifices needed to deal with the depletion of environmental resources that threaten life itself, again on account of electoral short-termism.

Yet, in addition to dangers of encouraging suboptimal policy outcomes, there are risks that competition in representative democracies may, in any case, only be imperfect at best. Those who believe that the aim of representative democracy should be to connect citizens' preferences to the political system have always had to contend with the objection that elections typically only offer infrequent choices between indivisible packages of policies (party manifestos) that many citizens would rather pick and mix (Dunleavy and O'Leary, 1987, p. 95). On top of this systemic constraint, political parties may further restrict choice through their own behaviour. European political parties have thus been depicted as cartels. One version of this argument has them colluding to avoid the uncertainties of competition, and to substitute in its place a predictable carve-up between themselves of the benefits of the political system: its offices and its policy outputs (Katz and Mair, 1995). Another has governing parties acting – this time unilaterally – to cut the range of alternatives that their opponents can offer voters. Into this category might be put the hiving off of responsibilities to new and quasi-autonomous regulatory bodies, to central banks, and to the European Union (Blyth and Katz, 2005).

The last three paragraphs might explain why the Eurobarometer data in Table 6.1 demonstrate that of all the components of representative democracy political parties are held in particularly low regard. However, another variant of the 'alienation argument' attributes the problem not so much to the structures of representative politics as to changes in society that apparently make it less supportive of mass democracy. Society, it is claimed, is becoming more individualistic and this, in turn, depreciates social capital and makes it harder for citizens to comprehend the relevance of the collective and the public.

Even if they are not becoming more individualistic, it may even be a problem for democracy that European societies are seemingly becoming more complex and fragmented. The difficulty here is that representative democracy may work best where the cleavages in society that struggle for representation in the political process are small in number and high in salience to citizens. Where cleavages are salient, citizens identify with a subgroup in society or have a high-stake interest in its political success (Rokkan, 1970). This reinforces motivations to participate that derive from a more diffuse sense of obligation to the democratic process as a whole. Where political cleavages are straightforward, political systems escape a dilemma between overburdening themselves and citizens by organizing democratic politics differently in relation to different dimensions of choice, or alienating those who feel the political system is insufficiently responsive to the kinds of choice they want to make (Schattsneider, 1960). Until recently other alignments have correlated so closely with left–right ones in many European countries that it has, on the whole, been possible to 'squeeze' and simplify choice into that one dimension of political competition. Other European democracies have been at most two-dimensional with linguistic–cultural differences cross-cutting left–right ones. Whilst this is not beyond the limits of what is possible in institutional design, the examples of Belgium and Switzerland might caution against attempting to accommodate much more complexity in a single structure of representative government.

Strengthened democratic constitutionalism?

The gloomy assessments we have considered so far are, however, open to the charge that they reflect dated and partial understandings of democracy. Thus the notion that we can no longer be confident that all those who make public policy can be knit together into a largely controllable chain of agency from a majority of voters, to parliamentary representatives, to elected government leaders, to the darkest recesses of bureaucracy was never attractive anyway to those who hold to a constitutionalist, rather than a popular, standard of democracy. For proponents of constitutional democracy it was always important to avoid building democracy on an assumption of a single controlling people and to aim, instead, for checks and balances exercised by different majorities at different times, or even by individuals exercising rights that are as constitutive of democracy as any popular sovereignty of the people as a whole (Habermas, 1996).

Given this difference of perspective, constitutionalists are as likely to claim that European democracy has been strengthened in recent decades as adherents of popular democracy are to believe that it has been weakened. Stone Sweet (2000) uses the extent of judicial review to test whether selected states have converged on constitutional democracy, and finds that they have.

New Governance?

Moreover the constitutionalist notion that judicial protection of the individual is as important to democracy as 'will-formation' by electoral and parliamentary majorities may mean that new forms of governance, depicted above as a menace to the state as an integrated instrument of public control, could yet turn out to be another promising innovation. Whilst they pose obvious challenges of public control (Lord, 2005), new patterns of policy-making that replace traditional hierarchies of government by policy-making in more informal networks between policy specialists and affected 'stakeholders' can, in principle, be controlled by the courts and by ombudsmen using publicly sanctioned administrative standards (Scott, 2000).

Provided that safeguards are in place, new forms of governance may offer original ways of structuring representation, participation and accountability. Where, as Adrienne Héritier puts it, policy networks consist of similarly informed but mutually suspicious actors (1997), they amount to mechanisms of 'horizontal accountability' in which different types of decision-maker have to justify their actions to one another. This may be most useful where it is hard to institutionalize the 'vertical accountability' of all decision-makers to the public as a whole, as, for example, would appear to be the case with the EU (Héritier, 1997). But even where vertical forms of public control are feasible, stakeholder networks can add value. They may, for example, give access and participation to a wider range of actor-types than those found in elected legislatures and, in contrast to fixed-composition parliaments, their composition can be varied on a case-by-case basis to fit those actors who are most likely to be affected by a particular policy (De Schutter *et al.*, 2001, p. 18). This helps counter the following shortcoming: in emphasizing the political equality of voters and representatives, formal democratic institutions do not provide for cases where some individuals are more intensively and personally affected by a policy than others. Nor need the involvement of informal policy networks in framing and implementing policy preempt the role of elected and accountable bodies, provided decisions still have to pass at some point through the 'filters' or 'sluice gates' (Habermas, 1996, pp. 371–2) of procedures structured for public control with political equality.

Second, traditional forms of representation and accountability can be deliberatively undemanding. A parliamentary majority may be able to shut down discussion on no other basis than that it is the majority, and that it has an electorally mandated programme, regardless of how well individual elements have been scrutinized in practice. Within networks, on the other hand, each policy has to be justified to independent actors whose only basis for agreement is mutual persuasion. As Christian Joerges and Jürgen Neyer (1997 p. 620) put it, they have to 'rely on persuasion, argument and discursive process rather than on command, control and strategic interaction'.

Communications Revolution?

Beyond such changes in how public decision-making is structured, another innovation has been the media revolution in communications between rulers and ruled (Bale, 2005). Although the European media hardly meets ideal conditions for a public space – equality of access for all points of view and reasoned, respectful and abuse-free reflection on the views of others – it is not devoid of those qualities either. Moreover, it allows for a vox pop in the literal sense of giving 'voice' on a daily basis to non-elite actors. It can also be relentless in ferreting out abuses of power, exposing policy failure and forcing significant policy change in response to public pressure.

New forms of participation?

A final example of how adaptations in democracy in the new Europe may be mistaken for evidence of decay concerns falls in the membership of political parties, and, in some countries, declining electoral participation. To set against both trends has been a growth in other associational activity. Citing evidence of a significant growth since the early 1990s in the numbers of French citizens who have signed petitions, participated in demonstrations or joined a civil association one commentator argues that 'electoral abstention may indicate a change, rather than a decline, in public life' (*Le Monde*, 21 June 2004). An interesting question is whether new forms of associational activity have an international nature. Limits on the sufficiency of domestic arenas for those seeking to influence global processes that affect ordinary lives may at least be spasmodically counter-balanced by opportunities for forms of 'round-the globe alliance between extra-parliamentary and parliamentary forces' (Beck, 2004, p. 69). Albeit that such opportunities – usually centred on protest and new social movements – cannot of themselves have the systematic procedural features needed to be democratic, they can feed into properly structured democratic systems and revive their sometimes flagging engagement with sections of the societies they represent.

A problem of joint supply?

In the last section we introduced the debate between those who believe that democracy in the new Europe is seriously challenged and those who, to the contrary, believe it is adjusting to a changing environment in ways that allow it to reproduce its core values in new ways. Not to be excluded though is that one of the biggest innovations of all lies in the increasing entanglement of democracy within the European state with developments beyond it. It is to the daunting challenge of suggesting a framework for analysing what might be involved here that we now turn in the remainder of the book. This section begins that process – whilst at the same time concluding the discussion of how best to assess democracy in Europe – by arguing that for at least that large part of the new Europe that is a part of the European Union it is no longer possible to evaluate the democratic performance of national democracies and that of European Union institutions apart. Rather, the two levels are linked together in the joint supply of standards of democratic performance. Since space does not permit an exhaustive analysis of this important phenomenon we will have to confine ourselves to a brief survey of its salient features.

In Chapter 4 we observed that the contemporary EU has repeatedly been justified to its citizens on the grounds that it represents them democratically twice over in its institutions: first, through the need of the governments meeting in the Council of Ministers to answer to national publics and parliaments; and, second, through the direct election by the public of representatives at Union level who share significant powers over the allocation of Union office and the determination of its policies. The first component self-evidently depends on national democratic politics and institutions. Yet it would be a mistake to underestimate how far the second also remains anchored in the national arena. The following paragraphs elaborate.

The quality of representation at Union level depends on linkages to the voter that run through national arenas

National electoral systems are used to administer European elections, to aggregate the votes and to allocate seats. National political parties structure voter choice. And national media provide most of the information during the campaign. Apparently trivial defects in particular national arrangements for administering European elections are often attributed with a cumulatively significant impact on turnout across the Union as a whole. Mikko Mattila estimates that just 'holding elections during weekends and having multiple constituencies in all countries could increase the turnout by approximately ten percentage points' (2003, p. 449).

More fundamentally, it is the use of member states as constituencies for European elections and of national parties to structure choice that give European elections the character of an unusual form of national general election: everyone votes at the same time for more or less the same menu of parties that dominate national politics, but without any risk that legislative or executive power will actually change hands. Even if this does not invariably force European elections back into a straightjacket of domestic political competition without any mention of Union issues, the unusual combination just described often means the elections are not anchored in an agreed understanding of the choice that voters are being called upon to make. Is a European election a mid-term plebiscite on the performance of national governments? An occasional opportunity to vote 'with the heart' for parties that are most expressive of voter values, rather than 'with the head' for those that are most likely to affect outcomes? A means of expressing views on European integration or even of attempting to influence the legislative outputs of the EP? European elections are probably all of these things, at different times, and for different groups of people (Bréchon, 1999).

The quality of Representation at Union level depends on incumbent actors in national arenas

National parties have been criticized for 'making a parsimonious effort' in polls to the European Parliament to the point at which one can ask whether there 'has really been an election at all' (Delwit, 2000, p. 310). Indeed, national parties may even benefit from restrained competition in European elections. As long as European elections are second-order in nature, MEPs have no special incentive to follow the preferences of an electorate that does not choose on EU – let alone EP – issues. Yet, they have every reason to follow the preferences of the national parties that reward or sanction their careers by deciding whether they are to be re-adopted as candidates for subsequent European Parliaments, or offered a route back into domestic politics (Andolfato, 1994). Pressure to please domestic parties is further intensified by the use of closed lists in European elections in most member states. Chances of political survival are not just dependent on being re-adopted, but on the order in which the party presents its candidates for election.

The pivotal role of domestic parties in shaping MEPs' career paths may, in turn, reinforce the 'grand coalition politics' of the EP, in which the centre right (EPP-ED), the centre left (PES) and even the Liberals (ELDR) and Greens often link up across the political divide to exercise the powers of the Parliament. A predictable carve-up of the Parliament's policy outcomes minimizes the risk of spill-back controversies to the domestic arena. The difficulty, as Pat Cox (President of the Parliament, 2002–4) has argued, is that consensus politics may make it difficult for MEPs to 'demonstrate to voters that preferring one set of candidates to another' in European elections will change policy outcomes (ELDR, 1999).

In so far as it reduces the pressure to align the exercise of the powers of the EP with public opinion, the restraint of political competition in both the parliamentary and electoral arenas exposes European Parliamentary politics to risks of 'rent-seeking' behaviour. Policy pay-offs from including a directly elected Parliament in the EU's representative structures that would be closer to the preferences of the represented in a more politically competitive system may, instead, end up being aligned more closely with the preferences of representatives themselves and of those who organize their election. Thus shortcomings of democratic 'responsiveness' may compound earlier observations (p. 000) about the difficulty of securing democratic 'responsibility' through present structures.

Yet representative politics at Union level may be trapped in at least some degree of reliance on national parties. Even those voters who switch their support from one election to another – and more of us do in an age of 'partisan de-alignment' – need to be able to float between parties with 'brand recognition'. Meanwhile the continued role for national parties in structuring voter choice is closely associated with use of member states as constituencies for European elections, and that, in turn, is unlikely to change for two reasons. First, it provides each country with an assured level of representation in the European Parliament, and, as such, is an important component of the Union's 'institutional balance'. Second, it allows European elections to benefit from feelings of civic obligation to vote that have developed through political socialization into the national arena. Any sudden substitution of pan-European for national parties as the means of structuring voter choice in European elections might even risk further declines in turnout.

The quality of representation at Union level depends on civic capabilities developed within national arenas

Although we have encountered many possible explanations for modest participation in European elections, there is one we have not so far mentioned. Citizens who feel they lack knowledge of the Union are less likely to vote. In one survey, those who feel they have little knowledge of the EU rank the probability of their participating at just 5.81 on a scale of 1 to 10, whilst those who think they know quite a lot about the Union rank the probability of their voting at 8.45 (Eurobarometer 57, 2002, p. 98). Indeed, citizens may even have only limited awareness of their own role as voters in the EU's political system. In a further survey (Blondel *et al.*, 1998, p. 93), answers to the question 'who elects the European Parliament?' were only slightly better than random.

There are at least two ways in which the national political environment affects understanding of the EU political system. First, content analyses conclude that national media coverage of European elections is often insufficiently sustained to pass a certain 'threshold of visibility' needed for 'cognitive mobilization' (Gerstlé *et al.*, 2000). Second, governments may vary in their willingness to inform their publics on Union matters. A rough and ready indicator of that willingness is the proportion of each national public that is aware at the end of its six-month term that its own government has held the rotating presidency of the Council of Ministers. On this score, large Member States are systematically less likely than smaller to inform their publics (Lord, 2004, p. 56).

Some of the foregoing problems may be self-perpetuating. Here the key point is made by James March and Johan Olsen (1995): both representatives and represented need 'political capabilities' that are only likely to develop with use. Elections that continue to have a heavily domestic content cannot perform the developmental role (Held, 1996) of improving citizens' understanding of how best to use the EU's political system to achieve their needs and values.

So far, then, we have suggested three reasons why the performance of EU democracy is heavily dependent on that of its member states. Yet, conversely, there are a number of grounds for believing that the quality of democracy within the national arena is affected by Union membership. Consider the following partially overlapping points.

Union membership affects executive–legislature balance within national democracies

Perhaps the most important – and least understood – aspect of European Union governance is that national governments are themselves amongst the main beneficiaries of delegations of power to Union institutions. They may give up some agenda-setting power to the Commission (though even the extent to which they do that is open to question) but they retain key decision-making in the Council of Ministers. Although they exercise those powers collectively rather than individually, and increasingly in conjunction with the European Parliament, it is surprisingly rare for decisions to be made against the wishes of any one government, even where the rules allow majority voting (Matilla and Lane, 2001). Whilst this suggests there is still significant scope to exercise democratic control of Union decisions through national institutions, it also implies that it is insufficient to leave that control to the executive branches of national governments. Since the latter are amongst the key power-holders in Union institutions, they are part of the very process that is in need of democratic control.

Union membership may affect the quality of democratic control and competition in national arenas

As seen in Chapter 2 democratic states have often institutionalized public control through integrated and hierarchical systems of public control in which citizens elect parliaments, parliamentary majorities form governments, and governments head up bureaucracies loyal to their political masters. To difficulties with sustaining this model that have little to do with European integration, participation in the European Union adds another. As Wolfgang Wessels puts it (1998), the Union typically works by encouraging actors from member states to 'fuse' their efforts and resources. Yet, crucially, it brings them together in a segmental political system. Even elected members of national governments meet in sectoral (that is, thematically distinct) formations of the Council of Ministers, whilst individual officials, experts and whole ministries communicate directly with their counterparts in other member states. The result is to peel particular actors and agencies away from at least some of the disciplines of collectively responsible government within member states (Dehousse, 1997), and provide them with an element of autonomy based, first, on the costs to their political principals and representative institutions of monitoring all their activities, and, second, on a need to give rein to transnational networking between technocrats with specialized knowledge if there are to be solutions to the problems that created a need for EU policies and institutions in the first place.

Indeed, there is a risk that using national elections to provide representation in relation to two very different political systems may reduce the representative qualities of domestic institutions, rather than increase those of the Union. In some member states, Union membership may have contributed to a drift towards cartel parties (Katz and Mair, 1995), whose main concern is to manage issues between themselves, rather than compete freely. This is, first, because Union issues may threaten the cohesion of parties that have developed around domestic issues; second, because opportunities to appoint to office and influence the policy outputs of two, and not just one, political systems (the national and European) can now be used to sustain any cartel of *status quo* parties in the domestic arena; and, third, because the transfer of powers to the Union provides precisely the opportunity to outflank opponents by putting some matters beyond domestic political competition (Blyth and Katz, 2005).

Union membership may create problems of 'moral hazard' in relations between represented and representatives in the national arena

The preceding points suggest two ways in which the transfer of policy from national to Union level may make it harder to achieve public control: decision-making will be at one further stage of delegation from the voter; and the costs to voters or their representatives of monitoring decision-making will rise if Union institutions are harder than their national counterparts to observe or follow. But these lower 'risks of being found out' may encourage complicity by national policy-makers in the de-democratization of their own states. They may create perverse incentives to shift decisions to the Union not for reasons of superior policy delivery, but to evade control, shift blame or dump unpopular tasks on another layer of government.

Union membership may affect constitutional balances within national democracies

It is often claimed that the Union strengthens the constitutional underpinnings of democracy within its member states. Thus conditions for accession to the Union require credible guarantees of individual rights, the rule of law and independent judiciaries. Yet European integration may also have more worrying implications for the inter-institutional balances and individual rights on which national constitutions are premised. In Joe Weiler's elegant phrase, the executive branch of each national government 'reconstitutes' itself as the legislative branch for the purpose of making laws delegated to the Union (1997, p. 274). Many national governments also end up exercising powers through the Council of Ministers that are assigned to regions and localities in their domestic systems. More, however, than changing vertical and horizontal distributions of power within national democracies, Union decision-making can, potentially, override national definitions of individual rights, as a consequence of the principle that Union law takes priority over national law, including national constitutional law.

Fritz Scharpf (1996) has made a similar argument, that the Union and its member states are becoming increasingly implicated in one another's democratic performance. But there is an important difference in our accounts of the problem. In his, it arises from a need to couple the two levels in a way that acknowledges that some of the output conditions for democratic rule can only be solved at Union level while some of the input conditions are only available at national level. In ours, the problem is to be found entirely on the input side. Scharpf may or may not be right about what policy outputs are needed for democracy to be effective in the new Europe. We make no special comment on that until the next chapter. For the moment we just note that all the disparate points in this section can be summarized as a single predicament: if public control of the Union through its own dedicated democratic institutions is attempted, the latter are still likely to be affected by the quality of democracy at national level. If national institutions are used to control the Union their democratic quality is likely to be affected by the sharing of their capabilities between the tasks of rendering two political systems responsible. Whether, then, democracy is imputed to the Union through its own institutions or those of its member states, the two levels are likely to be implicated in the democratic performance of the other.

Conclusion

In this chapter we have considered a number of possible measures of the quality of democracy in Europe. We began by noting survey evidence that suggests a seeming paradox: at the very moment it has achieved a near universal recognition as the only legitimate form of rule across a region that has had its fair share of disagreement about the nature of rightful government, there would seem to be little satisfaction with democracy. To some extent such ambiguities can be resolved by looking beyond subjective indicators of reported satisfaction with democracy to more objective indicators such as the willingness of citizens to support the democratic process through their active participation in elections, the proportion of offices open to competitive election, and the extent of the delivery of democracy's basic freedoms and of its minimum procedural conditions. Yet even the addition of such indicators does not resolve profound difficulties in evaluating democratic performance. Amongst them, the quality and reliability of aspects of democracy that are more or less measurable may depend on a complex range of other factors that are decidedly not quantifiable.

To this difficulty is added a further one in the conditions of the new Europe, namely that whatever method of assessment is chosen it will need to pick up a recent development of decisive importance: at least for that large part of the new Europe that is inside the European Union, democratic standards are no longer exclusively shaped by any one level of government. Rather they are jointly delivered – or jointly supplied – by institutions beneath, within and beyond the state. Whether this is an idiosyncrasy of the European Union as it is presently constituted, or a sign of deeper forces making for the mutual entanglement of democracy within and beyond the state in the new Europe is a question the next two chapters aim to help the reader to judge.

Chapter 7

Challenges to Democracy in the New Europe

In the remainder of the book we turn to our own argument that some combination of democracy within and beyond the state makes good normative and practical sense in the conditions of the new Europe. The main sections of this chapter offer a distinctive take on three familiar arguments: first, that democracy may have implications for international order; second, that it may need to be adjusted to pressures of globalization; and, third, that beliefs about democracy involve certain universal claims that have always sat uncomfortably with democracy delimited to the state. A concluding section then briefly considers implications for democracy beyond the state.

Chapter 8 follows through with a full statement of our claim that the prospects for democracy within and beyond the state are likely to be interdependent in the conditions of the new Europe. Throughout it should be borne in mind that by democracy beyond the state we mean some combination, first, of concerted efforts to manage the European part of the international system so that it only contains political systems that are democratic according to more or less internationally agreed standards; and, second, of attempts to apply democratic standards to shared institutions beyond the state.

The imperfect democratic peace

In 1795, one of Europe's most reclusive philosophers, Immanuel Kant, published a book which asked what conditions would be needed to bring 'perpetual peace' to the war-ravaged continent (Reiss, 1991). His proposal for a 'republic of republics' has come to be associated with the 'democratic peace theory' that democracies do not fight one another. As seen in Chapter 5, the governments and regional institutions of the new Europe have at least since 1989 sought to manage the European part of the international system so that it includes only democratic states. Indeed, in the view of some, democratic peace theory is more than policy. It is a part of the international identity of the new Europe (Manners and Whitman, 2003).

It might seem curious that democratic peace theory has assumed such a role. Using a database of all conflicts between 1800 and 1999, Sebastian Rosato (2003) argues that over the period as a whole peaceful behaviour cannot be attributed to features of democracy itself; and that since 1945 in particular it is impossible to tell whether peace between democratic states has been the product of their political systems or of the restraining effects of cold war and US hegemony.

What, in the face of such evidence, could possibly justify continued advocacy of democratic peace theory and, indeed, its inclusion in arguments for democracy beyond the state? The answer begins by clarifying what Kant actually said. Kant did not advocate democracy, but republican rule, as a means of promoting peace. By republicanism he meant a form of rule in which sovereignty is not absolute, but restrained and divided. The distinction is important, since not all democracies have republican features as defined by Kant. From a Kantian point of view, some are simply the 'wrong kinds of democracy', and should not be expected to behave as peacefully as those that avoid concentrations of power in a single person or institution.

Nor did Kant even argue that republican rule in single states would be sufficient for peace. In arguing for a republic of republics, he was clear that individual republics would need, in turn, to be restrained by a republic common to them all. This hardly amounts to a naive belief that states are likely to be more peace-loving by virtue of their domestic political systems alone, without regard for the nature of the international system. To the contrary, it implies quite clearly that domestic constitutions and the management of the international system interact with one another to shape the prospects for peace.

In sum, then, a democratic peace theory that is properly connected to its Kantian roots would not suggest that it is democracy on its own that promotes peace, but specific types of democracy and their conjunction with factors that extend beyond democratic politics themselves. Specifically, the probability of a state behaving peacefully will rise with:

(a) its transition from a non-democratic to a democratic system;
(b) its democratic deepening;
(c) its development of constitutionalist forms of democracy;
(d) the number of other states in its security environment that are democratic;
(e) the degree to which it and the other states in its security environment use the principles of constitutionalist democracy to regulate relationships between themselves.

We now set out in detail why each of these steps is important.

(a) The fact of democracy

Democratic states, it is argued, force their governments to account for their international actions. Governments can expect to be tested by subsequent domestic controversy on whether any decision to use force was justifiable, necessary, proportional and in the country's best interests. Not only is there a procedure for sanctioning poor answers to these questions – electoral defeat – but, historically, that punishment has on occasion been savage towards those who cannot justify their international behaviour or show due diligence in avoiding conflicts. Another feature is that democracies not only provide people with means of removing their leaders. They also limit the costs to their leaders of losing power. This reduces the risk of failed leaders creating failed states, with destabilizing consequences for the wider state system, in their attempts to cling to power.

(b) The degree of democracy

Yet we know from historical experience that the considerations mentioned in the foregoing paragraph will not restrain the international behaviour of democracies in all circumstances. At best, they will only work in conjunction with other factors. One problem, of course, is that the bare fact of public control, which we have repeatedly represented as the lowest common denominator of all political systems that are properly classified as democratic, will not restrain aggressive behaviour that is domestically so popular as to be rewarded, rather than punished, by electoral success. Is there hope, then, in the observation that democracy is a matter of degree and not just of kind? Are there, in other words, reasons for believing that states are progressively more likely to behave peacefully with each step they take to deepen their democratization beyond minimum conditions of electoral accountability?

One possibility is that it matters how far democratic peace values are themselves internalized into domestic political cultures. Such internalization could, for example, moderate identities and deliberative practices in ways that reduce risks of democracy being used to mobilize support for threatening forms of international behaviour. Relevant changes to identities might involve, first, a substitution of a 'soft' nationalism that seeks only a peaceful coexistence with others for a 'hard nationalism' that makes claims that are unlikely to be vindicated without aggression against outsiders; second, an acceptance that certain limitations on the way in which identities are held can even make those identities safer and more sustainable for the very people who value them most; or, third, a movement towards complex and multi-level identities in which neighbouring peoples are not seen entirely as 'others', even if they are not completely seen as 'us'. The differences such changes might conceivably make to the international behaviour of states is underscored by historical accounts of the role that very different approaches to the cultivation of national identities played in the enabling of the 1914–18 war:

> state power in the intensely competitive atmosphere of the late nineteenth century was military power, but military power involved the effective indoctrination of the entire population in a religion of nationalism. (Howard, 1983, p. 182)

(c) The form of democracy

Democracy, as we have repeatedly seen, can be constructed with different numbers of veto points that may, in turn, be differently distributed and more or less stubbornly entrenched. Executive power can be divided from legislative power, which can, in turn, be divided within itself. On top of all that, power can be further divided between central and regional governments, and arrangements put in place to increase the likelihood that different majorities will hold sway across the branches and levels of the system. Not only rules for initiating a conflict, but the practical demands of sustaining it with the resources and active cooperation of the wider polity, can then be used to harness the multiple veto points of a constitutionalist democracy to lower further the probability of a state settling its international disputes by conflict. The Western allies who in 1949 designed what is now the German state certainly believed that democratic constitutionalism would make a difference. But advocates of democratic peace theory would probably be wise to acknowledge that even the multiple veto points of democratic constitutionalism may be insufficient without the considerations of political culture reviewed in the last paragraph and an interface with quite particular international conditions which we now consider in the next two subsections.

(d) The number of democracies

To understand why the number of states that are democratic, and not just the depth and form of democracy in single states, may be critical to the prospects of a democratic peace, we need to appreciate that international systems are prone to security dilemmas (Jervis, 1976): it is hard to structure them so that any one state can make itself more secure without others feeling less so. Democracy may help states manage security dilemmas in two ways: first, an unintended consequence of their internal accountability procedures is that it is easier for other states to obtain information about their motives, capacities and preparations. Second, democratic states may develop distinctive norms of international behaviour. They may, for example, be constrained in their dealings with one another by the similarity of their own legitimacy claims. Governments which assume that popular election gives them a right to represent the views of a particular people on how its internal affairs and its international relations should be ordered can only dispute that other elected governments have the same right by implicitly calling their own legitimation claims into question (see Dixon, 1994, pp. 16–18; Russett, 1993, pp. 31–5). Thus it may be that the unlikelihood of 'democracy on democracy', rather than 'democracy on non-democracy', aggression is the core prediction of democratic peace theory.

Whether democracy moderates security dilemmas through improved information or more credible and constraining norms of international behaviour, the common implication of the foregoing claims is that the democratization of any one state provides a 'positive externality' for all the rest in an international system. If valid, democratic peace theory could well be expected to follow a pattern of increasing returns: its marginal benefits will rise with the number and importance of states in a system or a region that are suitably democratized. Indeed, the benefits may only kick in after some threshold at which all are confident that there is a critical mass of democracies to stabilize the system.

(e) The internationalization of democracy

The obvious policy implication of the systemic character of any democratic peace and of its susceptibility to increasing returns is that states should move towards – or seek to sustain – democracy as a group. This explains the attachment of the new Europe for coordinated democracy promotion and peer review (see Chapter 5). It also chimes with Kant's original argument for a shared framework of republican principles to regulate the individual republics. Yet all this presupposes at least some limitation on the sovereignty of participating states, which are expected to commit themselves to one particular form of government so long as they remain within the security community. Second, it also requires them to accept institutions as part of the commitment technology, including mutual monitoring according to standards that none control individually, and maybe even sanctioning of backsliders. Advocates of such a structure need to be able to answer Locke's famous question about polecats and lions: who would rationally attempt to escape one set of risks to their security by creating a still larger source of political power, without ensuring the latter is itself checked, balanced and controlled by those for whose benefit it is supposed to operate? This point completes the argument that any institutions or other processes set up to promote a democratic peace from beyond the state should themselves be controlled by principles of constitutionalist democracy.

Civilizing globalization

Whatever the state's past role in allowing democracy to be applied to the government of mass societies, commentators have questioned its continued capacity to deliver democracy under conditions of globalization. Claims that globalization makes it hard for states to maintain boundary relationships that allow democratic institutions to make distinct and autonomous choices have focused particularly on the role of financial markets, which are thought to be in a position to 'regime shop' until they are equally comfortable with the policies of governments. Even the technical term for this – 'arbitrage' – summons up an image of markets 'arbitrating', or standing as judge and jury, on elected governments, forcing them to align policy with their own preferences, rather than those of voters.

To make matters worse, this constraint may be far from symmetric. It may be felt particularly by small and less developed democracies; and even within developed democracies, it may be harder to exercise effective choice from some points of the political spectrum than others. Thus the debate as to how far states can practice social democracy under conditions of globalization is of particular significance to the condition of European democracy. Given that social democrats are one of just two or three mainstream political families in most European countries, limits on the programmes they can offer voters would amount to a significant narrowing of electoral choice and political competition in much of Europe.

Another suggestion is that globalization erodes feelings of 'community' that underpin democracy. Any sense that citizens of a democracy are all in the same boat – or that they share a community of fate – is challenged by what has been graphically described as a 'new Medievalism': monopoly provision by states of public goods and services, and even of authority and law, is apparently giving way to a patchwork of competing providers whose operations overlap the precise territorial demarcations of the state. Groups and individuals develop differential opportunities to opt out of the policies of their home state – whether through the tax haven, or welfare services and security purchased on international markets. The result is to erode the success of the state in creating congruity between ruler and ruled. Representative institutions no longer correspond to a body of citizens with more or less the same stake in the collective problem-solving covered by national democratic institutions.

Yet commentators diverge widely in their assessments of whether globalization really is a threat to democracy. For a start it is hard to measure the extent of the problem empirically. How far states are able to run different policies from one another might seem to be a fairly obvious indicator of their autonomy in the face of globalization. The evidence, though, on this score is mixed, as Layna Mosley explains: 'substantial cross-country variation remains in public consumption spending, government transfer payments, public employment, and taxation, whereas aggregate fiscal and monetary policies have increasingly converged' (2004, p. 183).

At a deeper level than these measurement problems are profound philosophical difficulties in specifying what is meant by autonomy in the first place. At one extreme, it is hardly attractive to suggest that a democratically elected government is autonomous wherever it is able to choose between more than one option, or wherever it is able to sustain a different policy to others. Choices, after all, may be between the devil and the deep blue sea, whilst differences in the policies that democracies are able to sustain in the face of globalization may not reflect their continued ability to choose freely as much as two other factors: first, variations in how those who hold power under conditions of globalization choose to discriminate between their victims; and, second, a path-dependent logic which dictates that even those who face identical and equally unforgiving systemic constraints will continue to respond differently if they started out from different points.

At the other extreme it would be unreasonable to consider any constraint on the democratic state as a loss of autonomy, since most actions of most agents are constrained in at least the minimal sense of having human causes external to themselves (Hume, 1902 [1777], p. 85). Indeed, it is neither coherent nor desirable to expect absolute autonomy of any liberal democracy. The liberal democratic state has, by definition, always been constrained by economy and society; and that, as seen in Chapters 2 and 3, has been responsible for its main qualities and successes. At the most globalization substitutes the constraints of international economy and society for those of national economies and societies, but even that is more a distinction of degree than of kind for European societies that have long been embedded in their international environments. Nor to be excluded is that certain kinds of international constraint may turn out to be as benign as their domestic equivalents for democracy. By increasing the visibility of societies to one another, globalization exposes states to new demands from their own citizens for democratic rights enjoyed by other peoples. Globalization also increases the probability that violations of rights will be found out and found out quickly. Whilst new and more global forms of communications pose problems of their own to democratic politics they do at least make it harder for states to restrict opinion formation amongst their own people to a pliant local media.

Yet, in our view, it is possible to anchor the discussion about the relationship between globalization and democratic autonomy. Our starting point is with a couple of fairly obvious observations. First, any body of citizens will have expectations of what they should be able to do together – or, in the jargon, what 'collective action problems' they will need to be able to solve – if they are to be meaningfully described as 'self-governing'. Second, in the discharge of those responsibilities, elected governments will come up against a number of other social systems – markets, the media, the law and so on – that they cannot dominate for reasons just discussed, but whose behaviour they will need within bounds to change and regulate if they are to meet their citizens' expectations of what it is to be a self-governing people.

Whether a democracy can coexist with other social systems as the latter go global, while meeting its citizens' expectations of what it is to be a self-governing people and still satisfying democratic values of public control with political equality is in our view, as sensible a test as any of democratic autonomy under conditions of globalization. We cannot deal with all. But in the paragraphs that follow we mention, first, some problems of public control and, then, some of political equality that arise when democracies attempt to solve collective action problems under conditions of globalization.

A useful starting point is to follow the example of David Held (1995) and consider what might be deficient in the view that globalization should remain ungoverned since it can, more or less, function as a 'spontaneous order'. A spontaneous order emerges as the cumulative unintended consequence of many individual actions, and not as the product of a guiding intelligence. As such it is (apparently) non-coercive, without institutional costs, without need of legitimation, and often capable of approximating staggeringly complex optimal solutions, although its participants might be simple to the point of ignorance in their understanding of their social contexts. Yet, even spontaneous orders require institutions to regulate such matters as property rights. They also need to combat the underprovision of those goods that are so diffuse in nature that no one is prepared to pay for them (public goods), and the overprovision of 'bads' that actors can inflict on others at little cost to themselves (negative externalities). Indeed, they can only remain spontaneous where they are safeguarded against the abuse of private forms of power, such as monopoly positions and anti-competitive behaviour. Even then, there is no guarantee their outcomes will correspond to widely shared notions of justice and individual rights.

Rather, then, than trust globalization to spontaneous order it is much more likely that public authorities will club together, where they cannot otherwise handle things individually, to regulate the stability of global transactions that would otherwise pose 'systemic risks'; to provide international public goods that cannot be generated by the self-regarding behaviour of individual participants in globalizing systems; and to prohibit or clean up the transmission of negative externalities across international boundaries.

The observation that 'globalization is negotiated' (Hay, 2002) is nowhere truer than in its tendency to spawn myriad international organizations and other coordination mechanisms beyond the state precisely as arenas where globalization can be negotiated. It is at this point, of course, that globalization becomes a problem of public control. Two preliminary points are in order. First, solutions to several of the coordination problems with which globalization confronts previously unlinked public authorities require legal certainty, including, for example, agreement to designate some 'goods' as proprietary rights and some 'bads' as criminal activities, no matter where they are acquired or perpetrated in the global village. This, in turn, means that even where frameworks of international cooperation do not enact law, they are an important source of it. They initiate and agree measures prior to transposition into the law of states, whose democratic institutions may only be able to have second thoughts by risking either the credibility of the international framework of rule-making as a whole or their own credibility as an individual participant perceived by others as a reliable partner. Second, decisions on what are 'goods' and what are 'bads' are allocations of value (except where 'pareto' decisions are possible). There are limits to how far states can club together to regulate globalization in a manner that is neutral between the reproduction of types of identity, or types of economic system or welfare state. Compulsory allocation of value is precisely a condition in which public control is thought to be a moral imperative: the only way in which we can possibly justify such a thing is where we can all see ourselves as acting through representatives to author the very laws by which we are ourselves bound.

But, even where governments are accountable for their individual contributions to international organizations or 'regimes' (informal norms of coordination: Keohane, 1984; Krasner, 1983), the cost to any one national democracy of monitoring all that is decided in such bodies or processes is high. On account of their opacity and the involvement of so 'many hands' in their decisions, it can be hard to discern who decided what and when in many international bodies; and, as just suggested, any one national democracy may feel constrained from unravelling agreements that are presented to them as faits accomplis painstakingly negotiated by many states. Worse, their governments may be able to abuse their privileged position at the interface between politics within and beyond the state by migrating decisions towards international frameworks, less for functional reasons of better policy delivery and more to shift blame and evade responsibility (Lord and Beetham, 2001). Indeed, delegations of power to international organizations often involve the executive branch of national governments taking decisions that would need parliamentary approval in domestic politics.

It is likewise claimed that globalization makes it harder for states to deliver political equality. Regardless of any role it has in increasing differentials of income and wealth, globalization may make it harder to sustain rules designed to ensure a level playing field in the democratic process, including rules of media ownership, campaign finance, and equal access to high places. The genius of democracy in proceduralizing political equality through the principle 'one person, one vote' would count for less if the incentive on those who compete for political power to adjust their policies to voters is compromised by an additional need to adjust them to globalized sources of media endorsement or campaign finance. If correct, this would be a weighty charge indeed against globalization. To the extent that procedures aiming at political equality allow democratic institutions to produce policies that do not merely mirror inequalities in the economic or social power of their policy addressees, they contribute to the autonomy of the democratic process itself.

Before concluding this discussion, we need to make two observations that are particular to the new Europe. First, for Europeans, much of what passes for globalization is refracted through a further process of Europeanization. Indeed, some commentators argue that the latter is the stronger force of the two for most countries of the region. By 'Europeanization' is meant a series of adaptations by national and subnational actors to economic, social and political change originating at the European level, some mediated through the institutions of the European Union, others not. Second, European states are, nonetheless, significantly unequal in how they are affected by globalization. The following are examples:

1. *Variations in size.* If larger democracies are more likely to be able to sustain the policies of their choice in the face of globalization, the average population of the ten largest European states covered by this book (France, Germany, Italy, Poland, Romania, the Russian Federation, Spain, Turkey, Ukraine and the United Kingdom) is more than 50 times that of the smallest ten (Albania, Armenia, Azerbaijan, Cyprus, Estonia, Latvia, Lithuania, Luxembourg, Macedonia and Slovenia).

2. *Variations in levels of economic development.* If globalization is an 'asymmetric constraint' that mainly only limits the freedom of economically less developed democracies to pursue the policies of their choice (Stiglitz, 2002), the new Europe contains states at several different levels of economic, social and political development.

3. *Variations in sensitivity/vulnerability to the international economy.* If freedom to choose policies in the face of globalization is less a matter of size or level of economic development than of 'sensitivity' or 'vulnerability' to policy 'shocks' from international markets, Europe has some countries that

are only imperfectly integrated to international capital markets, whilst others have thrown themselves open to flows of portfolio and direct investment that dwarf their 'real economies'. It also, of course, has some countries that have chosen to combine in a single currency, and others who have not.

4. *Variations in social cohesion and social capital.* If social cohesion and social capital affect how the forces of globalization are internalized into the domestic politics of democratic systems, as well as the capacity of those systems to adapt through democratically mediated social compromise, some European states are culturally homogeneous. Others are multinational yet harmonious political units. Still others are deeply divided societies with recent histories of violent conflict. Nor are all divisions cultural. They follow different cleavage lines from one European democracy to the next. Moreover European states, and even parts of states, vary in how far they have invested in the past in 'society building' (Putnam, 1993).

5. *Variations in type of democratic system.* If the margin of choice in the face of globalization depends in part on the mechanism of choice used, the new Europe, as we have seen, has consensus and majoritarian democracies, presidential and parliamentary ones, and systems that mix direct and indirect democracy in different ways.

The point about Europeanization operating as a kind of microclimate within globalization might suggest that the new Europe possesses unusual opportunities to develop a regional subgovernance of globalization. The observation that European states differ in their exposure to globalization might, conversely, suggest that they are likely to disagree on how far they need shared responses.

The normative insufficiency of democracy within the state

The argument for democracy beyond the state that we consider in this section is given urgency by globalization and new security challenges, but, unlike the arguments of the preceding two sections, it does not ultimately depend on what we believe about a changing world. Rather it implies that political thought and practice may have been deficient all along in associating democracy too closely with the state. The argument in question is that the particularistic and often communitarian forms into which human association – including, crucially, the practice of democracy itself – has largely been fragmented in the past has no answers for how human beings should fulfil certain moral obligations they have to one another. The gap can only be filled by complementing those communitarian forms with more cosmopolitan commitments and processes grounded in principles of democracy applied beyond the state.

As we discussed in Chapter 2, it was always odd, if not contradictory, that universality, which is at the core of democracy, should have become a prisoner of the particularity of the nation state. A possible explanation, as we also discussed, is that there are limits to how far people are prepared to accept rule by one another, summarized, for example, in Mill's claim that 'free institutions are next to impossible in a country made up of different nationalities', and his belief that each nationality should, accordingly, have a 'government to themselves and themselves apart' (Mill, 1972 [1861] p. 361). Indeed, the nation has historically incubated other belongings, and provided a means of learning democracy, as well as the community of mutual commitment that it, no less than any other common political project, requires (Jones, 2001, p. 152). All the beliefs associated with nationhood can be disputed, politically, ideologically, philosophically and historically. Nevertheless, at the present stage of human political development, it seems unlikely that we have any other form of collective identity that combines the subjective, objective and political as successfully as the nation that we could compare it with. This is rather a concession to nationalism's endurance than its defence.

Yet it is possible to protest the moral inadequacy of nation-statehood while at the same time acknowledging the difficulty of managing without it. The obvious difficulty is that it does not in itself provide any means of meeting any sense of moral obligation towards people beyond the state ('beyond the river bank' as Mole tried to explain to Ratty in *The Wind and the Willows*, cited, typically, by Miller in 'In Defence of Nationality', (Miller, 2000, p. 24). Isn't there a degree of moral ambivalence attached to a moral landscape that is delimited by something as banal as a border?

Actually the problem is worse than Mole suggests: it is impossible to deny that we have moral obligations to those beyond our own nations as long as we continue to believe that human beings have intrinsic worth by virtue of being human. All people share certain characteristics and needs which we all recognize: the capacity for love and relations with other humans, imagination and reflection, vulnerability and feelings of pain, use of language as a tool of communication, the need for recognition, hunger and thirst, the need for security, fear of the unknown, memory and a sense of beauty. We are also aware that, however much is relative in our needs and desires, there are also basic conditions in which all humans flourish, the absence of which leads to human misery.

Such characteristics and needs are not contingent on belonging to any particular culture, but constitutive of humanity (Parekh, 2003), of human relationships and of human rights. Indeed, Habermas makes the crucial distinction that we can justifiably get together in particular communities with those with whom we have common values amounting to a shared view of the good life. But the rights we owe one another are universal: we cannot claim them for ourselves in virtue of being human without recognizing that all other human beings have them too. We have duties to our fellow citizens, to the community of which we are members, but that does not discharge us from duties to our fellow humans (Parekh, 2003, p. 9). While we live in political communities, our morality has a *political content* on the basis of our humanity.

Its failure to address our moral obligations to those beyond national boundaries has always been a gap in the organization of democracy into particularistic communities, but the problem has become acute with globalization. Globalization, as we discussed in the last section, throws us more closely together into 'communities of fate' with human beings everywhere. The events are clear: ever more economic interdependence and social interaction, non-state actors' intervention into political and security spheres, rapid spread of diseases, pollution and overuse of global resources, the ever increasing concerns with societal security and human rights and increased legitimacy of regional and other organizations, at the same time as the increased polarization of the globe into 'poor' and 'rich' countries, the rise of the Right in Europe and of fundamentalism everywhere, globalization on a qualitatively unprecedented scale and monetary transnationalism. Globalization also removes alibis that might previously have given pragmatic justification to the focusing and delimitation of moral obligations to territorially bounded communities, namely limited awareness of wider humanity, and limited means to address its problems wisely. All of this, moreover, is increasingly acknowledged in political practice and discourse. When others are overwhelmed by events beyond their control, whether it is a natural disaster or a tyrannical regime, both public opinion and political leaders acknowledge that moral obligation does not stop at the river bank. If we have learned to value our fellow nationals, who have often become so by historical contingency (for no one is born a patriot, but everyone is born a human being), surely it is within our moral capabilities to build on this and extend beyond it. But by what institutions – and with what implications for the practice of democracy? – that is the question that we address in the rest of this section.

That the contemporary human condition is escaping the confines of the state may be clear, but how it affects democracy – the theory and practice of – is much less so. It is hardly an overstatement that we find ourselves in a paradoxical situation: the rule of the people is thought to be best exercised within the state, but people's lives are affected by powers exercised 'increasingly on a transnational, or even global scale' (McGrew, in Held and McGrew, 2000, p. 405). The foundations of nationhood and statehood on which democracy was theorized and built are less able to support it. Indeed, as we have repeatedly seen, the state is itself increasingly enmeshed in a vast and complex network of international organizations and regulative measures, which affect the daily lives of individuals, but go well beyond the national units into which the key democratic principles of public control with political equality are organized. How, then, is democracy to be rethought, so that it can produce a 'good political community' (McGrew, in Held and McGrew, 2000, p. 405) capable of meeting moral obligations beyond the state? Anthony McGrew (2000) has identified three theoretical paradigms of global democracy. We explore these as background to a discussion of what the new Europe might contribute to democracy beyond the state.

Liberal-democratic internationalism

Under this solution nation-states would remain the primary actors in world politics but ways would be found of moderating their behaviour so as to achieve a better balance than at present between the rights of people and the rights of states, the interests of nations and the interests of the 'global neighbourhood' (McGrew, 2000, p. 409). Such a solution would not require elements of 'global government'. It would suffice to have a pattern of interstate relations that are cosmopolitan and multilateral in spirit, and in relation to which governments are rewarded, or at the very least not sanctioned, by their publics for taking on international responsibilities. Indeed, the central problem of this solution is precisely that it is too statist in nature. It seems paradoxical to replicate an existing model of a state-centred liberal democracy on a transnational level when it is its very principle of state-centredness that needs reforming in the face of the changing national environment. Moreover, it does not of itself address the substantive preconditions of democracy or of how to avoid 'quasi democracies' amongst its component states.

If we want to be more radical and decouple 'community' altogether from territory we might look to 'Demarchy' (Burnheim, 1985; Dryzek, 1995; McGrew, pp. 410–13) where central to governance is the functional management of specific international problems, such as trade and the environment, and where authorities 'are directly accountable to the communities whose interests are directly affected by their actions' (*ibid.*). The communities would be represented by committees elected through a proportional system and their coordination supervised by over-arching committees, also drawn from non-state communities of interest. The idea here is very clear: the active direct participation of people across the boundaries represented by specific shared interests with a long-term aim of achieving equality through self-governing communities. This model draws on ideas of republicanism, direct and participatory democracy, global civil society and Marxism (self-managing communities of interest as practised in the former Yugoslavia operated on similar 'micro' levels). What is interesting about this model is that it is already partially practised within the EU, where structured and multinational consultation of stakeholder interests works in parallel with decision-making by institutions geared to more overarching interests.

Cosmopolitan Democracy

To a cosmopolitan the world is one of 'overlapping communities of fate', where inclusiveness, solidarity and equivalence can only be realized by transnational bodies and expanding frameworks of states bound by the rule of law, democratic principle and human rights (Held, 2004, pp. 382–3). The idea is not to reduce state power, but to develop legitimate political and administrative structures at regional and global levels as 'necessary supplements' to those at state level (Held, 2004, p. 387). The central claim here is that 'democratic autonomy' – an 'entitlement to self-determination within the constraints of community' (Held, 2004, p. 413) – must under conditions of globalization include some means of making cosmopolitan democratic law which, logically, must transcend the nation state and extend to all in the universal community. Since this form of governance would require a transnational common structure of political action, and thus a post-Westphalian conception of global order, cosmopolitanism is more radical than internationalism in seeking a reconstruction, rather than a mere reform, of the existing world order (Held, 2004, p. 416).

The cosmopolitan model reflects, in many ways, a European democratic tradition: autonomy of self, internationalism, participatory republicanism ('general will') and, particularly, the recognition of the importance of law and authority. In that respect, despite some concessions to direct democracy, it relies very much on liberal democracy as the foundation that would have to underlie this project. Cosmopolitanism seeks to improve the human condition by removing barriers among people which diminish their social and economic opportunities; it is only by first creating a democratic civic identity that these barriers can be removed and cosmopolitanism can thrive.

In sum, then, the cosmopolitan argument is that civilizing citizens means rescuing democracy from the nation state's monopoly on their moral obligation to fellow humans outside our 'imagined' community'. If democracy is to be adapted to our multicultural, multi-layered and multilateral world it has to shed this attachment to particularity and move, procedurally and normatively, beyond the borders of the state. Some means must be found of supplementing traditional symmetries between democracy and territory and of seeking governance that can deliver on the global scale (see also Held, 2004, p. 367).

The main criticism of cosmopolitanism is that its civilizing project presumes a degree of universality which is far from present at the global level and it is morally contestable whether it should be. Globalization does not start from a *tabula rasa* – nor is it based on democracy. Non-democratic states and regimes are equal participants and civic identity, if existing at all, is rather a result of democratization than its precondition. Cosmopolitanism stipulates a world order, but does not specify its institutions, and, finally, it says very little about the distribution of global resources and who is to police it. All in all, the cosmopolitan model lacks practicability and is politically unconvincing. However, its normative thrust remains worthy of continuing elaboration when it comes to civilizing states and citizens. If there are no intellectual reasons why it should be wholly impossible in the longer term, it is important that democratic citizenship should not, as it has too often in the past, close itself off in a particularistic fashion that prevents it developing a more cosmopolitan character over time. For example, one of the main conditions for global/cosmopolitan democracy – the emergence of a debate and coordinated political action that transcends political borders – could with the right spirit of openness quite plausibly be incubated within present structures (Habermas, 1999, pp. 46–59; for the literature on cosmopolitan democracy and cosmopolitan citizenship see also Held, 1995, 2004; Linklater, 1998). Such a development would at least extend imagination beyond the 'imagined community' of the nation-state.

Indeed, it is important to reiterate that cosmopolitanism seeks to supplement, and not replace, the state. Far from necessarily being a threat to identity and democracy at the level of the state, it is possible to imagine, with Richard Bellamy and Alex Warleigh (1998), a cosmopolitan communitarianism, in which essentially communitarian identities at a level of the state are held in a way that leaves national democracies open to taking on obligations beyond the state, and to engaging with other communities beyond the state with respect for the diversity of all. We are not looking to disregard 'thick' ethno-cultural identities at a level of the state, but supplement them by 'thinner' civic identity – rooted in loyalty to the common political institutions – at a level of any democracy beyond the state (Habermas, 1992). We develop this argument further in Chapter 8. Joseph Weiler has portrayed European integration as a restraint on the abuse of external and internal boundary relationships by states: on behaviour externally threatening to neighbours and internally repressive of citizens and their rights. Value commitments by states to the limitation of their own sovereignty have helped make statehood safe for states and those who live in them. On this interpretation, the ideological dimension of European integration, so scorned by those claiming that the real motives for European unification lie in the hard-headed calculations of national interests, is itself a part of the European 'rescue' of the nation-state (Habermas, 2001a).

Also implicit in many cosmopolitan writings is the notion that democracy may first reach beyond the state through regional rather than global organizations, certainly as part of the process of opening governance of the global order to greater public control with political equality, and maybe even as a permanent feature of it. However, cosmopolitanism can, of course, only justify the new Europe developing its own form of democracy beyond the state if the latter itself avoids the particularism that leaves democracy within the state with no obvious means of meeting universal obligations. Amongst the optimistic are those who claim that the European Union is already developing as a kind of crossroads – or connection point – between the communitarian and cosmopolitan values in the manner suggested by Bellamy and Warleigh. Whilst hugely different assessments of its success are possible, it is hard to deny that it is at least engaging with the issue of how governance, accountability, belonging and citizenship might be organized beyond boundaries.

Conclusion

When conducting an interview for an earlier study, one of the authors of this book was confronted by the claim that 'democracy can only live within the state'. For the reasons set out in Chapter 2, this is an understandable point of view. But what it omits, in our opinion, is any understanding that 'democracy within the state' may also be a problematic notion. In this chapter we have explored three reasons why it may be. First, the quality of democracy in any one state – and possibly even peace itself – may be affected by the degree of democracy elsewhere in the international order. Second, the shift of economic and social relations, and even of political allocations of value and sources of law, to sites other than the state may make it hard to deliver democracy's defining attribute of public control with political equality through the state alone. Third, democracy within the state has always been too much for some and too little for others: too much for those minorities that feel trapped within a democracy with which they do not identify; and too little for those who feel that there are some forms of rights delivery that cannot easily be confined to the state alone.

Now such shortcomings do not of themselves prove a case for democracy beyond the state. Whether that further move is warranted is as much as anything else a matter of preference and of judgement between a number of alternatives such as the following:

1. *Roll-back*. One possible response, of course, to activities beyond the state that outstrip the capacities of the democratic state is to scale back the former, rather than despair of the latter. This might be the argument of various anti-globalization campaigners, though curiously enough also of those who believe that the only problem with globalization is the urge to respond to it with unnecessary international institution-building, rather than policy competition between national democracies.

2. *Justifiable non-democracy beyond the state*. This response might start out from the observation that democracy is not the only desirable form of rule and that – precisely because the state provides the best conditions for democracy – it often does not even occur to us to apply it to other forms of human association (Bellamy and Castiglione, 2000, p. 65). So why not take the same attitude to beyond-state institutions, provided they can guarantee rights, standards of public administration and constraints on the arbitrary use of power? Indeed, the difficulty of extending democracy to institutions beyond the state may even be an opportunity to transfer to them precisely those decisions that are best not taken democratically. Thus for purposes as varied as pro-

tecting rights, ensuring fairness in the administration of policy and solving 'time-inconsistency problems' (where, for example, the timing of the political cycle is an obstacle to optimal policy-making), interest has been shown in 'non-majoritarian' use of institutions beyond the state to take decisions independently from any one set of points on the political spectrum (Majone, 1996).

3. *Reassertion of the role of the democratic states as 'principals'*. This solution implies that we simply have not tried hard enough – or not been inventive enough in designing institutional technologies – that would allow us to manage shared problems beyond the state through international institutions whilst retaining the state as the ultimate locus of democratic control. This is often described as an intergovernmental – as opposed to a supranational – position. However, that distinction is not always helpful in a new Europe that often seems to blend, fuse or even confuse 'intergovernmental' and 'supranational' structures (Weiler, 1997, pp. 276–7; Wessels, 1998). The tools of principal–agent analysis may therefore be a more helpful way of expressing the thought that activity beyond the state does not necessarily undermine the state as a site of democratic control. If mechanisms can be developed that allow national democracies to act as 'principals' in which they can specify, monitor, review and even recall the terms of delegation to beyond-state institutions regardless of whether they are supranational or intergovernmental (Bergman, 2000; Pollack, 1997b), there may be no reason why even ambitious international structures should not be anchored in the democratic politics of single states.

4. *Democracy beyond the state*. Some might make a positive case for some measure of democracy beyond the state as a means towards the reconciliation of peoples, or as a contribution to a more cosmopolitan sense of political community. Others, however, might prefer to make the case negatively by ruling out the alternatives set out in the preceding paragraphs. In answer to the first alternative it might be doubted that the need for collective action beyond the state can either be escaped altogether or reduced to a number of technical decisions that are so anodyne in their allocations of value as not to create any need for democratic control. In answer to

the second alternative it might be objected that only some needs for beyond-state action are likely to be of a kind that would justify non-democratic institutions. It may be impossible to limit beyond-state action to an agenda of rights protection and, once again, to technical efficiency improvements. In answer to the third alternative it might be doubted that beyond-state institutions are ever likely to be adequately controlled by within-state democacies alone, since the evidence to date suggests a number of structural problems in that relationship that are unlikely to be conjured away by improved agency alone (see pp. 146–9).

There is, however, a pattern to such arguments that is best understood by relating them to the core justifications for democracy set out on p. 2. To recall, the intrinsic justification for democracy is that people should as far as possible have control over decisions affecting their own lives; and that even where they have no alternative but to act collectively and under the coercive force of law they should ideally be able to see themselves as authoring such decisions through representatives (Habermas, 1996). In contrast, the consequential argument is that democracy has spin-off benefits other than those contained in its own definition; for example, for the protection of rights, the promotion of peace and the delivery of prosperity.

Now the crucial point is that the relative likelihood of democracy within and beyond the state satisfying these justifications is an empirical question once we have fixed what people value in the control of their own lives or what consequential values they want from democracy. Those who hold to either justification for democracy cannot therefore wed themselves too rigidly to its delivery through any one level of government. Instead they are committed by the logic of their own argument to considering moving its delivery up and down between levels of government – or dispersing it across many – depending, in the case of consequential justifications for democracy, on what is empirically most likely to deliver the international stability, economic and social welfare, and rights protections expected of democracy; and depending, in the case of intrinsic justifications, on whatever citizens believe is necessary for them to see themselves as authoring their own laws through representatives.

Indeed, any attempt to keep the state pure of any democracy beyond the state would have paradoxical implications if it could be demonstrated that some hybrid would better deliver democracy's values: it would effectively associate the state with a conscious decision to prefer less democracy to more, and thus require it to put less weight on democratic principle in its own legitimation. Not to be excluded then is that the democratic state may need to establish some relationship with democracy beyond the state as part of its own justification.

Chapter 8

Democracy Within and Beyond the State: a Complementary Relationship

In the last chapter we argued that democracy within the European state now requires some measure of democracy beyond the state. In this chapter we develop the converse argument that any democracy beyond the state is likely, nonetheless, to presuppose the continued success of democracy within the state. Our first claim is that if there is to be any democracy beyond the state it would be best constrained by democracy within the state. Our second is that any democracy beyond the state would best rest on a mix of 'cosmopolitan' and 'communitarian' identities (Bellamy and Warleigh, 1998) that presuppose a continued, though tamed, role for states and nations in nurturing political community. Cutting across these arguments is a third: any democracy beyond the state is unimaginable without civic capabilities that would need to be created within the state. Individually and cumulatively these arguments are shown in the first two sections of the chapter to suggest that it is profoundly mistaken to predict that any development of democracy beyond the state will stifle democracy within the state. A third section then anticipates an objection to the whole drift of our argument towards complementary forms of democracy within and beyond the state, namely that there has to be a clear locus of sovereignty in one or the other. A fourth section concludes both the chapter and the book.

Better to suffer the mischiefs of polecats than to be devoured by lions

The English philosopher John Locke (1650–1722) could never understand why his predecessor Thomas Hobbes (1588–1679) had proposed a sovereign with unlimited power as a solution to the disorders of the day. 'This', he argued, 'is to think that men are so foolish that they take care to avoid what mischiefs may be done them by polecats or foxes, but are content, nay, think it safety to be devoured by lions' (Locke, 1977 [1690], p. 163). In other words, Locke found it hard to believe there could ever be a rational basis for unlimited forms of rule: given the choice, individuals would never expose themselves to the risks of an unlimited sovereign and would prefer instead to safeguard their own well-being by dividing power between different power-holders.

For like reasons Kant insisted that in his proposed 'republic of republics' the individual republics should restrain the shared republic as much as vice versa. Thus one obvious reason for holding that democracy beyond the state presupposes the continued health of democracy within the state is that the second may be required to check the first. The fear that it would amount to an excessive concentration of power – and ultimately degenerate into an unbearable tyranny – has long been one of the most persuasive arguments for not seeking to exit the anarchy of international relations through some form of world or even regional government. Yet to find grounds for hesitation we do not need to go so far as to imagine that government beyond the state – democratic or otherwise- need develop into a Leviathan. It is sufficient to imagine the many human frailties that attend the exercise of political power – the cutting of corners, the covering up of errors, the denial of responsibility, the shifting of blame, the offloading of problems, the partiality that makes us poor judges in our own cases, the limitations of the imagination and the rigidities with which we interpret information that make it hard for even the well-intentioned to see a problem from another person's point of view – to worry about the significant exercise of power beyond settled mechanisms of democratic control that only developed slowly within the state and may take as long again to develop beyond it.

Indeed our arguments for maintaining a role for democracy within the state cover the possibility that beyond-state institutions may be troublingly weak and not just disturbingly strong.

Two propositions are central to our argument: first, that there is an intimate link between democracy and what has come to be known as a 'republican' commitment to minimizing arbitrariness in human relations; and, second, that the exercise of power from beyond the state involves its own distinctive risks of arbitrariness and it own original means of dealing with them. The following paragraphs explain.

Philip Pettit (1997) has documented how a lasting legacy of the European enlightenment was a profound and widespread belief that government should not be based on the arbitrary will of individuals, but on principles that are publicly agreed and defended, non-manipulable, known in advance and applied without fear or favour to all. Quoting the seventeenth-century English writer James Harrington (1992) he describes this goal as a substitution of the 'rule of law' for the 'rule of men'.

Although not in itself democratic, there has been a steady convergence between this commitment to minimizing arbitrariness in government (and human relations more generally) and selected strands of democratic thought. On the one hand, constitutional democrats have probably had the better of the argument that ideals of non-arbitrariness are inherent to any proper understanding of democracy itself. To the extent that the sovereignty of the people is enabled – and justified – by the rights of the individual it must also be constrained by those rights (Habermas, 1996).

On the other hand, democracy may itself be a powerful guarantee against the arbitrary exercise of power. Quite apart from any structural incentive it creates for power-holders and those who would challenge them for office to compete by anticipating the needs of the public, what could be less arbitrary than to have the people themselves judge whether their needs are, in fact, being met? Indeed, what could be less arbitrary than to have the people acting as political equals – on the basis of one person, one vote – judge whether their needs are being met? Anything else would involve drawing a distinction that would itself be arbitrary between those who are sufficiently worthy as human beings to be included in the franchise and those who are not.

The idea that political power should be divided between different holders provides an example of convergence between the search for non-arbitrary government on the one hand and democratic rule on the other. In a much-quoted passage the eighteenth-century French political thinker Montesquieu (1989) defined the concentration of political power as the very definition of 'tyranny itself'. What the likes of Montesquieu had in mind was that lawmakers (legislators) who are not also law-enforcers (executives) would be more likely to frame the law with the care of knowing that it could one day be applied to themselves; and that only where the interpretation of law (judiciaries) is independent can the law itself be constrained by the rights of the individual.

A somewhat different possibility, though, is that arbitrariness can be reduced by dividing powers according to characteristics of the governed and not just functions of government. If power is so dispersed that decisions cannot be made without the agreement of different institutions that are appointed by different elements of the governed in different ways and at different times, it is less likely that public decisions will be partial, and more likely that they will have to be justified as a source of common benefit to all the represented. Democracy is an obvious means of bringing about just such an outcome. Different electorates can be used to elect different institutions, or the same electorate can be used to elect different institutions but at different times.

If, then, it is a fair surmise that non-arbitrariness and democracy are twin standards that many of us expect to be coherently linked in contemporary systems of government, what are the implications for the exercise of power from beyond the state? A useful way to answer this question is by considering whether there are likely to be added risks of arbitrariness where decisions are made beyond the state. The following are three possibilities.

First, a weak and patchy sense of political community may well mean that decisions taken from beyond the state are inherently more likely to be felt by their addressees as arbitrary forms of outside interference, as opposed to the acts of a self-governing people authoring its own law. This will be all the more likely where such decisions run up against the problem of 'reasonable pluralism'. By reasonable pluralism is meant that we all have 'contradictory but equally reasonable' views of what is right and good in politics and society (Rawls, 1993, p. 36).

Now just moving decision-making powers beyond the state will not always add to the range of reasonable pluralism that is often already wide in national democracies. In some respects, though, it is bound to aggravate the difficulty. Some ideas of the 'right' and the 'good' are themselves wrapped up with national identity. Large parts of Europe have developed strong welfare states which – crucially for the prospects of agreeing even limited economic and social policies beyond the state – have been constructed on different assumptions of what is socially desirable and individually right. Nor to be discounted is that one value that is vulnerable to being traded off against others in any decision-making beyond the state is national identity itself – or certain constructions of it.

A particular difficulty is that, quite regardless of whether it is democratically controlled any exercise of power from beyond the state may well develop its own principles of legality and its own norms of what is right and fair. But in so far as these conflict with their equivalents within states – including conspicuously with the will of democratic majorities that are properly constituted according to the rules of the domestic arena – decisions from beyond the state may well be experienced as arbitrary even though on their own terms they are not arbitrary at all.

A second reason for fearing arbitrariness in the exercise of power from beyond the state relates to difficulties in engaging civil society with any form of public authority. The key insight here is that the social mobilization of constraints on the powerful is unlikely to be either frictionless or instantaneous. As seen, Mancur Olson (1965) successfully attacked the complacency of the assumption that all groups in society with an interest in the operation of a political system would organize to influence it. By pointing out that, to the contrary, engagement would be confined to those for whom the marginal return of organization exceeded the marginal cost, he highlighted the constant danger that political systems are likely to fall into the arbitrary pattern of paying more attention to the concentrated interests of rent-seekers and incumbents than to the diffuse interest of the public as a whole.

Given such difficulties, some of the shrewdest commentators on democratic politics have long understood the importance of 'spill-over conflicts' from elites to publics in stimulating democratic competition and choice (Schattsneider, 1960). What often saves political systems from a mixture of inertia and capture is that at least some elite actors have an interest in taking arguments public: that is to say, in putting their own time and resources behind stimulating new patterns of mobilization and constructing original interpretations of the diffuse public interest.

Moreover, the more this is done the easier it is to do. On the one hand, organization to influence any political system may involve high start-up costs but increasing returns thereafter. On the other hand, we have seen how far democracy depends on well-developed civic capabilities amongst both represented and the representatives: trust, rights, knowledge of shared problems and institutions, and an ability to deliberate (March and Olsen, 1995). Not only are these capabilities also likely to grow with use but they may even represent a social capital that affects the performance of institutions centuries after investment in its construction (Putnam, 1993).

If, then, specific features of society and democratic competition combine to limit arbitrariness in the political system it is not hard to imagine risks in transferring powers to settings beyond the state. Such transfers may open up disparities between concentrated interests that are able to cultivate the rare skills needed to influence a transnational political system and diffuse ones that cannot. Nor is the new setting likely to have the benefit of previous investments in building its own balanced infrastructure of civic engagement in which political parties, interest groups and different media complement one another, compensate for one another's defects, compete to avoid any of their number enjoying rents, and deepen their capacities over time to solve the coordination problems involved in linking groups and individuals together in efforts to influence the political system and understand the uses to which it can be put. Nor, finally, are institutions beyond the state likely to have accumulated social capital and civic capabilities of their own.

A third reason for being especially concerned by the problem of arbitrariness when power is exercised from beyond the state relates to the nature of arbitrariness itself. Political power is by no means the sole source of arbitrariness and may often be a solution to it (Pettit, 1997). In thousands of everyday ways we use political power to restrain what we consider the greater evil of arbitrary domination in economic and social relationships between ourselves. In other ways we use what we hope will be non-arbitrary forms of political power to restrain its more arbitrary forms.

Assume, for example, that the two dimensions of democracy beyond the state that we have delineated in this book are sought for the reasons suggested in the last chapter. That is to say, coordinated action to ensure all political systems are democratic according to international agreed criteria is sought as a means of promoting international order; whilst democratically controlled international organizations are sought to ensure that an otherwise spontaneous economic order is sufficiently regulated to avoid negative externalities and underprovision of public goods. Clearly these both involve protection against arbitrariness: against arbitrariness in interstate behaviour in the first case; against arbitrariness in the behaviour of economic actors in the second. Both are, moreover, onerous responsibilities that underscore the point that non-arbitrariness requires capable, yet restrained, political power. Already a difficult balancing act within the state, this may well be even harder to achieve beyond it.

If the foregoing all represent greater risks of arbitrariness associated with the exercise of power from beyond the state, there is something else they have in common: each could plausibly be mitigated through a continued role for national democracies in beyond-state decisions. Fears that national democracies – and values associated with them – might themselves be arbitrarily dominated in any democracy beyond the state could be countered by giving the first assured rights of representation in the second. Concern that individuals and groups in society might find it more difficult to organize to resist arbitrary domination when power is exercised from beyond the state could be countered through national democratic intermediaries – political parties and forms of 'interest' or 'value' representation such as advocacy coalitions – pooling their efforts to reap scale economies from organizing at transnational level. Anxiety that citizens might lack civic capabilities and social capital in relation to institutions beyond the state could be countered by constructing the latter on the assumption that even in the experimental setting of transnational democracy core 'virtues' may be best incubated within the state (Laborde, 2002, p. 591) even if more innovative virtues – such as a willingness to follow demanding deliberative public standards with those from other democracies – cannot. Apprehension that institutions beyond the state might be troublingly weak and not just overbearingly strong in relation to sources of arbitrariness might be best countered by requiring them to engage with other bodies with a potential to both enable and constrain them at the same time. In many well-documented ways national democracies often interface in just such a way with international bodies: at once changed in their own behaviour and yet able to determine the success or failure of the international structures by how far they are prepared to lend their policy instruments to them.

Identities

Our second argument for why we believe democracy beyond the state will depend on the continued success of democracy within the state has to do with identity. In the second chapter we argued that the controversial nature of the relationship between democracy and identity lies in the fact that they are locked in an intimate, but nevertheless tense, relationship. Indeed, the very result of this intimacy is that the nation state often betrays both democracy and identity by not quite fulfilling either. The tension, as we also argued, is rooted in uncertainty as to what it is the guardianship of the nation state should guard: should it protect the demos or the ethnos? No wonder, then, that the debate about how identity best relates to democracy, and thus to the legitimacy of political systems, is seemingly endless amongst students of politics.

For our part, we have argued that cultural identity for all its accomplishment in binding a community is not necessarily the most compatible with democratic principles in a well-functioning polity. The latter seeks a polity-based identity (see Chapter 2) which can, but does not need to, look far into the past for solidarity-forging events, because these are sought in the participation in the polity, compliance with its norms and rules that need not be rooted in traditions, and commitment to and cooperation with its institutions.

Yet, although polity-based identity is the most self-evidently compatible with democratic principle to the extent that it overlaps so substantially with it, we have also mentioned, but not elaborated, reasons why we think that it may not be sufficient. Something more akin to national identity will still be conducive to democracy (Canovan, 2000; Miller, 1995; Moore, 2001) . The 'coldness' of procedures, disappointment of compromise, confusion of choices and unpredictability of results – all characteristics of democracy – may need to be complemented by the legitimacy, faith and trust deriving from 'fellowship' in a core national community.

Of course, it goes without saying that many less than democratic regimes have used the same argument for legitimizing political processes that have harmed their own people and that belonging to a cultural community is not synonymous with cooperation or compromise (Harris, 2003). Indeed, it can be divisive precisely because the 'warmness' of belonging excludes as much as it binds together. Yet the solution is not to propose that uniquely amongst polities democracies should forgo the distinctive contribution of cultural forms of identity whilst leaving their appeals to be picked up and monopolized by opponents of democracy. Rather, it is to understand how an appropriately designed democracy can add value to cultural belonging by taming it, by making it 'safe for itself', by reconciling it with other values; and, indeed, by reconciling culturally diverse groups. The trick, as it were, is to retain cultural identities somewhere deep down in the substratum of democracy whilst using democracy's superstructures to pick and choose amongst possible consequences of cultural belonging: to retain its benefits as a source of motivation, of trust and of willingness to make at least some sacrifices in solidarity with others; and, yet, to curb its tendencies to aggression and exclusion.

Here it needs to be remembered that democracy is not a finite state of affairs, but an ongoing process guided by the principles of consent and participation, obligation and legitimacy, accountability and popular sovereignty. These principles are most effective and best maintained where their practice is reexamined and reconstituted according to societal, demographic, economic and even international changes.

We have discussed at length why we have arrived at a historical crossroads at which the continuation of democracy within the state is better secured by its exercise beyond it. Yet we also argue for the emerging dependence of democracy beyond the state on the continued success of democracy within the state. Just such interdependence between democracy within and beyond the state is already implicit in our general remarks about the need for democracy to pull off the trick of preserving cultural identity as part of its substratum whilst using its own overlay of values and institutions to select only what is best and discard what is worst in cultural identity. Only democracy within the state can draw on the motivational force of cultural identity and hand its benefits on as it were to the legitimation of laws and policies democratically agreed from beyond the state. On the other hand, a democracy beyond the state constructed around the related elements of democratic peace, the reconciliation of peoples, and 'supranationalization' of minority and individual rights would offer further safeguards against the abuse of cultural identity.

Beyond such a general answer, specific clues of what kind of identity may be needed to sustain democracy beyond the state are already apparent from the study of the European Union. Though, needless to say, the answer is not a simple one. A whole host of issues need to be addressed.

The limits of national identity in the new European polity

There is a degree of plausibility in arguing that the larger polity can be only as democratic as its constituent units. That is, however, too simplistic and does not answer the questions arising from the current concerns about the lack of identification with the EU project, so manifestly demonstrated by the EU Constitution fiasco following the French and Dutch referendums in spring 2005. Yet, a closer scrutiny of the domestic political situation in both France and the Netherlands hints at problems within those societies – whether it is the French dissatisfaction with their own government augmented by economic insecurities expressed in the fear of the influx of 'foreign' labour, or the Dutch unrest concerning the nature of their multiculturalism) – as much as at problems they may have with the EU. The relationship, even if in the rejection of its current form, is, however, clear – the EU is close enough to be considered an integral part of domestic politics, but not close enough to be seen as a way of solution (Balibar, 2004; Fossum, 2001; Habermas, 1992, 1999, 2001a).

If we for the moment stay with this claim it seems reasonable to argue that the nation state is finding itself in a precarious position: under pressure from beyond and within the state with a substantially reduced ability to influence either. This cannot be lost on the Europe-wide population who surely understand (and react accordingly to) the tight squeeze of their national states. It seems, however, to be lost on the conceptual vocabulary within which we address the issue of national identity. There is a tension between national identity and a European one, as there should be, considering the changes in the international environment generally, but more acutely within the EU.

The first point to stress is that we are finding ourselves in the area of collective identity whose substance and significance and value have always been highly contested and emotive. The greatest success of the nation state has been its ability to harness identity into a valuable political tool in the form of nationality. The true value of democracy is to elevate nationality into a democratic citizenship which entails rights, dignity and respect, but also obligations and expectations of those. That amounts to our perception of the world and our place in it and, not least, constitutes the point of departure from which we construct our identity. This identity, for there are many others that are possibly more immediate, such as our gender, profession, social status, age and family hierarchy, is a historical product related closely to the nation state, the same nation state that is either losing the ability to control, construct and guard it in the traditional way, or has willingly partially relinquished this capacity in order to provide more goods, such as greater prosperity, more freedom and peace, more equality and solidarity among more people. Why are we assuming that the 'new nation state' should be the object of the same identity as the classical nation state?

We have said enough about what kind of polity the EU is and about what it seeks to be and about the reasons for democracy beyond the state. It is time to state the obvious: if there is a tension between national identity and European identity, it is because there is a tension between the nation-state in its current form and perceptions about national identity. Interestingly, these perceptions reflect rather the 'pathology of identity' than identity as such (Cerutti and Rudolph, 2001, p. 6). The stress on a difference, whether cultural or ideological, and the inability to accommodate it is not an intrinsic feature of identity. If that were the case, we would not place our hopes for a better world in democracy and we would not have an EU of 25 states seeking a deeper integration. Paradoxically, it is the proponents of the unchanging identities that claim the loss of national identity as one of the major discontents with the EU, probably aware of how fluid identities are and how easily influenced by a changing political environment. Whilst national identity carries an honourable status associated with a cultural continuity of 'the nation', the obstinacy of non-adaptation is associated with rather less honourable historical events. We must therefore concede that national identities have been constructed and engraved in our political consciousness and rhetoric within the contours of the classical nation state and that it is time to acknowledge their passing.

It may also be the time to reiterate that the intrinsic value of democracy is not just in its procedures, implying the compromise of differing interests acceptable to the largest majority of citizens, but the accommodation of differences in order to produce a stable political community. Stability implies tolerance, acceptance of differences, unity of purpose and mutual constraint between individuals and groups, thus ensuring the greatest possible liberty within constitutional limitations. The achievement of the latter, where achieved, has been a long historical process (Habermas, 2001c, p. 768). There is no denying that the resolution of the alleged tension between national identity and the European one may be equally long.

Why EU identity should grow out of national democracy

What does this mean? Similarly to the nation state, this means a reconciliation of differences and the construction of a political community with a corresponding identity. The first reason why it is national democracy that lays the foundation for European identity to emerge is here: the Union can only provide an overarching 'umbrella' identity that corresponds to its political community. The EU community has its roots in national communities where politics are experienced in daily life. It is unrealistic in the extreme to expect that a disaffected citizen can find political content so far removed from its locality. The nation state has its own battles to fight to forge solidarity among its own citizens, before they can extend it beyond its borders. We have discussed the civilizing strategies of the EU in aiding this process earlier. Our concern here is with national democracies and that for a number of reasons.

First, in a multi-layered, multifaceted and multicultural polity such as the EU, every national group has a legitimate interest in how others conduct their policies. The EU is reliant on domestic competition in its member states to produce results that will not harm the other member states – this is particularly so with identity-related legislation which may jeopardize minority cultures and inhibit the necessary trans-border and transnational cooperation projects. Whilst the EU can provide a buffer for states' deficiencies, the excessive reliance on the EU to solve national problems is not a sensible way forward. Linking identity to the efficiency of the Union may increase the EU's legitimacy, but only up to a point. It is already somewhat disconcerting that some of the new member states view the EU as a 'corrector' of their own inefficiencies and the complement to otherwise less well defined democratic credentials. Such a relationship is bound to produce disappointment when, at the end, the national democracy does not improve and the EU does not provide. Disappointment leads to regression and regression in identity formation tends to revive the ethnic identity that has exclusionary tendencies.

Second, insecurity about one's own democracy feeds insecurity about identity and vice versa. This is particularly the case in contemporary societies where porous borders and global immigration tests national democracies to the limit. We contend that only a mature well-functioning democracy has enough mechanisms to find solutions to those problems at the domestic level so that their insecurities do not spread to levels beyond the state and pose a challenge to an emerging European polity. As we have argued in Chapter 5, it is apparent that democracy promotion finds its greatest challenge in states where identity issues have migrated into Euroscepticism.

Third, 'unity in diversity' has become a slogan for Europe. It is a polity of such originality (Weiler in Cerrutti, 2001) that we struggle to give it a name. It combines a number of identities. It is a political community with a high level of legal and economic legitimacy, far outstripping any international organization. Simultaneously, it is maintaining the political identity of sovereign nation states which defies a confederal model along whose lines it may appear to be structured. For the lack of better vocabulary we call it a multi-level governance model which nevertheless seeks an overarching identity to make this structure last and evolve. The question is: how diverse and how united should this Europe be? The truth about cultural identity is that it does not need to have a centre, whilst the truth about political identity is that it must have one (Cerruti, 2001, p. 16).

How 'thick' or 'thin' should this identity be?

The answer is: thin enough to allow others in, but thick enough to create a sense of common future and purpose with enough trust and motivation among culturally diverse groups to make decisions that may not directly concern them and possibly even benefit others. Where else is an individual to learn such practice if not within its own national democracy? Where else are the communitarian problems to be resolved and where should primary political identity be forged? We contend that it is at the national level.

The literature on national identities and their character in respect of democratic practice is vast and rich in terminology and arguments about the fundamental question as to what kind of identity sustains a democratic state. In the first place there is by now an exhausted and rightly almost discarded 'civic/ethnic nationalism' dichotomy (B. Yack, in Beiner, 1999). Then there is a huge body of work by 'liberal nationalists' – often stretching the concept of liberalism to its limits (Kymlicka, 1995; Miller, 1995, 2000; Tamir, 1993). Both camps seek to accommodate the state's propensity towards nationalism and curb it by strong liberal principles. Finally, building on the Kantian version of republicanism, there is the sophisticated and normatively very appealing notion of Habermas's 'constitutional patriotism' and its various critical adaptations, such as 'civic patriotism'; some giving more credence to cultural identity than others (for a review of all, see Laborde, 2002). This is not the place to argue the virtues and pitfalls of these theories. All concur on one point though: collective identity in a democratic state should draw its inspiration from institutions rather than culture – it should be a political identity.

The role of culture in its linguistic, ethnic or historical formulation and 'ways of life' is too particular to bind together a diverse society where there may be different groups with mutually incomprehensible 'ways of life', or groups struggling to resolve historical animosities. Democratic national identity must be underpinned by universal principles of civil liberties, equal rights, democratic self-government and all the other norms attached to the realization of these (Laborde, 2002, p. 599). Hence, the binding issue of a thus conceived political community is in civic virtues and respect for and commitment to institutions that safe-guard the continuation of a 'common existence' (Parekh, 2003, p. 9). So, the 'narrowness' of ethnic solidarity is juxtaposed by the 'broadness' of the unifying universal principles.

How much input from cultural identity is necessary for a democratic polity is a matter for discussion. It suffices to say that negligence of the importance of cultural identity opens space for nationalist demagoguery (as in France, Austria, Belgium, many Eastern and Central European countries, and so on). There is more than sufficient evidence that identity seeks recognition and that recognition is best found and secured in a political solution. Some cultural identities are better suited to remain private, but some, such as minority cultures cannot be easily pushed into private spheres as liberals would wish. It has never been easy to divorce culture from politics, but in our diversity- and rights-worshipping age it is increasingly more difficult, and less acceptable. On the other hand, coming back to the beginning of this section, the polity-based identity imbued with a deeper meaning of obligation, trust, motivation and commitment to one's community is what national democracies aspire to – with various degrees of success. The national level is the appropriate one to design a constitutional framework within which these aspirations can be fulfilled in a particular society.

It follows that nationally 'anchored' identity already covers a fairly wide spectrum of cultural markers, communitarian practices, institutional affiliations and universal norms. If we imagine an identity continuum, the direction of which would start with a very 'thick' ethnic/primordial affiliation, gathering universalist principles along the way and 'thinning' towards a cosmopolitan end, national polity-based identity would be, ideally, somewhere in the middle of this continuum – Ideally, because identity does not follow a linear continuum and 'thick' and 'thin' are also disputable: considering the 'gathering' effect, 'thinner' seems too modest for such a complex construction of belonging. It is, however, a well-established description, supposedly meant to denote the less immediate and personal, so we continue to use it.

What does all this mean for European identity? We suggest 'thicker' at the local level and 'thinning' out towards the European one. The existing European culture (for there are many historical, ideological and cultural commonalities among European peoples) has not been able to capture their citizens' imagination in such a way that it could provide enough political legitimacy for the European project. This is not to say that it will not do so in the near or more distant future. For the foreseeable future though, the European Union competes for legitimacy and collective identity with the nation state whose character may be changing, but in ethical and identificational terms remains paramount, if not, as we argue, fundamental in creating an identity that can extend to the European community – that is, in principle endorse a cosmopolitan project of democracy and human rights. We are imagining, with Richard Bellamy and Alex Warleigh (1998), a 'cosmopolitan communitarianism', in which Communitarian (national) identities at the level of the state are developed and held in such a way that opens national democracies to taking obligations beyond the state. We are looking for a combination of 'thick' cultural identity with 'thinner' civic identity, along the lines of 'constitutional patriotism' at beyond the state level – thus, communitarian foundations, normatively inspired and democratically expanded by cosmopolitan principles – a new form of identity that is not seeking to replace national identities, nor stretch it to fit all states. The intended outcome is twofold: first, a normative blueprint for the engagement of national democracies beyond the state with other communities with respect for diversity of all; and, second, states restrained from abusing their sovereignty by threatening neighbours and internally repressing their own citizens.

Indeed, there is a powerful movement in contemporary political thought that, far from regarding attachments to universal and particular values as incompatible with one another, emphasizes their interdependence. Universal values cannot on their own ground commitments to a particular political community or set of institutions. Yet they may require such commitments for their realization. Perhaps the most persuasive way of solving this dilemma is for particular political communities to see themselves as elaborating their identities around local interpretations of universal ideals (Waldron, 1993). That there is scope for this follows from the significant indeterminacy to be found in such ideals. Almost all of them – rights, democracy, liberty or equality – can be achieved in more than one way. As Matthias Kumm puts it, 'consensus on principles need not extend to their full specification' (p. 12). 'Abstract principles' may be too 'thin' to ground a sense of political community that is thick enough to sustain democratic politics, but local interpretations of those principles need not be (Kumm, p. 14). Thus conceived democracy beyond the state becomes a certain relationship between the way in which democratic rule is constructed at the two levels. A thin overlay of democratic principle held in common is combined with mutual respect for differences in local interpretations of democratic politics.

Whither sovereignty?

Before concluding we want to anticipate the objection that, however we define it, democracy beyond the state can never be more than an oxymoron. Since our answer has scope to take the discussion further, we develop it at some length. It is that the concept of a sovereign nation state as an ultimate bearer of both sovereignty and democracy is, in any case, in need of re-examination; and, indeed, of rescuing from perceptions rooted in historically accumulated discourses which do not reflect political developments of recent decades and are likely to gather momentum even further. Crudely put, democracy needs a 'playing field', presumed to be a sovereign nation state, but that state does not need to be sovereign to the point when it can harm democracy within, whilst democracy too may fare better when practised in tandem at all levels: subnational, national and beyond the state.

Rights and duties that states have *vis-à-vis* their own citizens require, logically, acknowledgement of equally important rights and duties towards each other and each other's citizens. This is the basic idea of international law and by extension the meaning of democratic peace ('perpetual peace', according to Kant). If peace is a common end, then democratic peace must combine democracy and international law at every level where rights and duties are exercised and fairness is expected – national and supranational. It is, hence, reasonable to agree on rules by which states and people can function with a degree of certainty that these rules will be adhered to. The minimum condition under which that degree of certainty can be reached is – 'peace among nations'.

In an anarchical system of sovereign states there are few guarantees for peace, and the idea of Democratic peace is no more than an untested aspiration (see Chapter 7). Yet, if democracy is to become a truly global ideology in pursuit of a democratic peace, it will require a mutual penetration of domestic and international politics. This, in turn, implies a degree of constraint to state sovereignty through self-imposed agreements among international actors and the institutionalization of peace within international organizations. Democratic peace, democracy promotion and state sovereignty form an intimate and at times tense relationship.

An equally obvious counter to any objection that the last two chapters have merely served to demonstrate that 'democracy beyond the state' is an oxymoron since it would itself undermine sovereign statehood is that 'sovereignty' and 'statehood' are not 'essences' but 'concepts'. Interconnected characteristics of sovereignty undermine the notion that 'democracy beyond the state' may be a contradiction in terms. First, sovereignty is a historical product. Its meaning and extent have always been tightly connected to normative and political developments within the domestic and international environment. Whether citizens' expectations of the state are of an economic or security nature, concepts of state sovereignty have, historically, had to adapt to the fulfilment of those expectations. Equally, the international community expects certain behaviour of states and has long abandoned the notion that any state is beyond international law.

Second, whatever form the concept of sovereignty has taken at any one time it has always been qualified in the name of other norms, such as human rights, minority rights, democracy, communism and security. This is true even of what Stephen Krasner (2001) terms the 'historically myopic' view of sovereignty associated with the Westphalian state. Transgressions of its claim that state sovereignty should amount to exclusive authority and autonomy within a defined territory include the Treaty of Versailles, the Yalta agreements which allowed for the imposition of the communist regimes in Eastern Europe, the Dayton Agreement, the IMF's structural adjustment programmes, the 'modern' protectorates whereby the state is de facto controlled by external powers (for example, Iraq, Bosnia), voluntary agreements of a partial relinquishment of state sovereignty by the member states in the European Union, and, most tellingly of all, the Peace of Westphalia itself (1648). The treaties did not abolish the Holy Roman Empire, but dictated the internal organization of it through the involvement of external actors.

Third, notions of sovereignty have been qualified in the past not only by other values, but, crucially, to ensure the performance of the state itself. Thus Robert Keohane questions the assumption that 'full sovereignty' is to be equated with the 'success' of states. Some of the states that are most sovereign in the Westphalian sense are conspicuously weak.

Fourth, the difficulty of maintaining absolute definitions of sovereignty, has been met in practice by taking sovereignty to pertain to equality among states in the system. Thus whatever qualifications to the authority and autonomy of states are thought to be justified by other norms of international arrangement ought in principle to apply equally to all states. This at once introduces flexibility and discipline: sovereignty can be qualified where that is thought to be desirable, but those wanting to introduce such constraints, need to be sure they are serious about their equal, and non-discriminatory, application, lest the legitimacy of the constraint be questioned.

Fifth, notions of state sovereignty do not just evolve; they are also negotiated. No generation of state leaders is able to negotiate the problems of its day without taking decisions that by implication confirm or reconfigure existing notions of sovereignty. The foundation of the European Communities in the 1950s and the 'return' of the Central and Eastern European states after 1989 has, arguably, strengthened norms that enjoin the states of the region to discuss the meaning of 'statehood' and 'sovereignty' with one another (Keohane, 2002). This is not to suggest those states have abdicated the definition of their sovereign statehood to others. It is only to suggest an expectation that the views of 'others' should be considered and an honest attempt made to reconcile domestic and international understandings of sovereign statehood.

Sixth, the inclusion of some negotiated dimension to sovereign statehood recognizes that sovereignty and statehood are necessarily relational concepts. As long as we take the view that all those whose needs and values are affected by an action have a legitimate interest in it we cannot also hold to the view that the manner in which states structure their sovereign statehood is a purely private concern. Indeed, as soon as a state seeks to rely on norms of good neighbourliness, as it is almost certain to do in parts of the world characterized by dense interdependence, it is likely that others will, in turn, expect it to meet any norms of the neighbourhood that concern the attitudes of states towards their own sovereignty. In any case, sovereignty and statehood often carry a heavy burden of domestic expectations – prosperity, security and the protection of identities – whose delivery depends on compatibility between the individual state and the system of states. Thus participation in the consensual definition of state sovereignty between neighbours may be as self-interested as it is normative.

Seventh, concepts of sovereignty have not just been historically constructed and negotiated; they have, at any one time, almost always been complex and multidimensional. Krasner (2001, p. 19), for example, identifies four kinds of sovereignty, as follows:

1. *Interdependence sovereignty* refers to the ability of states to regulate the trans-border movement of goods, people, capital and ideas. Not only is this the dimension of sovereignty that has, arguably, been most substantially eroded by globalization and European integration, but the fact it has often been ceded willingly by states in search of efficiency gains underscores the previous point that states often 'trade' sovereignty for performance.

2. *Domestic sovereignty* refers to authority structures within the state and their ability to regulate behaviour. Such sovereignty does not presume any particular kind of political system, since historically the authority structure (hierarchy) of the state has assumed many forms, from monarchies to republics, from communism to democracy, from unitary to federal, from centralized to decentralized.

3. *Westphalian sovereignty* denies any authority external to the state. It implies the state is the highest point of organized power within the international system, and that it is entitled to non-interference in its domestic affairs. This notion of sovereignty has enjoyed widespread support precisely because of its tight connection to the principle of national self-determination and thus gains legitimacy from both of the supreme values of our times: democracy and national identity (as discussed in Chapter 2).

4. *Legal sovereignty* follows as a logical extension of the previous three dimensions: any one state must be recognized by others as having the international legal sovereignty to enter into agreements with others if it is to have de facto and de jure control of its own affairs. Moreover, those agreements must be voluntary and not coerced.

These four dimensions are interlinked, but hardly ever are all four enjoyed in full. Less control of trans-border economic activity means less interdependence sovereignty. States may use their legal sovereignty to sign up to international agreements, which, as long as they are in force, diminish their own roles as authoritative allocators of value and source of law. By the same token, the international system may contain states that are internationally sovereign, but fail to control disintegration within, precipitated by the lack of authority and control over domestic politics (failed states in Africa, the former Yugoslavia, Warsaw Pact countries and so on). It is increasingly a fact of international life that peace, safety and economic prosperity are best achieved by a degree of compromise of state sovereignty. As Krasner puts it, 'sovereignty is a basket of goods that do not necessarily go together' (Krasner, 2001, p. 21).

Conclusion to the chapter and the book

It has long been the *cri de coeur* of a 'small is beautiful' brigade, whose members would prefer to return democracy to its roots in small communities, that we should (re-)discover ways of practising democracy in arenas other than the state. But – under conditions of globalization – it is nowadays also common to ask whether democracy needs to be applied to the exercise of political power from beyond the state. As David Held formulates this argument, 'to prosper' democracy needs to be aligned with 'the forces which actually shape everyday life' (1995, p. 15).

Globalization, the dependence of security provision on much more than the 'self-help' of individual states, and difficulties with the notion that our moral obligations to others stop at national frontiers have already combined to promote a dense and complex institutionalization of politics beyond the state. Nowhere is this more evident than in the new Europe. In addition to membership of worldwide international organizations, large parts of the new Europe participate in multilateral security organizations, such as the North Atlantic Treaty Organization (NATO) and the Organization for Security Cooperation in Europe (OSCE). Above all, some 500 million inhabitants of the region belong to member states of the European Union, which goes beyond the issue-specific focus of classic international organizations to provide something much more akin to a general governance structure, covering most of the issues with which public policy has classically concerned itself.

So, looking back over the book as a whole, what have we said and, as important, what have we not said? In summary form, our conclusions, with reference back to the three arguments that we set out to make in Chapter 1, are as follows.

Claim 1. A two-dimensional experiment in democracy beyond the state is currently being attempted in the new Europe. Our empirical chapters identified one dimension with attempts to extend democratic standards of public control to shared regional institutions, conspicuously those of the European Union (Chapter 4); the other with coordinated attempts to manage the European part of the international system so that it consists only of democracies that measure up to standards of democratic rule that have themselves to some extent been agreed internationally (Chapter 5). An important connection between these dimensions that arguably remains underdeveloped is that criteria and processes used in democracy promotion are themselves in need of democratic control and deliberation.

Claim 2. In the conditions of the new Europe the prospects for demococay within the state depend on democracy beyond the state. Our argument here was that if any of a number of further propositions are accepted core justifications for the democratic state can no longer be delivered through the democratic states alone. The further propositions are, first, that democracies need at least to some extent to co-ordinate their management of their part of the international order if they are to maintain conditions of peace and stability needed for democratic rule itself; second, that globalization requires at least some international co-ordination to provide public goods and constrain negative externalities; and, third, that there are normative difficulties with the delimitation of all rights delivery to politics within the state. The conclusion to Chapter 7 used the distinction between intrinsic and consequential justifications for democracy to set out our own judgement that if the three propositions are, indeed, a fair summary of prevailing conditions in the new Europe, democracy within the state needs to be complemented by democratically controlled structures beyond the state if it is to satisfy justificatory claims that have been made on its behalf.

Claim 3. The prospects for democracy beyond the state in the new Europe depend on the continued success of democracy within the state. Whatever the need to complement democracy within the state with the democratic control of political power exercised from beyond the state, we have argued in this concluding chapter that any democracy beyond the state should and will continue to rely on democracy within the state. Amongst reasons we have given for this judgement is that democracy beyond the state will need its counterpart within the state for a subtle balance between an enabling and a constraint of its own powers, for identity, and for the generation of social capital and civic capabilities.

Cutting across such unashamedly evaluative and speculative claims, we have, however, also reached a more analytical conclusion about the present condition of democratic rule in the new Europe. Building on the earlier analysis of Chapters 3 and 4, Chapter 6 concluded that for those denizens of the new Europe who live in the European Union in particular, national and European-level institutions are already mutually implicated in one another's democratic performance. It is hard to assess the overall quality of democracy in those countries without making some allowance for the joint supply (or otherwise) of core democratic standards by institutions within and beyond the state.

So where should the debate go from here? Our hunch is that it is precisely the possibility that democracy beyond the state will have to be nested in the ways we mention in a continuation of democratic statehood that opens the way for democracy to be differentiated at the two levels: for democracy beyond the state to be a distinctively novel form of democracy. Here it is worth briefly distinguishing the possibilities that democracy at the two levels might conceivably complement one another in how they meet the 'demos' conditions for democracy on the one hand and the 'polity' conditions on the other. As we have repeatedly seen, the former aspect has already been well thought through in the literature with many interesting ideas for how contrasting concepts of political community within and beyond the state might simultaneously stabilize one another and permit democracy to be practised at both levels.

In contrast, our understanding is more patchy of how 'polities' might interface most plausibly to produce different yet complementary approaches to democracy at the two levels. Whilst a great deal of creative thinking has highlighted how 'new governance' (see p. 140) when employed beyond the state might produce 'good governance', much of the existing debate is still floundering with what is, arguably, a core question: how can combinations of democracy within and beyond the state produce the minimum levels of institutional and legal unity required by any democracy?

Basically the problem of legal and institutional unity is this: however we divide powers in complex ways, however we introduce 'majority-restraining devices', however much we employ new forms of governance in which standards are owed to individuals and groups and not just the people as a whole, a democracy cannot be a democracy unless public decisions pass at some point through the 'sluices' (Habermas, 1996, p. 300) of institutions procedurally structured for public control with political equality. Moreover, those decisions will need to follow the rule-of-law principle of equal application to all if they are to comply with the attachment of democracy to political equality.

We can imagine some possible answers. For example, that any democracy beyond the state is likely to remain, in the final analysis, the agent of democracies within the state. Or, at the other extreme, that democracy beyond the state is likely to achieve a legitimacy and autonomy of its own and, because it operates at the highest level of all, it is likely to establish the priority of its democratically made decisions over those of national democratic institutions. Or a third possibility, to argue by analogy with the academic study of European Union law, is that democracy at the two levels will only be able to coexist if democratically empowered actors do everything possible to avoid pressing equally reasonable but mutually incompatible claims to supremacy or priority against one another (Weiler, 2002). In other words we should expect a legal and institutional unity between democracy within and beyond the state to emerge precisely through incremental steps in conflict avoidance that will eventually accumulate into a *modus vivendi* between the two levels. Which of these possibilities would – normatively and practically – best allow democracy within and beyond the state to stabilize one another in the new Europe would be a profitable direction for further research.

Bibliography

Abromeit, H. (1998) *Democracy in Europe: Legitimising Politics in a Non-State Polity*, Oxford, Berghahn Books.

Anderson, B. (1983) *Imagined Communities*. London, Verso.

Anderson, J. (2002) 'Europeanization and the Transformation of the Democratic Polity, 1945–2000', *Journal of Common Market Studies*, vol. 40, no. 5, pp. 793–822.

Andeweg, R. (1995) 'The Reshaping of National Party Systems', *West European Politics*, vol. 18, no. 3, pp. 58–78.

Andolfato, D. (1994) 'Les Euro-deputés en Question', *Revue Politique et Parlementaire*, no. 970.

Andreev, S. (2005) *Conceptual Definition and Measurement Indicators of the Quality of Democracy: an Overview*, EUI Working Paper 2005/05. Florence, European University Institute.

Arblaster, A. (1987) *Democracy*. Milton Keynes, Open University Press.

Aristotle (T. Sinclair translation) (1962). *The Politics*. Harmondsworth, Penguin.

Arter, D. (1996) 'The Folketing and Denmark's European Policy: the Case of an Authorising Assembly', in P. Norton (ed.), *National Parliaments and the European Union*. London, Frank Cass, pp. 110–23.

Axelrod, R. (1984) *The Evolution of Co-operation*. New York, Basic Books.

Bale, T. (2005) *European Politics*, Basingstoke, Palgrave Macmillan.

Balibar, E. (2004) *We, the People of Europe? Reflections of Transnational Citizenship*, Princeton, NJ, Princeton University Press.

Batory, A. (2001) 'Hungarian Party Identities and The Question of European Integration', Sussex European Institute, *SEI Working Paper* No 49 *www.sussex.ac.uk*

Bauman, Z. (1999) *In Search of Politics*. Cambridge, Polity Press.

Bauman, Z. (2003) *Liquid Love*, Cambridge, Polity Press.

Beach, D. (2005) *The Dynamics of European Integration, Why and When EU Institutions Matter*. Basingstoke, Palgrave Macmillan.

Beck, U. (2004) *What is Globalization?* Cambridge, Polity Press.

Beetham, D. (1991) *The Legitimation of Power*. London, Macmillan.

Beetham, D. (1993) 'Liberal Democracy and the Limits of Democratization', in D. Held (ed.), *Prospects for Democracy: North, South, East and West*. Cambridge, Polity Press.

Beetham, D. (1994) *Defining and Measuring Democracy*. London, Sage/ECPR.

Beetham, D. (2005) *Democracy: a Beginner's Guide*. Oxford, One World.

Beetham, D., Bracking, S., Kearton, I. and Weir, S. (2002) *International IDEA Handbook on Democracy Assessment*. The Hague, Kluwer Law International.

Beiner, R. (ed.) (1999) *Theorizing Nationalism*. Albany, NY, State University of New York Press.

Beissinger, M. (2002) *Nationalist Mobilisation and the Collapse of the Soviet State*. Cambridge, Cambridge University Press.

Bell, D. (2002) *French Politics Today*. Manchester, Manchester University Press.

 Bellamy, R. and Castiglione, D. (2000) 'The Uses of Democracy: Reflections on the European Democratic Deficit', in E. Eriksen and J. Fossum (eds), *Democracy in the European Union. Integration Through Deliberation*. London, Routledge, pp. 65–84.

Bellamy, R. and Warleigh, A. (1998) 'From an Ethics of Integration to an Ethics of Participation: Citizenship and the Future of the European Union', *Millennium*, no. 27, pp. 447–70.

Benner, E. (2001) 'Is there a core national doctrine?', *Nations and Nationalism*, vol. 7, no. 2, pp. 155–174.

Bergman, T. (1997) 'National Parliaments and EU Affairs Committees: Notes on Empirical Varation and Competing Explanations', *Journal of European Public Policy*, vol. 4, no. 3, pp. 373–87.

Bergman, T. (2000) 'The European Union as the Next Step of Delegation and Accountability', *European Journal of Political Research*, vol. 37, no. 3, pp. 415–29.

Berlin, I. (1969) *Four Essays on Liberty*. London, Oxford University Press.

Berlin, I. (1972) 'The Bent Twig', *Foreign Affairs*, vol. 51, no. 1, pp. 11–30.

Bibic, A. and Graziano, G. (1994) *Civil Society, Political Society, Democracy*. Ljubljana, Political Science Association.

Blaug, R. (2000) 'Outbreaks of Democracy', *Socialist Register*, pp. 145–60.

Blondel, J. (1990) *Comparative Government: an Introduction*. London, Philip Allan.

Blondel, J. Sinnott, R. and Svensson, P. (1998) *People and Parliament in the European Union: Participation, Democracy and Legitimacy*. Oxford, Clarendon Press.

Blyth, M. and Katz, R. (2005) 'From Catch-all Politics to Cartelisation: the Political Economy of the Cartel Party', *West European Politics*, vol. 28, no. 1, pp. 33–60.

Bobbitt, P. (2002) *The Shield of Achilles: War, Peace and the Course of History*. London, Penguin.

Bogaards, M. and Crepaz, M. (2002) 'Consociational Interpretations of the European Union', *European Union Politics*, vol. 3, no. 3, pp. 357–76.

Bogdanor, V. (1986) 'The Future of the European Community: Two Models of Democracy', *Government and Opposition*, vol. 22, no. 2, pp. 344–70.

Bostock, D. (2002) 'Coreper Revisited', *Journal of Common Market Studies*, vol. 40, no. 2, pp. 215–34.

Bréchon, P. (1999) 'L'Europe face au déficit démocratique', *Revue Politique et Parlementaire*, no. 1001, pp. 5–15.

Brubaker, R. (1996) *Nationalism Reframed*. Cambridge, Cambridge University Press.

Budge, I., Newton, K. *et al.* (1997) *The Politics of the New Europe: Atlantic to Urals*. London, Longman.

Burke, E. (1975 [1774]) 'Speech to the Electors of Bristol', in B. Hill (ed.), *Edmund Burke on Government, Politics and Society*. London, Fontana.

Bútora, M. (1999) *Kto? Prečo? Ako?*, Bratislava: IVO.

Calhoun, C. (ed.) (1992) *Habermas and the Public Sphere*. Cambridge, MA, MIT Press.

Canovan, M. (2000) 'Patriotism is not enough', *British Journal of Political Science*, vol. 30, no. 2, pp. 413–432.

Cederman, Laer-Erik (2001) 'Nationalism and Bounded Integration: What It Would Take to Construct a European Demos', *European Journal of International Relations*, vol. 7, no. 2, pp. 139–74.

Cerutti, F. and Rudolph, E. (2001) *A Soul for Europe*, Vol. 1. Leeuwen, Peeters.

Chryssochoou, D. (1994) 'Democracy and Symbiosis in the European Union: Towards a Confederal Consociation?', *West European Politics*, vol. 17, no. 4, pp. 1–14.

Clergerie, J.-L. (1995) 'L'improbable censure de la Commission Européenne', *Revue de Droit Public et de la Science Politique*, vol. 111, no. 2, pp. 205–20.

Collier, D. and Levitsky, S. (1997) 'Democracy with Adjectives: Conceptual Innovations in Comparative Research', *World Politics*, vol. 49, no. 3, pp. 430–51.

Connor, W. (1972) 'Nation-Building or Nation-Destroying?', *World Politics*, vol. 24, no. 3, pp. 319–55.

Copsey, N. (2005) 'Popular Politics and the Ukrainian Presidential Election of 2004', *Politics*, vol. 25, no. 2, pp. 99–106.

Corbett, R., Jacobs, F. and Shackleton, M. (1995) *The European Parliament*. London, Catermill.

COSAC (2001) *Summary of Proceedings, XXIV COSAC.* Stockholm, 20–22 May 2001.

Council of the European Union (2000) *Council's Rules of Procedure.* Brussels, General Secretariat of the Council.

Council of the European Union (2003) *A Secure Europe in a Better World: European Security Strategy.* Brussels, Council of the European Union.

Cowles, M., Caporaso, J. and Risse, T. (2001) *Transforming Europe.* Ithaca, NY, Cornell University Press.

Crombez, C. (1996) 'Legislative Procedures in the European Community', *British Journal of Political Science*, vol. 26, no. 2, pp. 199–218.

Crombez, C., Steunenberg, B. and Corbett, R. (2000) 'Understanding the EU Legislative Process: Political Scientists' and Practitioners' Perspectives', *European Union Politics*, vol. 1, no. 3, pp. 363–83.

Crombez, C. (2003) 'The Democratic Deficit in the European Union. Much Ado about Nothing', *European Union Politics*, vol. 4, no. 1, pp. 101–20.

Dahl, R. (1971) *Polyarchy: Participation and Opposition.* New Haven, CT, Yale University Press.

Dahl, R. (1989) *On Democracy.* New Haven, CT, Yale University Press.

Davies, N. (1996) *Europe, A History.* Oxford, Oxford University Press.

Debeljak, A. (2003) 'European Forms of Belonging', *East European Politics and Societies*, vol. 17, no. 2, pp. 151–66.

Dehousse, R. (1997) 'European Integration and the Nation-State', in M. Rhodes, P. Heywood, and V. Wright (eds), *Developments in West European Politics.* London, Macmillan, pp. 37–57.

Delwit, P. (2000) 'Participation électorale et scrutin européen: une légitimité minimale', in G. Grünberg, P. Perrineau, and C. Ysmal (eds), *Le Vote des Quinze: les elections européennes du 13 Juin 1999*, Paris, Presse de Science Po, pp. 295–316.

De Schutter, O., Lebessis, N. and Paterson, J. (2001) *Governance in the European Union.* Brussels, European Commission.

Detlef, J. and Storsved, A.-S. (1995) 'Legitimacy through Referendum? The Nearly Successful Domino Strategy of the European Referendums in Austria, Finland, Sweden and Norway', *West European Politics*, vol. 18, no. 4, pp. 18–37.

Dewey, J. (1927) *The Public and its Problems.* London, George Allen & Unwin.

Diamond, L. (2002) 'Elections without Democracy: Thinking about Hybrid Regimes', *Journal of Democracy*, vol. 13, no. 2, pp. 21–35.

Dixon, W. (1994) 'Democracy and the Peaceful Settlement of International Conflict', *American Political Science Review*, vol. 88, no. 1, pp. 14–32.

Döring, H. (ed.) (1995) *Parliaments and Majority Rule in Western Europe.* Frankfurt, Campus Verlag.

Doyle, M. (1983) 'Kant, Liberal Legacies and Foreign Affairs', *Philosophy and Public Affairs*, vol. 12, no. 3, pp. 205–35.

Doyle, M. (1986) 'Liberalism and World Politics', *American Political Science Review*, vol. 80, no. 4, pp. 1151–69.

Dunleavy, P. and O'Leary, B. (1987) *Theories of the State: The Politics of Liberal Democracy.* London, Macmillan.

Dunn, J. (2005) *Setting the People Free: the Story of Democracy.* London, Atlantic Books.

Eriksen, E. and Fossum, J. (2000) 'Post-national Integration', in E. Eriksen and J. Fossum (eds), *Democracy in the European Union: Integration Through Deliberation.* London, Routledge, pp. 1–28.

Eriksen, E., Fossum, J. and Menéndez, A. (eds) (2004) *Developing a Constitution for Europe.* London, Routledge.

Eurobarometer: *Public Opinion in the European Community* (two issues per year). Brussels, Office for Official Publications of the European Communities.

European Commission (1992) *The Treaty on European Union.* Luxembourg, European Commission.

European Commission (1997) *Evolution in Governance: What Lessons for the Commission? A First Assessment*, Working Paper compiled by Notis Lebessis and John Paterson. Brussels, European Commission.

European Commission (1999) *Better Lawmaking 1998: A Shared Responsibility. Commission Report to the European Council.* Brussels, European Commission.

European Commission (2001) *Perceptions of the European Union: A Qualitative Study of the Public's Attitudes to and Expectations of the European Union in the 15* member states *and the 9 Candidate Countries* (The Optem Report). Brussels, European Commission.

European Commission (2004) Treaty Establishing a Constitution for Europe. *Official Journal of the European Union*, OJ C 310/1–474, 16 December 2004. Luxembourg, Office for the Official Publications of the European Communities.

European Convention (2002) *Working Group IV.* Paper by Andrew Duff. Brussels, Secretariat of the European Convention.

European Council (1993) *Conclusions of the Presidency*, Copenhagen June 1993. *Bulletin of the European Communities*, vol. 26, no. 6. Luxembourg, Office for Official Publications of the European Communities.

European Liberal and Democratic Reform (ELDR) Group of the European Parliament. (1999) Press Release, *Constitutive Agreement – Not a Political Coalition*, Brussels, 15 July 1999.

European Parliament (1983) *Report on the Preliminary Draft Treaty Establishing the European Union.* Brussels, European Parliament.

European Parliament (1997) *Report on Relations between the European Parliament and National Parliaments* (Neyts-Uytterbroeck). Brussels, European Parliament.

European Parliament (1998) *Report on the Moderation of Procedures for the Exercise of Implementing Powers – Comitology* (Aglietta Report). Brussels, European Parliament.

European Parliament (2000) *Report on the European Parliament's Proposals for the Intergovernmental Conference* (Dimitrakopoulos-Leinen). Brussels, European Parliament.

European Parliament (2001) *Report on Proposal for a Regulation on the Protection of Individuals with Regard to the Processing of Personal Data by the Institutions and Bodies of the Community* (Paciotti report). Brussels, European Parliament.

European Parliament (2003) *On the Proposal for a Council Regulation adapting the Provisions Relating to Committees Which Assist the Commission in the Exercise of its Implementing Powers* (Frassoni Report). Brussels, European Parliament.

Fink-Hafner, D. (1999) 'Dilemmas in Managing the Expanding EU: the EU and Applicant States' Point of View', *Journal of European Public Policy*, vol. 6, pp. 783–801.

Fink-Hafner, D. and Lajh, D. (2003) *Managing Europe From Home: The Europeanisation of the Slovenian Core Executive*. Ljubljana, FDV (Faculty of Social Sciences).

Forster, A. (1999) *Britain and the Maastricht Negotiations*. London, Macmillan.

Fossum, J. (2001) 'Identity-Politics in the European Union', ARENA Working Papers WP 01/17.

Franklin, M. (2001) 'How Structural Factors Cause Turnout Variations at European Parliament Elections', *European Union Politics*, vol. 2, no. 3, pp. 309–29.

Franklin, M., Marsh, M. and McLaren, L. (1994) 'Uncorking the Bottle: Popular Opposition to European Unification in the Wake of Maastricht', *Journal of Common Market Studies*, vol. 32, no. 4, pp. 455–72.

Freedom House data available at www.freedhomhouse.org/research.

Fukuyama, F. (1989) 'The End of History?', *The National Interest*, vol. 16, pp. 3–18.

Fukuyama, F. (2005) *State Building, Governance and World Order in the Twenty-First Century*. London, Profile Books.

Gallagher, M. (1996) 'Conclusion' in M. Gallagher and P. Uleri (eds), *The Referendum Experience in Europe*. London, Macmillan, pp. 226–52.

Gallagher, M., Laver, M., and Mair, P. (1992) *Representative Government in Modern Europe. Institutions, Parties and Government*. New York, McGraw-Hill.

Gellner, E. (1994) *Conditions of Liberty: Civil Society and its Rivals.* Harmondsworth, Penguin Books.

Gerstlé, J., Semetko, H., Schoenbach, K. and Villa, M. (2000) 'L'Européanisation défaillante des campagnes nationales' in P. Grünberg, P. Perrineau and C. Ysmal (eds), *Le Vote des Quinze: les elections européennes du 13 Juin 1999,* Paris, Press de Science Po, pp. 95–120.

Giddens, A. (1984) *The Constitution of Society: Outline of the Theory of Structuration.* Cambridge, Polity Press.

Giddens, A. (1991) *The Consequences of Modernity.* Cambridge, Polity Press.

Giddings, P. and Drewry, A. (1996) *Westminster and Europe: the Impact of the European Union on the Westminster Parliament.* London, Macmillan.

Glenn, J. (2004) 'From Nation–States to Member States: Accesion Negotiations as an Instrument of Europeanization', *Comparative European Politics,* 2, pp. 3–28.

Gray, J. (2002) *Straw Dogs: Thoughts on Humans and Other Animals.* London, Granta Books.

Green Cowles, M., Caporaso, J. and Risse, T. (2001) *Transforming Europe.* Ithaca, Cornell University Press.

Greenfeld, L. (1992) *Nationalism: Five Roads to Modernity.* Cambridge, MA, Harvard University Press.

Greenfeld, L. (2005). 'Nationalism and the Mind', *Nations and Nationalism,* vol. 11, no. 3, pp. 325–41.

Habermas, J. (1992) 'Citizenship and National Identity: Some Reflections on the Future of Europe', *Praxis International,* vol. 12, no. 1, pp. 1–19.

Habermas, J. (1996) *Between Facts and Norms.* Cambridge, Polity Press.

Habermas, J. (1999) 'The European Nation-State and Pressures of Globalization', *New Left Review,* vol. 235, pp. 46–59.

Habermas, J. (2001a) *The Postnational Constellation: Political Essays.* Cambridge, MA, MIT Press.

Habermas, J. (2001b) 'A Constitution for Europe?', *New Left Review,* vol. 11, pp. 5–26.

Habermas, J. (2001c) 'Constitutional Democracy: a Paradoxical Union of Contradictory Principles', *Political Theory,* vol. 29, no. 6, pp. 766–81.

Habermas, J. (2005) 'Why Europe Needs a Constitution', in E. Eriksen, J. Fossum and A. Menéndez (eds), *Developing a Constitution for Europe.* London, Routledge.

Hall, J. (1985) *Powers and Liberties.* Oxford, Blackwell.

Hardt, M. and Negri, A. (2000) *Empire.* Cambridge, MA, Harvard University Press.

Harrington, J. (1992) *The Commonwealth of Oceana and a System of Politics*. Cambridge, Cambridge University Press.

Harris, E. (2002) *Nationalism and Democratisation Politics of Slovakia and Slovenia*. Aldershot, Ashgate Publishing.

Harris, E. (2003) 'New Forms of Identity in Contemporary Europe', *Perspectives on European Politics and Society*, vol. 4, no. 1, pp. 13–33.

Harris, E. (2004). 'Europeanisation of Slovakia', *Comparative European Politics*, vol. 2, no. 2, pp. 185–211.

Hay, C. (2002) 'Globalization, "EU-isation" and the Space for Social Democratic Alternatives: Pessimism of the Intellect: a Reply to Coates', *British Journal of Politics and International Relations*, vol. 4, no. 3, pp. 452–64.

Hechter, M. (2000) *Containing Nationalism*. Oxford, Oxford University Press.

Hegeland, H. and Neuhold, C. (2002) 'Parliamentary Participation in EU Affairs in Austria, Finland and Sweden: Newcomers with Different Approaches', *European On-Line Papers*, vol. 6, no. 10, pp. 1–18.

Held, D. (1991) 'Democracy, the Nation State and the Global System', in D. Held (ed.), *Poltical Theory Today*. Stanford, CA, Stanford University Press.

Held, D. (1995) *Democracy and the Global Order: From the Modern State to Cosmopolitan Governance*. Stanford, CA, Stanford University Press.

Held, D. (1996) *Models of Democracy*, 2nd edn. Cambridge, Polity Press.

Held, D. (2004) 'Democratic Accountability and Political Effectiveness from Cosmopolitan Perspectives' in Held, D. and Koenig-Archibugi, D. (eds) Special issue on Global Governance and Public Accountability, *Government and Opposition*, vol. 39, no. 2, pp. 364–91.

Held, D. and McGrew, A. (eds) (2000) *The Global Transformations Reader*. London: Polity Press.

Henderson, K. (2004) 'Developments in the Applicant States', *Journal of Common Market Studies*, Annual Review, vol. 42, pp. 153–67.

Héritier, A. (1997) 'Policy-making by Subterfuge: Interest Accommodation, Innovation and Substitute Democratic Legitimation in Europe – Perspectives from Distinctive Policy Areas', *Journal of European Public Policy*, vol. 4 , no. 2, pp. 171–89.

Hill, C. (2003) *The Changing Politics of Foreign Policy*. Basingstoke, Palgrave Macmillan.

Hix, S. (1999) *The Political System of the European Union*. London, Macmillan.

Hix, S. (2001) 'Legislative Behaviour and Party Competition in the EP', *Journal of Common Market Studies*, vol. 39, no. 4, pp. 663–89.

Hix, S. and Lord, C. (1996) 'The Making of a President: the European Parliament and the Confirmation of Jacques Santer as President of the Commission', *Government and Opposition*, vol. 31, no. 1, pp. 62–76.

Hobsbawm, E. (1994) *Age of Extremes: the Short Twentieth Century 1914–1991*. London, Abacus.

Holmberg, S. (2001) *Swedish Voting Behaviour*. Göteberg, Swedish Electoral Studies Programme.

Horowitz, D. (1985) *Ethnic Groups in Conflict*, Berkeley, Univesity of California Press.

House of Lords (1996) *27th Report on the Scrutiny of European Business*. (Select Committee on European Legislation). London, HMSO.

Howard, M. (1983) *The Causes of Wars*. London, Counterpoint.

Hroch, M. (1993). 'From National Movements to the Fully-Formed Nation', *New Left Review*, vol. 198, pp. 3–20.

Hume, D. (1902 [1777]) *Enquiries Concerning the Human Understanding and Concerning the Principles of Morals*. Oxford, Oxford University Press.

Huntington, S. (1991) *The Third Wave, Democratization in the Late Twentieth Century* (Norman Oklahoma, University of Oklahoma Press).

Issacharoff, S. (2004) 'Constitutionalizing Democracy in Fractured Societies', *Journal of International Affairs*, vol. 58, no.1, pp. 73–93.

Jervis, R. (1976) *Perception and Misperception in International Politics*. Princeton NJ, Princeton University Press.

Joerges, C. and Neyer, J. (1997) 'Transforming Strategic Interaction into Deliberative Problem-solving: European Comitology in the Foodstuffs Sector', *Journal of European Public Policy*, vol. 4, no. 4, pp. 609–25.

Jones, C. (2001) *Global Justice Defending Cosmopolitanism*, Oxford, Oxford University Press.

Katz, R. and Mair, P. (1995) 'Changing Models of Party Organisation and Party Democracy: the Emergence of the Cartel Party', *Party Politics*, vol. 1, no. 1, pp. 5–28.

Kelly, J. (2004) 'International Actors on the Domestic Scene: Membership Conditionality and Socialization by International Institutions', *International Organisation*, vol. 58, no. 3, pp. 425–258.

Kemp, W. (2001) *Quiet diplomacy in Action: the OSCE High Commissioner on National Minorities*. Den Haag: Kluwer Law International.

Keohane, R. (1984) *After Hegemony: Cooperation and Discord in the World Political Economy*. Princeton, NJ, Princeton University Press.

Keohane, R. (2002) 'Ironies of Sovereignty: the European Union and the United States', *Journal of Common Market Studies*, vol. 40, no. 4, pp. 743–65.

Kielmansegg, P. (1996) Integration und Demokratie', in M. Jachtenfuchs and B. Kohler-Koch (eds), *Europäische Integration*. Opladen, Leske and Budrich.

Kirchheimer, O. (1966) 'The Transformation of the Western European Party System', in J. Palombara and M. Weiner (eds), *Political Parties and Political Development*. Princeton, NJ, Princeton University Press.

Kitschelt, H., Mansfeldová, Z., Markowski, R. and Tóka, G. (1999) *Postcommunist Party Systems, Competition, Representation, and Inter Party Cooperation*. Cambridge, Cambridge University Press.

Koenig-Archibugi, M. (2004) 'International Governance as New Raison d'état? The Case of the EU Common Foreign and Security Policy', *European Journal of International Relations*, vol. 10, no. 2, pp. 147–88.

Kopecký P. and Mudde, C. (2002) 'The Two Sides of Euroscepticism', *European Union Politics*, Vol. 3, no. 3, pp. 297–326.

Krasner, S. (ed.) (1983) *International Regimes*. Ithaca, NY, Cornell University Press.

Krasner, S. (2001) 'Rethinking the Sovereign State Model', *Review of International Studies*, vol. 27, December, pp. 17–42.

Krause, K. (2003) 'Slovakia's Second Transition', *Journal of Democracy*, 14:2, pp. 65–79.

Krehbiel, K. (1991) *Information and Legislative Organization*. Ann Arbor, University of Michigan Press.

Kreppel, A. (2000) 'Rules, Ideology and Coalition Formation in the European Parliament: Past, Present and Future', *European Union Politics*, vol. 1, no. 3, pp. 340–62.

Kritizinger, S. (2005) 'European Identity Building from the Perspective of Efficiency', *Comparative European Politics*, vol. 3, no. 1, pp. 50–76.

Kumm, M. (2005) 'To be a European Citizen, Constitutional Patriotism and the Treaty Establishing a Constitution for Europe', in E. Eriksem, J. Fossum, M. Kumm and A. Menéndez (eds), *The European Constitution, The Rubicon Crossed?* Oslo, Arena, pp. 7–63.

Kydland, F. and Prescott, E. (1977) 'Rules Rather than Discretion: the Inconsistency of Optimal Plans', *Journal of Political Economy*, no. 85, pp. 137–60.

Kymlicka, W. (1995). *Multicultural Citizenship*. Oxford, Oxford University Press.

Laborde, C. (2002) 'From Constitutional to Civic Patriotism', *British Journal of Political Science*, vol. 32, no. 2, pp. 591–612.

Laffan, B. (2001) 'The European Union Policy: a Union of Regulative, Normative and Cognitive Pillars' *Journal of European Public Policy*, vol. 8, no. 5, pp. 709–27.

Laver, M. and Shepsle, K. (1996) *Making and Breaking Governments: Cabinets and Legislatures in Parliamentary Democracies*. Cambridge, Cambridge University Press.

Lequesne, C. and Rivaud, P. (2001) 'Les comités d'experts independents: l'expertise au service d'une démocratie supranationale', *Revue Française de Science Politique*, vol. 51, no. 6, pp. 867–81.

Lewis, J. (1998) *The Institutional Problem-Solving Capacities of the Council: The Committee of Permanent Representatives and the Methods of Community*, Discussion Paper 98/1. Köln, Max-Planck-Institut.

Li, Q. and Reuveny, R. (2003) 'Economic Globalization and Democracy: an Empirical Analysis', *British Journal of Political Science*, vol. 33, pp. 29–54.

Lijphart, A. (1979) 'Consociational Democracy', *World Politics*, vol. 32, pp. 207–25.

Lijphart, A. (1984) *Democracies: Patterns of Majoritarian and Consensus Government in Twenty-One Countries*. New Haven, CT, Yale University Press.

Lijphart, A. (1997) 'The Puzzle of Indian Democracy: a Consociational Interpretation', *American Political Science Review*, vol. 90, no. 2, pp. 258–68.

Linklater, A. (1998) 'Cosmopolitan Citizenship', *Citizenship Studies*, vol. 2, no. 1, pp. 23–43.

Linz, J. and Stepan, A. (1996) *Problems of Democratic Transition and Consolidation: Southern Europe, South America, and Post-Communist Europe*, Baltimore, MD and London, Johns Hopkins University Press.

Locke, J. (1977 [1690]) *Two Treatises of Government*. London, Everyman.

Lord, C. (1995) *Absent at the Creation: Britain and the Foundation of the European Community, 1950–2*. Aldershot, Ashgate.

Lord, C. (1998a) *Democracy in the European Union*. Sheffield, Sheffield University Press.

Lord, C. (1998b) 'The Untidy Right in the European Parliament' in D. Bell and C. Lord (eds), *Transnational Parties in the European Union*. Aldershot, Ashgate.

Lord, C. (2001) 'Les partis politiques au niveau européen: quel type de concurrence imparfaite', in P. Delwit, E. Külachi and C. van de Walle (eds), *Les fédérations européennes de partis. Organisation et influence*. Brussels, Université Libre de Bruxelles, pp. 39–56.

Lord, C. (2004) *A Democratic Audit of the European Union.* Basingstoke, Palgrave Macmillan.

Lord, C. and Beetham, D. (2001) 'Legitimizing the EU: Is there a "Post-parliamentary Basis" for its Legitimation', *Journal of Common Market Studies*, vol. 39, no. 3, pp. 443–62.

Lord, C. and Magnette, P. (2004) 'E Pluribus Unum? Creative Disagreement about Legitimacy in the EU', *Journal of Common Market Studies*, vol. 42, no. 1, pp. 183–202.

Magnette, P. (1999) 'L'Union européenne: un régime semi parlementaire', in P. Delwit, J.-M. DeWaele and P. Magnette (eds), *A quoi sert le Parlement européen?* Bruxelles, Editions Complexes.

Magnette, P. (2003) 'When does Deliberation Matter? Constitutional Rhetoric in the Convention on the Future of Europe', in C. Closa and J. Fossum (eds) *Deliberative Constitutional Politics in the EU*. Oslo, ARENA Report No. 5/04.

Magnette, P. (2005) *What is the European Union? Nature and Prospects.* Basingstoke, Palgrave Macmillan.

Majone, G. (1996) 'The European Commission as Regulator', in G. Majone (ed.), *Regulating Europe*. London, Routledge, pp. 61–79.

Mann, M. (1995) 'A Political Theory of Nationalism and its Excesses', *Notions of Nationalism*. Budapest, Central European Press.

Mann, M. (1986, 1993) *The Sources of Social Power*, Vols I/II. Cambridge, Cambridge University Press.

Manners, I. and Whitman, R. (2003) 'The "Difference Engine": Constructing and Representing the International Identity of the European Union', *Journal of European Public Policy*, vol. 10, no. 3, pp. 380–404.

Mansbridge, J. (2003) 'Rethinking Representation', *American Political Science Review*, vol. 97, no. 4, pp. 515–28.

March, J. and Olsen, J. (1995) *Democratic Governance*. New York, Free Press.

Markell, P. (2000) 'Making Affect Safe For Democracy? On Constitutional Patriotism', *Political Theory*, vol. 28, no. 1, pp. 38–63.

Marx, K. (1973) *The Revolutions of 1848*. Harmondsworth, Penguin Books.

Mason, A. (1999) 'Political Community, Liberal-Nationalism, and the Ethics of Assimilation', *Ethics*, vol. 109, pp. 261–86.

Mattila, M. (2003) 'Why Bother? Determinants of Turnout in European Elections', *Electoral Studies*, vol. 22, no. 3, pp. 449–68.

Mattila, M. and Lane, J.-E. (2001) 'Why Unanimity in the Council? A Roll-Call Analysis of Council Voting'. *European Union Politics*, vol. 2, no. 1, pp. 31–53.

Maurer, A. (2003) 'The Legislative Powers and Impact of the European

Parliament', *Journal of Common Market Studies*, vol. 41, no. 2, pp. 227–47.

Maurer, A. and Wessels, W. (2001) 'National Parliaments after Amsterdam: From Slow Adapters to National Players', in A. Maurer and W. Wessels (eds), *National Parliaments on Their Ways to Europe: Losers or Latecomers?* Baden-Baden, Nomos Verlag, pp. 425–76.

McKelvey, R. (1976) 'Intransitivities in Multidimensional Voting Models and Some Implications for Agenda Control', *Journal of Economic Theory*, vol. 12, no. 3, pp. 472–82.

Mény, Y. (2002) '*De la démocratie en Europe*: Old Concepts and New Challenges', *Journal of Common Market Studies*, vol. 41, no. 1, pp. 1–13.

Michels, R. (1949 [1911]) *Political Parties: a Sociological Study of the Oligarchical Tendencies in Modern Democracy*. New York, Free Press.

Migdal, J. (2004) 'State Building and the Non-Nation-State', *Journal of International Affairs*, vol. 58, no. 1, pp. 17–46.

Mill, J. S. (1972 [1861]) *Utilitarianism: On Liberty and Considerations on Representative Government*. London, Dent.

Miller, D. (1993) 'Deliberative Democracy and Social Choice' in D. Held (ed.), *Prospects for Democracy: North, South, East, West*. Cambridge, Polity Press.

Miller, D. (1995) *On Nationality*. Oxford, Clarendon Press.

Miller, D. (2000) *Citizenship and National Identity*. Cambridge, Polity Press.

Milward, A. (1992) *The European Rescue of the Nation State*. London, Routledge.

Moberg, A. (2002) 'The Nice Treaty and Voting Rules in the Council', *Journal of Common Market Studies*, vol. 40, no. 2, pp. 259–82.

Montesquieu, C. de Secondat (1989) *The Spirit of the Laws*. Cambridge, Cambridge University Press.

Moore, M. (2001) 'Normative Justifications for Liberal Nationalism: Justice, Democracy and National Identity', *Nations and Nationalism*, vol. 7, no.1, pp. 2–19.

Moravcsik, A. (1998) *The Choice for Europe: Social Purpose and State Power from Messina to Maastricht*. London, UCL Press.

Moser, R. (1999) 'Independents and Party Formation: Elite Partisanship as an Intervening Variable in Russian Politics', *Comparative Politics*, vol. 31, no. 2, pp. 147–65.

Mosley, L. (2004) 'Government–Financial Market Relations after EMU: New Currency, New Constraints?', *European Union Politics*, vol. 5, no. 2, pp. 181–209.

NOP (National Opinion Poll) (2001) *British Election Survey*.

Norman, P. (2003) *The Accidental Constitution: The Story of the European Convention*. Brussels, EuroComment.

Olson, M. (1965) *The Logic of Collective Action*. Cambridge, MA, Harvard University Press.

O'Donnell, G. (1996) 'Illusions about Consolidation', *Journal of Democracy*, 7:2, pp. 34–51.

Olsen, J. (2002) 'The Man Faces of Europeanization', *Arena Online Working Papers* WP 01/2. http://www.arena.uio.no/publications/wp02_2htm

Organization for Security Cooperation in Europe (2001) *Republic of Belarus: Presidential Election 9 September 2001*. Warsaw, OSCE.

Organization for Security Cooperation in Europe (2003) *Republic of Azerbaijan: Presidential Election 15 October 2003*. Warsaw, OSCE.

Organization for Security Cooperation in Europe (2004a) *Russian Federation: Presidential Election 14 March 2004*. Warsaw, OSCE.

Organization for Security Cooperation in Europe (2004b) *Elections to the European Parliament 10–13 June 2004*. Warsaw, OSCE.

Organization for Security Cooperation in Europe (2004c) *Republic of Belarus: Parliamentary Elections 17 October 2004* Warsaw, OSCE.

Ostrom, E. (1998) 'A Behavioural Approach to the Rational Choice Theory of Collective Action: Presidential Address APSA 1997', *American Political Science Review*, vol. 92, no. 1, pp. 69–93.

Özkirimli, U. (2000) *Theories of Nationalism*. Basingstoke, Palgrave Macmillan, pp. 20–1.

Parekh, B. (2000) *Rethinking Multiculturalism*. Basingstoke: Palgrave Macmillan.

Parekh, B. (2003) 'Cosmopolitanism and Global Citizenship', *Review of International Studies*, vol. 29, pp. 3–17.

Patomäki, H. (2003) 'Problems of Democratizing Global Governance: Time, Space and the Emancipatory Process', *European Journal of International Relations*, vol. 9, no. 3, pp. 347–76.

Pennings, P. (2000) 'Parliamentary Control of the Executive in 47 Democracies', paper presented to ECPR Joint Sessions, April 2000.

Peterson, J. (1995)'Decision-Making in the European Union: Towards a Framework for Analysis', *Journal of European Public Policy*, vol. 2, no. 1, pp. 69–93.

Pettit, P. (1997) *Republicanism: a Theory of Freedom and Government*. Oxford, Oxford University Press.

Phinnemore, D. (2004) 'And not forgetting the rest . . . : EU (25) and the changing dynamics of EU enlargement'. Paper presented at UACES Conference 'The EU: New Neighbours, New Challenges', Birmingham 6–8 September 2004.

Plamenatz, J. (1973) *Democracy and Illusion: an Examination of Certain Aspects of Modern Democratic Theory*. London, Longman.

Polity IV Project: Political Regime Characteristics and Transitions 1800–2003, available at www.cidcm.umd.edu/inscr/polity.

Pollack, M. (1997a) 'Delegation, Agency and Agenda Setting in the European Community', *International Organization*, vol. 51, no. 1, pp. 99–134.

Pollack, M. (1997b) 'Representing Diffuse Interests in EC Policy-Making', *Journal of European Public Policy*, vol. 4, no. 4, pp. 572–90.

Pollack, M. (1998) 'The Engines of Integration? Supranational Autonomy and Influence in the European Union', in W. Sandholtz and A. Stone Sweet (eds), *European Integration and Supranational Governance*. Oxford, Oxford University Press, pp. 217–50.

Powell, G. B. (1989) 'Constitutional Design and Electoral Control', *Journal of Theoretical Politics*, vol. 1, no. 2, pp. 107–30.

Powell, G. B. (2000) *Elections as Instruments of Democracy: Majoritarian and Proportional Visions*. New Haven, CT, Yale University Press.

Pridham, G. (2001) 'Uneasy Democratisations – Pariah Regimes, Political Conditionality and Reborn Transitions in Central and Eastern Europe', *Democratization*, vol. 8, no. 4, pp. 65–94.

Pridham, G. (2003) 'The Slovak Parliamentary Election of September 2002: Its Systemic Importance' *Government and Opposition*, 38(3), pp. 334–55.

Putnam, R. (1993) *Making Democracy Work: Civic Traditions in Modern Italy*. Princeton, NJ, Princeton University Press.

Radaelli, C. (2000) 'Whither Europeanization? Concept Stretching and Substantive Change', *European Online Papers, vol.* 4, no. 8.

Raunio, T. (2002) 'Beneficial Co-operation or Mutual Ignorance? Contacts between MEPs and National Parties', in B. Steunenberg and J. Thomassen (eds), *The European Parliament: Moving Towards Democracy in the EU*. Lanham, MD, Rowman & Littlefield.

Rawls, J. (1993) *Political Liberalism*. New York, Columbia University Press.

Reif, K. and Schmitt, H. (1980) 'Nine Second-Order National Elections: a Conceptual Framework for the Analysis of European Election Results', *European Journal of Political Research*, vol. 8, no. 1, pp. 3–45.

Reiss, H. (1991) (ed.) *Kant: Political Writings*. Cambridge, Cambridge University Press.

Rhodes, R. (1996) 'The New Governance: Governing without Government', *Political Studies*, vol. 44, no. 4, pp. 652–68.

Riker, W. (1982) *Liberalism against Populism*. San Francisco, Freeman & Co.

Rijshøj, S. (2004) 'Europeanization and Euroscepticism – Experiences from Poland and the Czech Republic', *Stredoevropske politicke studie* (Central European Political Studies review) 4 http://www.iips.cz/seps/clanek.php?ID=2211

Rokkan, S. (1970) *Citizens, Elections, Parties: Approaches to the Comparative Study of the Process of Development.* Oslo, Universitetsforlaget.

Rosanvallon, P. (2004) 'Le Mythe du Citoyen Passif', *Le Monde*, 21 June 2004.

Rosato, S. (2003) 'The Flawed Logic of Democratic Peace Theory', *American Political Science Review*, vol. 97, no. 4, pp. 585–602.

Rose, R. (2004) 'Voter Turn-Out in the European Union Countries', in *Voter Turn-Out in Western Europe since 1945.* Stockholm, International Institute for Democracy and Electoral Assistance, pp. 17–25.

Rousseau, J.-J. (1968 [1762]) *The Social Contract.* Harmondsworth, Penguin.

Ruben, D.-H. (1998) 'The Philosopy of the Social Sciences', in A. Grayling (ed.), *Philosophy 2.* Oxford, Oxford University Press, pp. 420–69.

Russett, B. (1993) *Grasping the Democratic Peace: Principles for a Post Cold War World.* Princeton, NJ, Princeton University Press.

Russett, B. (1995) 'The Democratic Peace', *International Security*, vol. 19, no. 1, pp. 164–75.

Ryan, A. (1974) *J. S. Mill.* London, Routledge.

Ryan, A. (1998) 'Political Philosophy', in A. Grayling (ed.), *Philosophy 2.* Oxford, Oxford University Press, pp. 351–419.

Scharpf, F. (1996) 'Democratic Policy in Europe', *European Law Journal*, vol. 2, no. 2, pp. 136–55.

Scharpf, F. (2003) *Problem Solving Effectiveness and Democratic Accountability in the EU*, MPIFG Working Paper 03/01. Bonn, Max Planck Institut.

Schattsneider, E. (1960) *The Semi-Sovereign People: A Realist's View of Democracy in America.* New York, Holt.

Schedler, A. (1998) 'What is Democratic Consolidation', *Journal of Democracy*, 9:2, pp. 91–103.

Schimmelfennig, F. (2003) *The EU, Nato and the Integration of Europe, Rules and Rhetoric.* Cambridge, Cambridge University Press.

Schimmelfennig, F., Engert, S. and Knobel, H. (2003) 'Costs, Commitment and Compliance: The Impact of EU Conditionality on Latvia, Slovakia and Turkey', *Journal of Common Market Studies*, vol. 41, no. 3, pp. 495–518.

Schleiter, P. and Morgan-Jones, E. (2005) 'Power to the Presidents, Democracy and Constitutional Innovation', *The World Today*, vol. 61, no. 4, pp. 5–6.

Schmitt, H. and Thomassen, T. (2000) 'Dynamic Representation: the Case of European Integration', *European Union Politics*, vol. 1, no. 3, pp. 340–63.

Schmitter, P. (1992) 'Representation and the Future Euro-Polity', *Staatswissenschaften und Staatspraxis*, vol. 3, no. 3, pp. 379–405.

Schmitter, P. (1994) 'Dangers and Dilemmas of Democracy', *Journal of Democracy*, vol. 5, no. 2, pp. 57–74.

Schmitter, P. (2000) *How to Democratize the EU . . . and Why Bother?*, Lanham, MD, Rowman & Littlefield.

Schmitter, P. and Schneider, C. (2003) 'Exploring a New Cross-regional Time Series Data Set on the Key Concepts of Democratisation, Liberalisation, Transition and Consolidation', paper delivered to the Annual Meeting of the American Political Science Association, 28–31 August 2003.

Schoenman, R. (2005) 'Captains or Pirates? State-Business Relations in Post-Socialist Poland' *East European Politics and Societies*, vol. 19, no. 1, pp. 40–75.

Schönlau, J. (2001) 'The EU Charter of Fundamental Rights: Legitimation through Deliberation', unpublished PhD thesis, University of Reading.

Schraeder, P. (2003) 'The State of the Art in International Democracy Promotion: Result of a Joint European–North American Research Network', *Democratization*, vol. 10, no. 2, pp. 21–44.

Schumpeter, J. (1943) *Capitalism, Socialism and Democracy*. London, George Allen & Unwin.

Scott, C. (2000) 'Accountability in the Regulatory State', *Journal of Law and Society*, vol. 38, pp. 38–60.

Searle, J. (1990) *Speech Acts*. Cambridge, Cambridge University Press.

Searle, J. (1995) *The Construction of Social Reality*. Cambridge, Cambridge University Press.

Shackleton, M. (1998) 'The European Parliament's New Committees of Inquiry: Tiger or Paper Tiger?', *Journal of Common Market Studies*, vol. 36, no. 1, pp. 115–30.

Shaw, J. (1999) 'Postnational Constitutionalism in the European Union', *Journal of European Public Policy*, vol. 6, no. 4, pp. 579–97.

Skinner, Q. (1978) *The Foundations of Modern Political Thought*. 2 vols. Cambridge, Cambridge University Press.

Soysal, Y. (1998) 'Towards a Postnational Model of Membership', in G. Shafir (ed.), *The Citizenship Debates: a Reader*. Minneapolis, Minnesota University Press.

Starr, H. (1991) 'Democratic Dominoes: Diffusion Approaches to the Spread of Democracy in the International System', *Journal of Conflict Resolution*, vol. 35, pp. 356–81.

Stepan, A. and Linz J. (1996) *Problems of Democratic Transition and*

Consolidation. London, Baltimore, The Johns Hopkins University Press.

Stiglitz, J. (2002) *Globalization and its Discontents.* London, Penguin.

Stone Sweet, A. (2000) *Governing with Judges: Constitutional Politics in Europe.* Oxford, Oxford University Press.

Stuart, G., Knowles, V. and Pottebohm, S. (2003) 'Zwischen Legitimät und Effizienz: Ergebnisse der Arbeitsgruppen "Einzelstaatliche Parlamente" und "Verteidigung" im Konvent', *Integration,* vol. 1, no. 3, pp. 10–17.

Sverdrup, U. (2002) 'An Institutional Perspective on Treaty Reform: Contextualizing the Amsterdam and Nice Treaties', *Journal of European Public Policy,* vol. 9, no. 1, pp. 120–40.

Sveriges Riksdag (2001) *Synthesis of Answers to Questionnaire to European Union Affairs Committees.* Available at

Szczerbiak, A. (2001) 'Polish Public Opinion: Explaining Declining Support for EU-membership' *Journal of Common Market Studies,* vol. 139, no. 1, pp. 105–22.

Szczerbiak, A. and Taggart, P. (2002) 'The Party Politics of Euroscepticism in EU Member and Candidate States', Sussex European Institute, SEI Working Paper No 51, www.sussex.ac.uk

Szczerbiak, A. and Taggart, P. (2003) 'Theorising Party-Based Euroscepticism: Problems of Definition, Measurement and Causality', Sussex European Institute, SEI Working Paper No 69, www.sussex.ac.uk

Tesser, L. (2003) 'Geopolitics of Tolerance: Minority Rights under EU Expansion in East/Central Europe, *East European Politics and Societies,* vol. 17, no. 3, pp. 483–532.

Tamir, Y. (1993) *Liberal Nationalism.* Princeton, NJ, Princeton University Press.

Therborn, G. (1977) 'The Rule of Capital and the Rise of Democracy', *New Left Review,* vol. 103, pp. 3–42.

Tocqueville, A. de (1968 [1839]) *Democracy in America,* Vols 1 and 2. London, Fontana.

Trechsel, A. and Kriesi, H. (1996) 'Switzerland: the Referendum and Initiative as a Centrepiece of the Political System', in M. Gallagher and P. Uleri (eds), *The Referendum Experience in Europe.* London, Macmillan, pp. 185–209.

Trondal, J. (2001) *Administrative Integration Across Levels of Governance. Integration Through Participation in EU Committees.* Oslo, ARENA Report No. 7/2001.

Tsebelis, G. (1994) 'The Power of the European Parliament as a Conditional Agenda-Setter', *American Political Science Review,* no. 88, pp. 128–42.

Tsebelis, G. (1995) 'Decision-Making in Political Systems: Veto Players in Presidentialism, Parliamentarism, Multicameralism and

Multipartyism', *British Journal of Political Science*, vol. 25, no. 3, pp. 289–326.

Tsebelis, G. (1999) 'Veto Players and Law Production in Parliamentary Democracies: an Empirical Analysis', *American Political Science Review*, vol. 93, no. 3, pp. 591–608.

Tsebelis, G. and Garrett, G. (2000) 'Legislative Politics in the European Union', *European Union Politics*, no. 1, pp. 9–36.

van Biezen, I. (2005) 'On the Theory and Practice of Party Formation and Adaptation in New Democracies', *European Journal of Political Research*, vol. 41, no. 1, pp. 147–74.

Vermeersch, P. (2004) 'Minority Policy in Central Europe: Exploring the Impact of the EU's Enlargement Strategy', *The Global Review of Ethnopolitics*. vol. 3, no. 2, pp. 3–19.

Waldron, J. (1993) 'Special Ties and Natural Duties', *Philosophy and Public Affairs*, vol. 22, no. 1, pp. 3–30.

Wälti, S., Kübler, D. and Papadopoulos, Y. (2004) 'How Democratic is "Governance"? Lessons for Swiss Drugs Policy', *Governance*, vol. 17, no. 1, pp. 83–113.

Walzer, M. (1983) *Spheres of Justice*. Oxford, Blackwell.

Weale, A. (1999) *Democracy*. London, Macmillan.

Weiler, J. (1997) 'Legtimacy and Democracy of Union Governance' in G. Edwards and A. Pijpers (eds), *The Politics of European Union Treaty Reform*. London, Pinter.

Weiler, J. (2002) 'A Constitution for Europe? Some Hard Choices', *Journal of Common Market Studies*, vol. 40, no. 4, pp. 563–80.

Weiler, J., Haltern, U. and Mayer, F. (1995) 'European Democracy and its Critique', *West European Politics*, vol. 18, no. 3, pp. 4–39.

Wessels, W. (1998) 'Comitology: Fusion in Action. Politico-Administrative Trends in the EU System', *Journal of European Public Policy*, vol. 5, no. 2, pp. 209–34.

Westlake, M. (1997) 'Mad Cows and Englishmen: the Institutional Consequence of the BSE Crisis', *Journal of Common Market Studies*, vol. 35, Annual Review, pp. 11–37.

Whitehead, L. (1996) (ed.) *The International Dimensions of Democratisation: Europe and the Americas*. Oxford, Oxford University Press.

Wiener, A. (1998) *'European' Citizenship Practice: Building Institutions of a non-State*. Boulder, CO, Westview.

Woldendorp, J., Kernan, H., and Budge, I. (2000) *Party Government in 48 Democracies 1945–1988*. Dordrecht, Kluwer Academic Publishers.

Wolf, M. (2005) *Why Globalization Works*. London, Yale University Press.

Zakaria, F. (2003) *The Future of Freedom: Illiberal Democracy at Home and Abroad*. New York, W. W. Norton.

Index